POOR RICHARD'S ECONOMIC SURVIVAL MANUAL

By Alfred W. Munzert, Ph.D.

Published by HEMISPHERE PUBLICATIONS, INC.
20 Elm St.   Franklinville, New York 14737

First Hemisphere Publications, Inc. Edition, 1982
Copyright © 1982 by Hemisphere Publications, Inc.
All Rights reserved, including the right of reproduction in whole or in part in any form.
Illustrations and Cover Design by Kim K. Munzert.
Published by Hemisphere Publications, Inc.
Library of Congress Card Catalog Number—82-82499
ISBN: 0-917292-03-0
Second Printing

TABLE OF CONTENTS

iv

PART III

DEDICATION

I dedicate this book to the illustrious Benjamin Franklin, one of the greatest and wisest of our republics founding forefathers. With his deep beliefs in the self-reliance and dignity of the individual, I am certain that this is the kind of book he would have written to aid his fellow countrymen in these troubled and turbulent times.

Alfred W. Munzert

INTRODUCTION

This book was written as a practical survival guide for the average person struggling to cope with the destructive ravages of taxes and inflation. The wealthy have long known how to protect what they have and with the skilled advisors—attorneys, accountants, etc.—at their command, they require no further advice. The political leadership of the country, which has been both the cause and the beneficiary of our national inflation has even less interest in bringing inflation under control—despite their protests to the contrary.

But for the man in the street, laboring to support his family, to educate his children—to secure his share of the American dream—the continuing inflation and taxation makes a mockery of his efforts and viciously robs him of his future. As he earns more dollars, he pays more taxes, and the dollars he has left buy less and less. He works harder and harder—not to advance, but just to stay even. And he is losing the battle. In the last twenty years these twin rapists—taxation and inflation—have confiscated 80% of the accumulated wealth of the working middle class which constitutes the backbone of this nation. For the poor lower class, inflation alone makes survival increasingly precarious. These two groups account for 95% of the country's population and their standard of living will continue to decline because of inflation and taxes.

Make no mistake. Each of us today is in a deadly battle for survival and our entire way of life in these United States is literally at stake. Looming just over the horizon is the threat of a monetary and economic collapse that by comparison will make the depression of the 1930's seem like a picnic. What most Americans do not realize is that we are now being handed the bill for 50 years of fiscal mismanagement by our political leadership, who have squandered our wealth and mortgaged all of our futures. The horror of the situation can be illustrated by a simple comparison of several recent statistics:

(1) The estimated value of all property in the United States today, i.e., every home, building, automobile, home furnishing, equipment, machinery, etc.—every material possession owned by you, me and our fellow citizens is approximately 7.2 Trillion dollars.

(2) The total indebtedness of the U.S. Federal government both funded and unfunded is approximately 7.6 Trillion dollars—meaning that Uncle Sam has already mortgaged everything we own.

In a word—the nation is today insolvent—bankrupt. And this is only for committments already made in the past! The only asset we have left is our future productivity.

And who will pay for this monstrous indebtedness?

Unfortunately—you will. The government has no money of its own—only what it takes from its citizens in the form of taxes. In fact, your share of the national debt is already $32,740! And this is true of every man, woman and child in the country.

How long will it take you to pay this off? How long is forever? Total taxes today already take $.51 of every dollar you now earn and will continue to take the majority of your earnings far into the future. Moreover, the enormous and growing structure of government itself constitutes yet a further hideous burden upon the back of every taxpayer. It is estimated that just maintaining this army of regulators now cost in excess of $5,000 a year for every family in the country!

A government has two ways of raising the money it spends. It can tax its citizens for a portion of their earnings and—since it controls the coinage of money—it can simply start up the presses and print more money—which is precisely what our leaders have done and which is the true reason for our inflation.

We are continuously treated to the spectacle of government asking business and labor to hold down prices and wage demands in order to "control inflation."

This is sheer, unadulterated nonsense. Whoever controls the money supply controls inflation—and it is that simple. When the government prints extra money for which there is no backing in any form, prices rise because there are more dollars in circulation bidding for the supply of goods and services which have not increased since before the extra dollars were printed. The poor businessman and worker must ask for more dollars because each one they receive now buys less. They are simply trying to stay even when they ask for more. They are the victims—not the creators—of inflation. The real perpetrator is the government —who benefits nicely by being able to pay its obligations in cheaper dollars which it simply creates from paper and ink.

To compound the horror, the individual now gets hit with a double whammy—as his income rises in terms of dollars (each of which now buys less)—he gets pushed into a higher income bracket and pays out a greater percentage of his income in taxes than he did before. Between the higher taxes and the shrinking value of each dollar—his purchasing power actually declines, even though he earns more dollars. For the poor and those on a fixed income, the result is even more devastating. In fact, it is nothing short of a catastrophe.

This is the real horror of inflation. And for each 1% of inflation, the government collects an additional 7 Billion dollars in taxes through the "ratchet" effect of forcing people into higher income brackets. For the free spending politicians at the helm of our ship of state this further confiscation of individual wealth gives them an enormous windfall of extra funds to spend without having to legally raise taxes. It should be noted that Congress in the past has consistently refused to adjust or "index" taxes to the inflation rate to protect the individual from this growing confiscation of his earnings. Every such proposal has been quickly voted down or buried. While such a measure would not relieve the individual of the staggering burden he is now carrying—it would at least prevent the load from getting heavier. But it would place a restriction on our free-spending politicians and they are not easily going to surrender this great bonanza. In the recent tax legislation, an indexing provision finally was enacted. However, it is not scheduled to take effect until 1985 and already it is under strong attack from a growing number of Congressmen, who, highly displeased that it even managed to be enacted at all, are working diligently to have it canceled. Whether it will ever actually be allowed to take effect is at this point highly questionable.

Not only is this incredible transfer of wealth invisible to the individual citizen, it has literally brought this great republic of ours to the brink of self-destruction. Over the last 50 years, our government leadership, well intended but naive—has tried to be all things to all people—something no nation in history has ever achieved. Magnificent new schools, hospitals and highways have been built, home ownership has doubled and the standard of living has risen dramatically to the highest level in the history of civilization. On the surface, the illusion of wealth seems endless.

But it is just that—an illusion. It has all been created from nothing by borrowed money. We now discover that the bank account is overdrawn, the mortgage on the house is being foreclosed and we must now pay the bill for years of living beyond our income.

With a shock we also now discover that there never really was a "free lunch." Under the guise of social benefit and happiness for all, our governing elite have maintained themselves in office by trading benefits for votes. These "free" gifts so generously bestowed upon us by our benefactors have actually been billed to our credit card. We are left with a choice of bankruptcy or economic bondage. Alexander Tyler, an astute 19th century statesman once observed,

"Democracy will only survive until its citizens discover that they can vote themselves largess (gifts) out of the public treasury. The entire structure will then collapse through sheer fiscal irresponsibility."

We have now arrived at the eleventh hour—and the bill <u>must</u> be paid or we shall preside over our own destruction.

But even as the nation teeters on the brink of chaos—as the currency deteriorates, the banking system falters and the entire structure begins to crumble—the recent political change in Washington gives rise to a cautious optimism. The American people have finally realized that something is radically wrong with our direction. Without completely understanding the causes, they have sensed the deterioration and in their concern, have dictated one of the sharpest political changes in the nation's history. The new leadership, which understands full well the reality of our decline, and that we are facing economic disaster—has courageously pulled no punches. In an attempt to restore the nation to fiscal sanity, they have designed tremendous cuts in government spending and embarked upon a program of reducing the legion of regulators who not only consume a growing share of our taxes but who, by their very existence, continue increasingly to restrict and destroy our individual freedoms.

To reduce the unconscionable seizure of individual wealth, the new administration has proposed a long range tax reduction program which will not only allow the individual to retain a greater portion of his earnings but which will rekindle the private initiative and productivity that enabled our forefathers to build this great republic of ours.

No other solution is possible. Government growth and spending must not only be halted—it must be reversed. And quickly. If the new administration in Washington can make the program stick, perhaps—just perhaps—we may be able to work our way out. However, we can afford no further extravagance and this is our final chance for survival.

But have no illusions—the cure will indeed be bitter medicine. A fifty year binge of unrestrained spending has produced a psychology of affluence that will be difficult to temper. Two-thirds of our citizens—those under 40—have no memories of the last depression and have been raised in a society that virtually guaranteed health, wealth and happiness as a birthright.

With only 4% of the world's population, we annually consume

40% of its resources. To a society that throws away enough food in its garbage cans to feed several other nations and that gives the 16 year-old his or her own automobile as part of the coming-of-age ritual, the announcement that the well is running dry will generate about as much enthusiasm as the bubonic plague. Large segments of our population who do not perceive the danger of our crisis and certain political and social groups who have vested interests in preserving the status quo, will strongly resist the rescue efforts now evolving in Washington.

In the end, I believe we shall succeed in restoring the nation to its former levels of economic soundness and individual freedom. We are a great and productive people whose individuality and productivity have created a society unique in the history of civilization. We have overcome other threats to our survival and I am optimistic that if we truly understand the nature of our current crisis—that we shall again succeed.

But even granted complete success in the restoration of economic soundness through the current political program, it will take many years to accomplish the goal. In particular, it will take throughout the eighties to control and ultimately reduce inflation. It is a factor that the individual must thoroughly understand and come to grips with in his or her own battle for survival over the next decade.

That, specifically, is the objective of this book—to give the individual a thorough and complete understanding of inflation and taxes—in laymans terms—and the techniques to master them in battle.

Can the individual really fight these destructive forces and actually win?

The answer is a surprising YES!

But first he must acquire a basic but simple understanding of money and economics—not what the conventional wisdom would have him believe—but the actual realities. If he attempts to fight them with the traditional methods—he cannot win.

Second, he must learn to evaluate both his actual capabilities and true objectives.

Finally, he must learn a number of unorthodox techniques

that will allow him not only to survive, but even to prosper.

During a childhood of poverty in the great depression of the 1930's, I became a survival specialist and my adult life is almost a textbook example of successful economic survival. Despite an income that rarely exceeded $7–8,000 a year, I raised and college-educated eight children, all of whom are now highly productive citizens. Moreover, I myself enjoyed the benefits of world-wide travel and a superb education, becoming proficient in economics, money and banking, international trade, psychology and languages. I did not accomplish this by following the conventional wisdom. Quite the contrary—for I learned that reality is often far different than that which we are taught to believe. I became, in essence, an "economic guerilla fighter." I learned to take the strategic "high ground" and to dictate the terms of my own survival rather than allowing them to be thrust upon me by outside forces. Each man is, after all, the master of his own destiny and the architect of his own success or failure in this brief and troubled existence.

In the midst of very little money, my family and I have lived a rich and productive life. Because of our knowledge and unconventional approach to money and wealth—we have prospered. And therein lies the secret—for knowledge is power. You cannot devise solutions until you first understand the problems.

In the first section of this book—which is a distillation of the many unconventional approachs learned over the years—the real nature of money, wealth, productivity, etc. is carefully explained and defined.

In the second section I have outlined highly successful techniques for productive economic survival in all the major areas such as food, housing, transportation, etc. Whether you use all or even just a few, these methods will save you thousands of dollars in the future.

Finally, in the third section of this book, a series of evaluation charts will enable the reader to develop his or her own individual "battle plan" for fighting and winning the struggle for economic survival.

The knowledge contained herein has enabled me to lead a

rich and satisfying life and the writing of this book has given me a distinct pleasure. If it enables the reader to better cope with his or her own embattled existence, then this writing has fulfilled its purpose.

PART I

THE KEY TO SURVIVAL-
UNDERSTANDING
THE MAJOR
ECONOMIC CONCEPTS

THE FIVE MAJOR ECONOMIC CONCEPTS

Most people are victims of the conventional wisdom designed by the society into which they have been born. Insofar as these conventions develop a moral and social set of values such training is sound and productive, for it allows us to live in civilized harmony with each other. We are, for example, taught as children not to lie or steal, how to work and to respect authority.

But in the area of economics—a knowledge of which is vital to the survival and prosperity of every single individual—we are kept in abysmal ignorance. The average person has only the vaguest idea of what money, capital, wealth, productivity, and inflation really are. Nor is it anywhere taught in our educational system. The idea is fostered and perpetuated that "economics" is an exotic and mysterious science best left to the experts and government officials.

Convinced by the "experts" that the subject is far too complex to understand, the vast majority of people abandon their own self interest and accept as "fact" the economic absurdities thrust upon them by their governing officials. In their ignorance, they are asking to be exploited and every government—whether capitalistic, socialistic or communistic—willingly obliges.

The word "economics" is derived from the old Latin "oeco" meaning "household." Economics then is literally the act of managing your household—your money, wealth and capital. With something so vital to one's life, who but a fool would knowingly leave its management to some distant bureaucrat?

Obviously, it is imperative that each individual not only learn —but master—the basic fundamentals of a subject so important to his survival. Let us now proceed to some of these basic realities not taught by the conventional wisdom.

3

CAPITAL

The first major loss to the individual occurs through a lack of understanding of his or her real capital value. The traditional definition of capital is that it is:

—a stock of accumulated goods or money.
—accumulated possessions calculated to bring in income.

Capital then—accumulated goods or money—is left in the bank to draw interest or invested in a business, building, etc. The objective in its use is to produce further capital for the individual who accumulated it in the first place.

This is the conventional understanding of the term "capital" and is correct within its narrow scope of definition.

For the average man or woman, however, the narrowness of this concept is devastating.

They come unconsciously to assume that capital is something possessed by only the wealthy and something they themselves will not easily acquire. If they relate the term to themselves at all, they negatively visualize the meager several hundreds of dollars in their bank account and dismiss themselves as owners of any meaningful amount of capital.

It is here that the conventional wisdom obscures reality and prevents the individual from ever realizing or assessing the tremendous capital resource which everyone possesses.

Let us here set aside this limiting definition of capital and demonstrate how wealthy the individual actually is.

First, you must learn to "capitalize" yourself as an individual. Industry, for example, has long ago learned to "capitalize" its plants and equipment—to set a "value" on each item. A generator for instance, will be determined to have a capital value dependent on its capacity and length of production life, as will a fork lift, vehicle, etc.

But what is the "capital value" of an individual? And when—if ever—will society teach this knowledge to its individual members?

The fact is that each individual possesses an incredible capital reserve but is taught neither how to evaluate nor how to utilize this store of wealth.

Contrary to popular belief, the individual's real wealth lies not in money, jewels and goods, but in his or her TIME AND LABOR!

To illustrate how vast is this capital reserve, one need make only a few simple calculations:

(1) The average man or woman's working span will cover 45 years, and approximately 90,000 working hours.

(2) The capital value (or capital reserve) of the individual is 90,000 hours X his or her level of labor speciality(s).

For example, if one were to work a lifetime as even a simple laborer at say $4.00 per hour then he or she would have a capital value of $4.00 X 90,000 hours or $360,000.00!

If the same individual were to become let us say a technician —at $8.00 per hour—then his or her capital value would rise to $720,000.00!

If this person continued further up the ladder and became a doctor or lawyer at say $50.00 per hour, then his or her capital value would rise to $4,500,000.00!

It becomes immediately obvious that education or training of any kind has an enormous dollar value to the individual and will affect the level of survival or lifestyle throughout his or her lifespan. We will discuss this aspect in further detail in a later section of the book.

The essential point to bear in mind is that your real capital is your time and labor, and that you begin your adult life with a very substantial "bank account"—your capital value. You must also be aware that this capital is limited and irreplaceable. Once you have used it—once you have spent an hour of your precious time and labor—it is gone forever. You must watch it carefully and as you spend your "capital"—you must get the maximum value in return. You cannot afford to be cheated, for your capital can never be replaced. All wealth in this world—buildings, automobiles, products, goods, etc.—was created by someone's time and labor. If part of that labor was yours, then you should have received an adequate return for the "capital" you invested.

Each of us then, has a real capital value—regardless of age, sex or occupation—that is far greater than we assume. Whether you are just beginning a working career, middle-aged or retired —you have a capital value that can be calculated. In a further section of this book you will be shown how to determine your current value and how to use this knowledge as a valuable tool in your battle against inflation.

The traditional definition of "capital" then still has validity, but for the average person, real capital is his or her time and labor. The more the individual can evaluate the cost of each specific item such as food, housing, clothing, etc. in terms of their hours they must trade for them—rather than the dollars necessary—the less they will be victimized by "money,"—which can be manipulated—and by inflation, which is the result of that manipulation.

MONEY AND CURRENCY

No economic terms are more misunderstood by people than money and currency. Ask the average person what he believes money is and he will promptly show you a dollar bill. The vast majority of individuals honestly believe that if they are holding a bundle of bills in their hand that they have money. They are able to walk into a store, hand one of these bills to a clerk and obtain some tangible product in return. These pieces of paper have a magical element to them and since the individual possessing them has seen that they will secure the things he desires, it is not at all surprising that he comes to believe that these pieces of paper in themselves have a value. They are money in his view and nothing can persuade him otherwise.

This, however, is a deadly serious error. By believing that these pieces of paper that he possesses are actually money and by putting his confidence in them, he becomes a prime target for exploitation.

Real money was one of man's greatest inventions and one of the most powerful forces in the development of civilization. Before the concept of money was created, commerce or trade of any kind was quite difficult. Prehistoric men, living alone in caves, existed on a simple survival level, foraging and hunting for food and clothing. As skills developed, a simple barter system arose—and one type of product or goods was traded directly for another. This however, was often extremely inefficient. For example, if a sword maker wanted a pair of sandals, he would have to search out a sandal maker who wanted a sword and was willing to make the exchange. Over a period of time, communities decided that one particular product or commodity was generally acceptable in exchange for all goods and services, and thus the concept of "money"—a common and recognizable medium of exchange—was born.

Probably the earliest "money" were domesticated animals, such as sheep, cattle and pigs. A cow, for example, was the unit of valuation with which one could buy say 20 swords, 50 pair of sandals, 30 bushel of wheat, etc., etc.

Throughout the further history of mankind many things have been used as money. Usually, the items or objects used were substances that were rather scarce and therefore, highly valued. For example, in early Rome, salt was considered quite valuable and army wages were paid in salt. This, in fact, is the origin of the modern term "salary"—which is money paid for work. Certain South Seas communities used shells for money, and American Indians used intricately woven belts of beads called wampum.

Whatever the medium of exchange, or "money" decided upon, the existence of such a commonly accepted and recognized unit of exchange greatly spurred the growth of trade, expanded individual productivity and helped to raise the standard of living in the society.

Ideal or sound "money" serves the individual and society in several very important ways:

(1) It is a medium of exchange. Instead of bartering say a cow for four pigs or seven haircuts for one chair—we pay for each of these in "money". By simplifying the exchange of goods and services, "money" increases the volume of trade and permits society to be much more efficient.

(2) It is a unit of value. If each item or service has a specific value or "price" in terms of the money, it is mucy easier to relate the value of one to the other. For example, the "price" of a haircut is $3.50, and the "price" of a chair is $10.00. Those are their values as expressed in terms of money. It is much less difficult than in trying to determine how many haircuts equal a chair if two parties were trying to barter. Sound money then serves as a method of determining a specific value of any given item.

(3) It is a store of value. If the "money" is sound—if it maintains a constant value—it can be saved for later use. If it will buy the same quantity of goods and services next year or five years from now as it will buy today, then we can set aside any surplus we accumulate for future use—retirement, emergencies, vacations, etc. We are encouraged to save for the things we will need later.

Sound money then, possess these three characteristics and is of enormous benefit to society. Of all the various forms of money used by mankind throughout the centuries, the soundest and most ideal have been gold and silver. They possess all three requirements of good money and throughout the rise and fall of civilizations, they have retained their unique soundness as "money."

We come now to "currency", particularly paper currency, which all too tragically is mistaken by most people for "money." Currency—the paper bills and coins which we handle everyday —is not really "money"—but rather money substitutes. It is extremely important to understand this basic and critical difference.

During the Middle Ages, when gold had become the dominant form of money, wealthy merchants, traveling from city to city in pursuit of trade, would deposit their precious metal with the local goldsmith for safekeeping until they had completed their transactions in that city. The goldsmith, in turn, would issue the merchant a warehouse receipt for his gold.

As the volume of trade increased, the merchants discovered that it was far more convenient to simply sign over the receipts to each other rather than physically move the gold. Eventually, the goldsmiths began to issue "bearer receipts"—which meant that whoever possessed the receipt could present it to the warehouse and pick up the gold. These receipts were literally the first "banknotes" or paper currency. The practice was a tremendous success since it was a lot easier to carry around these receipts—money substitutes—than it was to lug the heavy gold around. And the merchant placed great confidence in this new and convenient "currency." After all, it was backed 100% by the actual "money" in storage at the goldsmiths. That piece of paper was literally "as good as gold."

However, the paper money substitutes—"currency" as it is now called is not money. It is vital to bear this fact in mind—that currency—paper dollars and coins in our society—are not money, but merely substitutes for money. It is through not understanding this fundamental economic fact that the average person becomes a victim in times of inflation. As long as real money—gold, silver, etc. is on deposit or stored somewhere as backing for this paper money substitute—then the paper money actually facilitates trade and commerce and the individual is protected. If he can at any time take his paper receipt to the warehouse (bank) and ask for the real money which it represents then he can feel secure in the knowledge that his wealth is safe.

Unfortunately, there is today no such real money on deposit as backing for our currency—nor is it possible in any way to redeem our paper currency for money. The horrible fact is that instead of money—we now have only the paper substitute—which is nothing more than just that—paper.

For most of our history as a nation this certainly was not true.

In our U.S. Constitution, written two hundred years ago, our founding forefathers stated very specifically:

"Congress shall have the power to coin money" and
"Gold and silver shall be the only legal tender (money)."

These wise leaders understood that sound, reliable money was the basis of a prosperous society. They definitely and firmly wrote into law that <u>only</u> gold and silver could serve as money in our society.

Accordingly, for the first 150 years of our existence as a nation, the soundness of our money was beyond question and it was the underpinning of the greatest national growth in the history of civilization. Each coin that was minted contained in itself the precise amount of gold or silver as the value printed on its face. Paper currency could be redeemed at any time for its full value in gold or silver from the nearest bank. So great was the confidence in our American currency that the expression "sound as a dollar" became a part of our culture.

All this changed abruptly in 1934, when under President Roosevelt, Congress forbid Americans to any longer own gold. Paper currency could no longer be redeemed for gold and the destruction of our great financial system was begun.

From 1934–1963, paper currency could still be redeemed in silver and coins continued to be minted with a silver content. However, in 1963, even the exchange of silver for the paper currency was discontinued and in 1964, all coins containing silver were also removed from circulation.

The final debasement and destruction of U.S. money had been completed.

Since 1964, the U.S. has had no <u>real money</u>. What we have instead are merely the <u>money substitutes</u>. Our paper currency cannot be redeemed for anything and the coins have been utterly debased. A fifty-cent coin, for example, has actually $.02 worth of metal in it. The quarter and dime have even less. All are now made from copper with a nickel covering bonded to the surface to give them the appearance of silver.

We have now arrived at a ludicrous point where we trade each other pieces of paper and call it money—as if we were all playing a game of Monopoly. As the theme for a stage play—the situation would make hilarious comedy. As a real life situation, however, it is nothing short of tragic.

But if, in fact, there no longer is any real money—only money substitutes—than why and how does this system continue to function?

The answer to this very logical question is quite simple and basically there are two reasons:

(1) It functions primarily because people still <u>believe</u> that they are dealing with real money. The medieval merchant who traded his gold warehouse receipts had absolute confidence in their value because he <u>knew</u> that the real money (gold) was on deposit and there for the asking. In a similar manner and because historically our currency also had the same secure backing, we still <u>believe</u> that it has and accept and trade it with complete confidence.

(2) The second reason why the system continues to function —even for those who understand the reality—is that we simply have no other choice. It is the only medium of exchange allowed by law. And as long as people are willing to accept this paper money substitute in exchange for valuable goods and services then the system will continue to function.

But have no illusions—these paper substitutes are <u>not</u> money and understanding this difference is vitally important.

In our present society, this paper money may be the medium of exchange, but it is also the medium of confiscation. It is the vehicle through which the individual's wealth and productivity are siphoned off by taxes and inflation. The <u>avoidance</u> of money is thus one of the key defenses against such confiscation and will later be discussed in detail.

INFLATION

Inflation is at once the most destructive and cruelest of all economic situations. It is also the least understood by the average person.

For years, the general public has been bombarded by a flow of information in the news media relating to the national concern over the destructive effects of rising inflation. Economists from the many government agencies and universities somberly discuss its effects upon the man-in-the-street and earnestly debate such high sounding concepts as the cost-push and wage-price spiral theories. In the former, as the theory goes, rising costs push up prices—and hence inflation. In the wage-price spiral, rising demand for higher wages force up prices and goods and services, and this is yet another contributor to inflation. The government's Consumer Price Index regularly alerts the citizen of the past months rise in cost of various commodities, and our politicians vow a fight to the death with this horrible monster.

Of all the scapegoats indicted for the crime the favorite villains are big business and labor unions. The basic cause of our misery—we are told by our leaders—is the mercenary lust of business for excessive profits and hence exhorbitant prices. The relentless drive of the unions for ever higher wages is also equally guilty. Government leaders, shaking an admonishing finger, warn that if they do not cease such inflationary behavior that they will have wage and price controls forced upon them.

The result is devastatingly effective and the public is led to believe that these two culprits—business and unions—are indeed the major villains in creating inflation.

In fact, not only are all of these forgoing theories and accusations complete absurdities—they are unadultered hogwash. Rising prices and rising wages are <u>results</u> of inflation, not the causes.

The <u>real</u> cause—and the <u>only</u> cause of inflation is an <u>increase in the money supply</u> (in our case, the paper money supply)—without a corresponding increase in the production of goods and services. Since the government controls the money supply —the government controls inflation and it could stop it overnight if it so desired.

To demonstrate just how an increase in the money supply creates inflation, we shall use a simple illustration:

Let us suppose that you live in a small town of, say 500 people. The town is quite self-sufficient, and everyone is gainfully employed in one of the small local businesses or industries. No one is wealthy, but the cost of living is reasonable and everyone is quite comfortable. It is a very desireable place to live.

On the south side of town are twenty very desireable building lots. You plan to buy one in the future and build a new home upon it. These are the last remaining lots in the village, but there is no cause for hurry. The population is quite stable and is not expected to grow. These beautiful one-acre lots sell for $500.00 each and this price has also been stable for many years.

Suddenly, however, a large and wealthy group of visitors arrive. They like the town and decide to stay. The price of the 20 lots begins to rise dramatically—from $500 to $1000, to $2000 and up as these new arrivals begin to bid against each other.

This rise in the price of the lots—inflation—is due to the fact that you have had a sudden <u>increase</u> in the supply of money in town <u>without</u> an increase in the number of lots to be purchased.

Inflation, then, is simply an <u>increase</u> in the money supply without increased production. More dollars chasing fewer goods automatically causes prices to rise.

Looking at it yet another way, each dollar <u>you</u> have now has less purchasing power and it therefore takes <u>more</u> dollars to buy that same item than it did earlier.

If the number of lots in your town could have been increased to meet the demand—then the price would have remained stable at $500 and there would have been no inflation. However, because of the increased money supply now flowing through your town, your $500 is no longer sufficient to buy a lot as you had planned. In brief, your purchasing power has been dramatically reduced.

Inflation then is nothing more than an increase in the money supply without an increase in productivity to balance it. In short, there is an excess of dollars floating through the society and bidding up the cost of every item. It is the governments calculated printing and distribution of millions of excess paper dollars that is the sole cause of our growing inflation and the destruction of each individual's purchasing power.

In W.W.II, German economists, well aware of the catastrophic effects upon a nation when large volumes of excess money is distributed through a society, developed a bold and devious scheme to destroy the economy of England.

In the spring of 1943, a top secret project was begun to develop printing plates for the counterfeiting of British pound-sterling notes. Over a six-month period, master German craftsmen developed plates that were so incredibly precise that the finished counterfeit money was totally indistinguishable from the original British currency. Millions upon millions of this counterfeit currency was then packaged and smuggled into previously determined locations in England. The plan called for agents to flood the country with this huge volume of money at a given signal and according to a prearranged schedule. At the last moment, the plot was discovered and the counterfeit currency was seized by British agents.

Had the project succeeded—and this huge excess supply of money been distributed—England would have erupted in chaos and its economy would have been severely damaged, if not destroyed. The inflationary effect would have been so overwhelming that it would have torn the country apart.

Consider for a moment what would happen if tomorrow morning everyone in your city suddenly discovered $10,000 in cash in his or her mailbox.

Rest assured that the result would be sheer pandemonium!

There would be an orgy of buying that would clean out the

shelves of every store, automobile showrooms would be emptied and offices and factories would close because no one would show up for work.

As the supply of goods in the city dwindled, the prices of the remaining products would skyrocket!

It should by now be clear that whenever a government tampers with the economy by increasing the money supply—that national inflation and the destruction of individual purchasing power is the inevitable result.

While the U.S. governments continuing creation of excess paper money may not appear as sudden or dramatic as the forgoing examples—it has, in fact, been relentless and incredibly destructive, as evidenced by several eye-opening statistics:

(1) From 1945–1980, the population of the U.S. rose from 140,000,000 to 226,000,000—an increase of slightly more than 60%.

During this same 35 year period, however, the amount of money put into circulation by the government rose from 27 Billion dollars to nearly 190 Billion dollars—an increase of more than 700%!

Based on population, there is now eleven times more dollars in the hands of every person in the country.

This mind-boggling increase in the money supply in turn, produced the absolutely predictable result:

(2) From 1945–1980, prices of ordinary goods and products rose dramatically from 800–1300%. The average price increase was 1200%!

A typical home cost, for example, rose from $4500 to $79,500, a newspaper from $.02 to $.30, a movie from $.25 to $3.50, a cup of coffee from $.05 to $.50, a pair of sneakers from $1.49 to $16.95, etc., etc.

It is immediately obvious that there is a direct relationship between the increase in dollars put into circulation and the amount of inflation. The money supply has been increased 11 times since 1945 and inflation, accordingly, has increased 12 times.

While this shocking 1200% inflation of prices is in itself mind numbing, just as significant is the fact that it also lays bare the tremendous loss of purchasing power of each dollar. Specifically, from 1945–1980, the dollar has actually lost 92% of its purchasing power and in comparison to 1945, a dollar now is worth only $.08! Logically, if this rate of destruction continues, in 3–4 years, it will completely lose its remaining purchase power and be utterly worthless.

But why, one would ask, would a government deliberately bring about such insane self-destruction?

There are, of course, a number of reasons:

(1) For the politicians and bureaucrats who run the nation—control of the money supply gives them vast political power.

As long as government is restricted from printing any more paper currency than there is gold or silver to back it—the currency remains sound and stable. And as long as the government is further confined to spending only what it takes in taxes—there is a limit to waste and irresponsible spending, for there is a limit to the amount of abuse the citizens will suffer when they know they are being taxed. In fact, our American Revolution was in essence a tax revolt against the British crown for what was considered heavy and unfair taxes.

So great was the concern of our founding forefathers about anyone tampering with the money supply of the nation that they wrote into the Constitution provisions specifically limiting politicians from such tampering.

Between 1934 and 1963, however, those Constitutional safeguards of the nations money were completely circumvented and the politicians were freed to print as much currency as they chose. We are now witnessing the tragic results.

The simple fact is that a large number of our Congressmen are elected and re-elected on promises of securing greater federal aid for their local voters. If I were to promise every citizen of our town a new automobile if I were elected mayor—I would probably be swept into office by a unanimous landslide vote.

It is, of course, more subtle at the national level. A congressman, for example, will propose a bill for a dam or a military base to be built in his area, items which would insure large sums of federal money flowing into his district, from which his voters would benefit through jobs and business purchases. Further, one Congressman will agree to vote for a colleagues bill if he will vote for theirs. And collectively, they will vote for massive expenditures for a vast array of projects, programs, grants, etc.—all of which are purported to be "for the general welfare of the people." It is easy to rationalize and justify such actions—particularly if the project is one of a social or idealistic nature. Many of these representatives are, I am sure, sincere in their conviction that what they are doing is good and just.

The bottom line, however, is that they are returned again and again to office to continue creating projects for which there really is no money and which must be paid for ultimately by the very people whom they were supposed to "benefit" and who naively consider them "free gifts" from a benevolent government.

As if this orgy of spending were not in itself destructive enough of our wealth—the vast bureaucracy it has spawned is even more appalling. Every new program legislated by the Congressmen now gives birth to another large and expensive bureau of technocrats to administer the project. In effect, these unelected regulators have become the real rulers of the nation, for they reach into every nook and cranny of our life, slowly chipping away at our individual freedoms. So cumbersome and inefficient has this vast and growing bureaucracy become that it is estimated that only $1.00 out of every $4.00 actually trickles down to the intended beneficiary of a program. The other $3.00 goes to operating the bureaucracy itself. Once established—this bureaucracy takes on a life of its own and it is nearly impossible to disband or abolish it.

An example is the Rope-Twisting Agency, established in the 1880's for the purpose of supplying hemp rope for the sailing vessels of the U.S. Navy. Although we ceased to use sailing vessels shortly after the turn of the century—the agency until recently still had a staff of over 40 people and an annual appropriation of nearly $2,000,000.

So vast and sprawling has been the growth of this bureaucracy that it is now estimated that at all levels of government, nearly one out of every four people now is employed by the structure.

We have, by our indifference, allowed the growth of a Frankenstein that will strangle us all.

Collectively, while the legislators and bureaucrats enjoy the tremendous power this system has given them—they are reluctant to incur the wrath of the voters by raising taxes to pay for these programs. If the voters really understood that they themselves would have to pay for these "benefits"—and that they would have to pay steeply higher taxes—they would reject most of these programs immediately. No legislator wishes to be the target of angry voters for having raised their taxes.

There is, of course, a safer way of securing the necessary funds—simply inflate the money supply. By printing extra paper currency, funds are made available for these grandiose projects and there is no need to raise taxes. The voters are thrilled at being the recipients of this wonderful government benevolence, the legislator is enthusiastically returned to Congress, and everyone is ecstatic over our affluent and humanitarian society which provides such a marvelous life for all of us.

The fact that flooding the country with more unbacked paper dollars creates greater inflation—thus reducing individual purchasing power for all of us—is conveniently swept aside as irrelevant. The general public doesn't understand it anyway—so why confuse them with such ugly facts.

The fact that inflation can be used as an instrument for the retention of political power by the politicians and bureaucrats who thoroughly enjoy their positions is one of the major reasons for its creation by a government—however self-destructive it may be.

(2) The second major force behind the creation of inflation is of course the voters themselves and the pressure they put upon the government for an ever-increasing range of "benefits."

The vast majority of the general public hasn't the vaguest

notion of the realities of money or economics—nor do they understand that the government has no money of its own—that it must ultimately come back to them for the cost of whatever "benefits" it bestows upon them. Instead, they place a blind and often unreasoning faith in government to "do something" about their problems. Currently, nearly 60% of all Americans receive government financial assistance in one form or another. This represents a clear voting majority and virtually ensures that such pressures and demands upon the government will continue. Washington today is, in fact, swarming with powerful citizen lobbies, all seeking federal assistance for their respective groups.

Accordingly, the government obliges and provides them with funds by simply printing more money.

It is these two factors then—politicians seeking political leverage and voters naively seeking "free benefits"—that are the major forces behind our continuing and destructive inflation. No nation's economy—even one as powerful as that of the United States—can sustain such prolonged assault and debasement of its currency without ultimately collapsing.

Inflation then, is created soley by an increase in the paper money supply—for whatever the reasons—without a corresponding increase in productivity. Understanding this fact is the first vital step in learning how to correct it and to defend yourself against its ravages.

In reality, it is a simple but ingenious form of further taxation: increasing the supply of paper dollars decreases the purchasing power of dollars in the hands of the citizens—thus allowing the politicians to retain a greater share of the basic wealth.

V. I. Lenin, the early champion of world communism and founder of the modern Soviet Union, once quite accurately predicted that,

"the best way to destroy the capitalist system is to debauch the currency".

PRODUCTIVITY

Productivity is an important term in the study and understanding of economics.

Essentially <u>productivity</u> is the amount of <u>goods and services</u> (wealth) that can be created in a <u>given unit of time</u>—usually an hour. When we speak of man-hour productivity, we mean the level of production a man (or woman) is capable of producing in one hour.

One of the major reasons for the high standard of living in the United States is that historically, the man-hour productivity of the American worker has been one of the highest in the world. Such productivity has a vital impact economically on a nation.

In creating wealth—whether it be buildings, automobiles, etc. —the two major costs are the materials and labor. If, for example, it takes five men two months to build a house—then the cost of that house to a buyer will be the combined cost of the materials, the wages of the five men plus a percentage of profit for the contractor or builder.

But now suppose that these five men are given better tools to work with and instead of it taking two months—they can now build the same house in only <u>one</u> month. Their man-hour productivity is thus <u>doubled</u>.

To use yet another example, in a factory making widgets— each worker is able to turn out say, five widgets an hour. Management now introduces new equipment that enables each worker to turn out <u>ten</u> widgets per hour.

In both instances, this dramatic increase in productivity has a profound impact on the society.

20

First of all, the increase in production provides a greater abundance of available goods. Secondly, since each worker is now producing twice as much in the same time—the cost of producing each unit drops sharply and the sale price to the public is far lower.

Even assuming that the worker receives no increase in wages —the dollars he receives for his work will now buy more because of the lowered price of the goods on the market. This increased productivity then benefits the society by providing a greater abundance and benefits the individual worker by increasing the purchasing power of the money he receives for his labor.

In societies with the highest standard of living, every person, from the youngest to the oldest produces goods and services to the level of their ability—and this total productivity creates an abundance for all and raises everyones standard of living.

Anything which interferes with—or decreases productivity lowers the standard of living. Because there are fewer goods and services available, the price of each of them rises—making everyone poorer.

This is the inflexible Law of Supply and Demand—the most basic of all economic realities and no nation in history has ever been able to repeal or change it. Whenever a government tampers with this iron law of economics—the result is shortages, rising prices and a lowering of living standards.

Contrary to popular opinion—and hand-in-hand with the destruction of our montary system—government tampering over the last 50 years with the productive economic system that originally built this great nation has created a situation where we are all beginning to witness a steady decline in our standard of living. The massive social welfare programs designed to provide a better life for the citizens of our society are backfiring—not because they are not good or moral in their objectives—but because they ignore the basic realities of economics.

Not only have these programs not accomplished their objectives—the form and method of their implementation by the government has dramatically decreased national productivity, thereby increasing everyone's cost of living, including beneficiaries of the programs.

A few brief examples will serve to illustrate how the government decreases productivity:

(1) Social Security—Currently more than 30,000,000 older, retired citizens receive monthly retirement payments. Not only is this group a large and growing segment of our total population—but the total payments received represent one of the largest of all public expenditures. Many billions of dollars each month are thus introduced into the economy as they spend these dollars for housing, food, clothing, etc.

Since these people are retirees—and thus have no productivity, the huge volume of dollars they introduce into the flow of the economy thus leads to inflated prices. You will recall that inflation is primarily due to an increase in the supply of money without a corresponding increase in the supply of goods and services.

Incredibly, the government not only prohibits these skilled older people from producing—it actually punishes them financially if they do so. If, for example, a social security retiree is healthy and ambitious and decides to work—if he or she earns over an arbitrarily small sum of money—for every extra dollar earned a percentage is deducted from the base pension payment!

It has been estimated that possibly 35–40% of our older citizens would continue productive work—either full or part-time if they were not so penalized. Because of the experience and skill possessed by many of these older citizens, they constitute one of the nations most valuable resources and the talent thus discarded represents an appalling loss to the nation.

Not only does this destructive government policy prevent the individual retiree from raising his own income and living standard if he so chooses—but the nation loses a tremendous productivity which would have helped to offset the flow of dollars and thus reduce inflation.

In brief, by destroying the productivity of our older citizens —the government punishes both the retiree and the society in general by creating greater inflation and a lower standard of living.

(2) Welfare—Again, welfare recipients also represent a large non-productive segment of the society and the billions of dollars paid out monthly represent yet another inflationary infusion which is not offset by productivity. Restrictions similar to those of social security retirees are again imposed by the government. If the welfare recipient earns extra money from employment—an equal sum is then deducted from his welfare payment.

Not only does this government restriction thus create a powerful incentive not to work, but it virtually guarantees the permanent existence of a large, non-productive group of citizens dissatisfied with themselves and collectively constituting a tremendous inflationary pressure on the entire society.

Such enforced idleness is destructive of human dignity and no one will ever convince me that an unemployed person would not vastly prefer to be gainfully and productively involved.

Were the government to remove these destructive restrictions from the social security and welfare recipients—allowing them to retain additional earnings without reducing their initial benefits—not only would individuals of both these large groups be given powerful incentives for raising their own standard of living—but the tremendous additional productivity that would result would dramatically help restrain inflation and raise everyone's standard of living.

(3) Youth And The Minimum Wage Catastrophe—One of my first jobs as a young teenager was that of "call boy" at one of the large railway stations near my home. Every evening after school and on Saturdays, I would ride my bicycle over to the railway yards where the station-master would give me a list of train crews that needed to be advised of their reporting schedules for the trains leaving the yards that night. I would then bicycle around the city, advising the crews of their reporting times.

In between crews, I learned many of the intricacies of the railyard from the station-master. I learned to operate the turntable and even had an opportunity occasionally to drive one of the engines under the watchful eye of a gruff old engineer. I loved the work and at 14, I became a confirmed lifelong railroad buff.

For the 24 hours I spent each week at the yards I received a pay envelope containing $12.00—from which I bought all my clothing, schoolbooks and entertainment and about half of which I saved for future schooling.

On another occasion, the public school nearby hired me, my brothers and several friends to wash windows and polish the school floors. We worked all summer long for $.25 per hour and by the time school was ready to open each of us had earned the princely sum of nearly $200.00 and were quite proud of the fact of not only having acquired status as wage earners, but of having graduated into the "adult" world.

In those days, at the end of the depression and just before W.W.II, every teenage I knew—both male and female—had some kind of a part-time job. They delivered groceries, worked in gas stations, babysat, washed windows, clerked in stores and performed a hundred useful little jobs. Not only did they cumulatively produce a greater abundance of valuable goods and services for the community—but they learned to grow into productive adulthood. Many received an apprentice-like training that shaped the course of their future lives as adults.

In those days of the free enterprise system, there was no minimum wage law, no government regulators to bedevil the little merchant and shopkeeper and there was a job of some sort for every young man and woman. Every one found his own niche and the system worked beautifully to everyone's benefit.

Today, however, this system which once provided the youth of the country with gainful employment and invaluable learning experience has been completely destroyed by government "reformers" determined to prevent the "exploitation" of youth and the poor.

With great political fanfare and an almost Marxist zeal, the bureaucracy has now imposed the "Minimum Wage Law" upon the nation. No business, shop or individual may any longer hire an employee for less than an arbitrary wage set by the regulators.

In addition, the employer must contend with a growing volume of regulatory paperwork, including the withholding taxes, social security taxes, insurance contributions, etc., etc. The hiring of even a part-time stock-boy or even a babysitter has thus become a prohibitively expensive and incredibly burdensome task for the small shop or business.

The result is, of course, completely predictable. Tens of thousands of businesses no longer hire people for marginal jobs because of the expense and hassle created by government regulation.

The Minimum Wage Law has indeed stopped the "exploitation" of the young and the poor. That's because most of them are now no longer working.

Not only has this destructive restriction created an unemployment rate among our youth that reaches as high as 50% in some areas—but there is a direct correlation between this enforced idleness and the rising crime rate and drug usage.

Again, we have in these effects of the Minimum Wage Law a classic example of how government interference with the economic system has accomplished the exact opposite of what it had intended. In addition to destroying job opportunities for millions of our youth—the lost productivity of still another large group is further detriment to the economic health of the entire nation.

One brief analysis will dramatically illustrate just how appalling is the waste and inefficiency in the programs intended to help the poor and disadvantaged of the nation:

By official government figures there are some 25 million poor people in the United States today. If we were to equally distribute among these people just the increase of monies appropriated for social welfare programs between 1965–1980—we could have given every poor person in the United States a tax-free income of $10,400 a year or $41,600 for a family of four!!!

Poverty in the United States would have been totally abolished! There would, in fact, no longer be any poor people.

Instead, these vast sums of taxpayers money went primarily to support a sprawling, parasitic bureaucracy which not only did very little to help the poor, but which further helped to reduce the freedom and dignity of the individual by imposing an ever increasing welter of regulations and restrictions.

If we take the combined total of these three large and important groups, i.e., the senior citizens, the poor and the youth—we are talking about virtually 40% of the country's population. If a sizeable portion of these citizens were allowed to contribute their productivity the impact upon the national economy would be both immediate and dramatic. The increase in productivity would help immediately to offset the excess amount of currency in circulation—thus reducing inflation. Purchasing power of everyone's dollars would rise and so would everyone's standard of living.

It follows then that increased man-hour productivity should be a primary goal of each individual—whatever his or her age or occupation—cummulatively because it increases the wealth of the society through a greater abundance and individually because it increases the purchasing power of money received in exchange for labor. Increased productivity is, in fact, one of the major weapons in combatting and off-setting inflation and we shall again review this positive force in our "battle plan" in the next section of the book.

TAXATION

No review of survival economics would be complete without an understanding of the tax structure under which we live. Since current taxes now consume the greater portion of our gross national productivity (GNP) it is vital for the individual to understand what a significant role they play in our everyday existence.

For the average person, taxes now constitute the single greatest expense—surpassing the expenditures for food, shelter, clothing, etc., so that the avoidance and reduction of one's taxload will have a significant impact upon individual survival strategy. While taxes have been a part of mans entire civilized history, never have they been as oppressive or destructive as they are today nor have they been as threatening to the high standard of living we have previously enjoyed in this great nation of ours.

Historically, no nation has ever survived when the government taxed its citizens beyond a certain point of endurance. The Roman Empire collapsed when taxation reached the 52% level and the decline over the last two hundred years of its existence is directly paralled by the progressive rise in taxes levied upon its citizens.

During the Middle Ages, the serfs were forced to contribute 25% of their crops to the feudal lords and in the later days of colonial empire building, the kings "fifth"—or 20% of all goods and money had to be paid in taxes to the crown. Both were considered excessive taxes and in fact, our American Revolution —which was essentially a tax revolt against the British Crown— occurred when overall taxes in the colonies reached a 23% level. The fuse that ignited the French Revolution just a few years later was a combination of oppressive taxes capped by the imposition of the "gabelle"—or salt tax—which caused the masses of workers to rise in a bloody insurrection. In brief, a government which progressively takes an ever-increasing share of its citizens wealth virtually insures its own self-destruction.

Ominously, taxes today, federal, state and local—take 51% of the earnings of our citizens and that percentage will continue to rise in coming years. While the massive new tax-bill just passed in Washington will lower federal taxes, for the average person the reduction will be more than offset by the rise in Social Security taxes and increased levies by the state and local authorities seeking to make up for lost federal revenues.

A brief examination of the major tax forms will give a revealing insight into just how destructive these exactions have been to the basic principles upon which this republic was founded.

INCOME TAXES:

The most visible and probably best understood by the average citizen is the direct tax levied on income. This tax, levied upon the income of both corporations and individuals, is the greatest current revenue producer for the government. Corporations are required to pay 46% of their profits as income tax and individuals are taxed on a steeply progressive or "graduated" scale ranging from 14–50% on earned income (from work or labor) and up to 50% on unearned income (interest, dividends, etc.).

No government in history has ever before effected such a level of direct confiscation of its citizens wealth. Not only is it increasingly destructive of the very foundations of our society, but it is in direct opposition to the principles laid down by our founding forefathers.

There are elements in this system that are very little understood by the vast majority of our citizens.

In the case of corporations, for example, the 46% levy paid directly by a company is only the tip of the iceberg. The remaining 54% of the companies profits, if paid out in dividends, is again taxed as income when received by the individual stockholders. If the corporation attempts to hold onto a sizeable portion of the 54% rather than paying it all out in dividends—perhaps for a variety of good business reasons—these retained earnings are subject to a second taxation by the government as a penalty for holding onto them. Of the total earnings of a corporation, as much as 78–80% of all profits may thus end up in the governments hands as taxes!

Under such a system, the concept of private ownership and free enterprise is a myth. The so-called "owners" of our national business structure are merely caretakers for the tax collectors. Whoever collects the lions share of profits from an enterprise is actually the owner, no matter in whose name it is technically registered. While the outward facade of private ownership remains, the government, through its taxation policy has, in effect, actually "nationalized"—or brought under state control—a vast portion of our capitalistic corporate business structure, without having to concern itself with the bothersome details of actual management. In socialist and communist societies, the government takes over actual title and ownership of industries. In essence, we have accomplished the same thing through taxation while still maintaining the fiction that we are a capitalistic free enterprise system.

Not only is this confiscation in itself destructive of our national private business sector—it produces yet a second result even more deadly:

As a general rule, an industry or business must annually set aside a reserve fund of 2.9% of its gross sales for the replacement of equipment and technology in order to maintain productivity and competiveness in the marketplace.

Over the last 20 years, however, because of the increasing and crushing taxation, the private business sector has been able to set aside only 2.1% as a reserve.

The result has been a growing obsolescence nationally in our productive capacity. We are now no longer able to successfully compete with foreign steel, automobiles and a growing range of other products. We have thus begun to suffer a catastrophic loss of jobs in a growing number of industries. Taxes thus are no longer just skimming off the cream of corporate operations— they are literally cutting into the muscle of our national indus- trial structure—which in the past has created most of the em- ployment for our citizens.

In the case of the individual taxpayer, our present system, of the withholding of income tax from the workers weekly pay- check was begun during W.W.II as a "convenience" for the worker, so that he needn't be bothered with the details except to file at the end of the year.

The fact that he was deprived of the use of his money through- out the year without interest or compensation was conveniently never mentioned. The procedure was only supposed to be a wartime emergency measure, but it proved to be such a roaring success for the tax collector that it became a permanently en- shrined institution in our society.

Few people are aware of the fact that our income tax is actually in direct violation of our original Constitution. So opposed were our founding forefathers to such taxation that they expressly forbid any such enactment:

"Congress shall levy no head tax lest it be proportional ac- cording to the census."

In other words, a head (income) tax was expressly forbidden unless it was a flat tax—say $50 or $100—and that it be the same for every individual. Just as appalling and understood by even fewer people is the fact that the use of a graduated income tax —such as that in the United States today—is one of the principal planks in the Communist Manifesto. Karl Marx was highly en- thused over the use of a graduated income tax as an effective instrument for "communizing" a society.

By "leveling" all incomes through such taxation, he believed it would reduce everyone to an equal status. This would destroy the middle class—whom he hated passionately since they were the founders and chief defenders of democracy.

We now have such a graduated income tax and the destruction of our middle class is already well advanced—precisely as Marx had anticipated.

Ben Franklin, Thomas Jefferson and the rest of that venerable body of geniuses who framed our magnificent Constitution would weep in anguish if they could see our present system of taxation. They fully understood that the power to tax was the power to destroy. Through such a tax, the ruling elite could confiscate the common man's wages—thus denying him the fruits of his labor and limiting his ownership of property—both of which rights were prime objectives of the American Revolution and the very foundations of democratic freedom in the new republic. They correctly preceived that an income tax in the hands of the ruling politicians was a powerful instrument of political repression and destruction. For that very reason, as a safeguard for future generations of Americans, they wrote this clause into the Constitution specifically prohibiting the politicians from levying such a tax on income.

Until W.W. I, this far-sighted Constitutional provision protected our citizens from the tyranny of confiscation so correctly feared by our founding forefathers. Over the years, one attempt after another to destroy this clause was beaten back by Supreme Court judges upholding the worthiness of our founders wishes. And under its protection, the common man prospered and the United States became the strongest, most advanced democracy in the history of civilization. The revolutionary experiment of government of the people, by the people and for the people, begun in 1786 had come to full fruition and the first real democracy of average, middle class citizens had been accomplished.

Then, in 1913, on the eve of W.W. I and under the guise of patriotic support for "democracy", the Sixteenth Amendment—which imposed an income tax in direct violation of the original Constitution—was whisked through Congress by powerful political interests. Karl Marx and the other opponents of middle class prosperity and freedom had finally won and the worst fears of our founding forefathers had now been realized. Today, stripped of the original Constitution's protection, the middle class—the strongest defenders of our democratic principles—

are slowly and systematically being destroyed through the horrors of the graduated income tax.

Just as chilling is the fact that the Sixteenth Amendment is the only amendment which abridges and takes away one of the cherished safeguards and guarantees of individual freedom in our original Constitution. All of the other amendments expand upon and further strengthen the individual's freedom; the Sixteenth imposes a violation of individual rights directly forbidden by the Constitution. Even the language of the amendment makes no attempt to hide its purpose. It is a blunt, undisguised repeal of one of the most vital of Constitutional rights. Below is a comparison:

> ORIGINAL CONSTITUTION—"Congress shall levy no head (income) tax lest it be proportional according to the census."
> SIXTEENTH AMENDMENT—"The Congress shall have power to lay and collect taxes on incomes, from whatever source derived, without apportionment among the several States, and without regard to any census or enumeration."

With such a precedent, which allows the simple cancellation of a major Constitutional safeguard of freedom—who is to guarantee that some future Congress will not just as simply eliminate our other Constitutional guarantees of freedom? Freedom of speech perhaps, or freedom from search and seizure or the right to trial by jury. Are they not all just as vulnerable, since the precedent has already been set?

There are, in fact, serious challenges today to others of our Constitutional guarantees—such as the right to keep and bear arms, freedom of the press and the right to assemble. These are serious questions for every reader to ponder and they are not to be taken lightly—for the future of our democratic society may well be hanging in the balance.

Suffice it to say that we shall continue to pay income taxes on an ever increasing scale. While the rate at the federal level has recently been reduced, all but a few of the fifty states now level state income taxes and a growing number of cities either already level or are considering leveling still a third level of taxation on the incomes of individuals and corporations.

REAL ESTATE TAXES:

The second most visible of taxes is that levied against an individual's home or property. The principal source of revenue for local cities and counties, real estate taxes have, in fact, become so repressive that they have virtually destroyed the concept of private ownership, one of the most cherished ideals of our American society.

Originally conceived as a nominal levy on the estates of the landed gentry to help defray the costs of nominal local government services, real estate taxes today have risen to an almost unbearable level to cover the costs of schools, garbage pickups, local civil activities and an ever expanding range of local bureaucracy and services.

For the individual, the result has been catastrophe and home ownership a farce. While he technically may hold title to the property, if he is unable financially to pay his real estate taxes for 3–4 years, his property is seized by the community and sold for just the taxes due. He is not compensated for his ownership beyond the due amount and his equity is lost forever. Even if the individual is fortunate enough to have completely paid off his mortgage he will, over the next twenty years, again pay out in taxes a sum equal to the full value of the home.

In essence, the individual does not really "own" his home. He merely "leases" it from the community and is allowed to remain only as long as he continues to pay the ever-increasing taxes.

Throughout the nation today, millions of senior and poorer citizens, having struggled a lifetime to build or pay for a home, are being forced to sell their homes because they can no longer meet the unconscionable levels of real estate taxation.

SALES TAXES:

Of all visible taxes levied, one of the most punishing is the sales tax, imposed by all but a few states in the union. Originally a nominal—1–2% imposed on just the purchase of certain goods—it has been creatively expanded by our legislators to cover all goods and services and now ranges from 7–9% on virtually everything we purchase, from a product to a plumbing installation or a minor auto repair.

While the sales tax was originally designed to raise revenue for the individual state, it has proven so lucrative that almost all counties in a state now levy an additional sales tax of their own and a growing number of cities are adding still a third layer to the tax. The sales tax produces enormous sums of money for the tax collector and it falls with terrible severity on the poor and elderly who must spend all of their income for goods and services in order to survive. Such taxes therefore take a very large portion of their smaller incomes and have a dramatic negative impact on their standard of living.

Of all the aspects of the sales tax however, probably the most upsetting is the discussion in Congress of the imposition of a national "ad valorem" (according to the value) sales tax. Originated by European nations, where it is called the V.A.T. (value added tax)—it would impose a tax on every stage of manufacture or service of a product.

Let us take, for example, the simple illustration of the manufacture of a wooden kitchen table. At stage one, a log removed from the woods by a lumberjack has say, a $10.00 value. He sells the log to a saw mill and adds a 10% VAT tax, so that the saw mill pays $11.00 for the log. After sawing up the log, the finished boards now have a value of $30.00, which the saw mill operator now sells to a furniture company and adds another VAT of 10% for a total of $33.00. The table built from the boards rises to a value of say $100.00 plus another VAT of $10% or a total of $110.00 when it is delivered to the retail furniture store. The store owner finally sells the table for $200.00 plus another

10% VAT for a total of $220.00 to one of his customers.

It is conservatively estimated that the imposition of such a national VAT tax would raise the cost of all goods and services some 25–30% for the consumers of the nation. For the poor lower classes, it would be an absolute catastrophe. In spite of this, there is powerful support in Congress for the imposition of such a tax and there is a strong possibility of its enactment over the coming decade.

SOCIAL SECURITY TAXES:

Of all taxes currently imposed upon the citizens of our nation, none is more controversial than the Social Security tax—which is causing a bitter and growing devisiveness among large and important segments of our society.

There is, first of all, a large and growing population of retired senior citizens numbering upwards of 30,000,000 who are dependent upon Social Security benefits for their very survival. Throughout their long working years, these people contributed to the system and were promised a minimum level of security in their later years.

They have good reason to be concerned. A number of years ago, while working for a large insurance company, I was part of a team that developed some frightening statistics:

Of every 100 men reaching the retirement age of 65,

—7 were financially self-sufficient and could live comfortably without outside assistance;
—26 had some small savings or investment, but were dependent on outside assistance for at least 50% of survival necessities;
—67 were totally dependent on outside assistance for survival!

93% of these retiring males then, were either partially or totally dependent on Social Security for survival. For females, while the percentage was slightly lower due to the fact that a certain number were widows with insurance and estate settlements, the overall picture was nearly as grim.

The picture has not changed appreciably since then and if anything, it has gotten worse.

With the announcements in recent years that the system is going broke and that drastic cutbacks in benefits will be necessary, the explosive reactions of anger and frustration by our million of senior citizens should not at all be surprising—their very survival is at stake. The fact that the running and management of the Social Security system is now shaping up as one of the greatest financial boondoggles in the history of our nation is certainly no fault of the retirees who in good faith contributed to it. They are completely justified in demanding that the federal government honor its commitment.

As one who will shortly join these legions of retired citizens, I am personally in complete agreement with their demands and am just as indignant at having been led down the primrose path by our political leadership.

But no matter how righteous or justified the anger over the sorry mess of the system itself, we are still forced to face the grim economic realities of the situation.

In direct opposition to the needs and honest claims of our retired citizens is the grim and worsening plight of the younger working population now being taxed to support the system.

When the Social Security system was first enacted during the 1930's, there were sixteen workers for each retiree and contributions were a nominal 1% of wages with an equal amount contributed by the employer. It was assumed that these sums would be held in a fund and reinvested to obtain additional earnings for the worker upon retirement. This is the normal procedure practiced by insurance companies to create retirement annuities.

This however, was never done. Instead, contributions were paid into the general slush fund and retirement benefits simply paid out of current taxes taken from those still working. No investment earnings were ever accumulated and over the years

Congressmen seeking political leverage added benefit after benefit with no concern over where the ultimate funds would come from.

The net result today is one of the greatest financial catastrophes in American history.

There are today only three workers for every retiree and the rate of contribution for both worker and employer is nearly 7% each and rising steeply. By 1990, there will be only two workers for each retiree and if the present rate of tax increase is continued, each worker would be forced to pay 25–30% of his earnings in just Social Security taxes!! Incredible as it may seem, what we really have is a gigantic pyramid club run by our own government.

Such a situation obviously is impossible. For the worker on the lower end of the earnings scale Social Security taxes are already more burdensome than his income taxes and there are growing indications of a massive and open revolt by the working population if such taxes continue to increase.

The younger worker then has different, but equally as valid reasons for bitterness as does the senior citizen. Burdened by increasingly oppressive taxes to support a system from which he hasn't the remotest chance of ever collecting benefits for his own ultimate retirement, he is close to the point of open defiance.

If the system had actually been managed as a true retirement annuity fund, the results would have been vastly diff.erent today. Again, while working for the insurance company previously mentioned, we calculated that if the Social Security contributions of both the worker and employer had actually been placed in a true retirement fund—the earnings from reinvestment would actually give the retiree three to four times the benefits currently received by senior citizens under the Social Security system!

As a further proof of the soundness of such a proposition, federal employees, who have their own private pension fund (they refuse to join the Social Security system because they know better) into which they contribute a similar 7% of wages—draw retirement benefits three times greater than Social Security retirees!

As a final point, the reserve investment capital that would have been created had Social Security contributions been paid into an actual retirement fund would have fueled the greatest economic boom in history. This incredible amount of capital could have provided enough mortgage funds so that every family in the country could have owned their own home and it could also have financed such an unprecedented business expansion that unemployment in the nation would have been virtually wiped out.

Instead, these incredible sums of money were largely consumed by a monstrous bureaucracy and all of us—young and old —are now facing the possibility of a financial Armageddon.

The only ultimate solution to old age security is a real retirement pension fund managed by competent financial agencies who will invest these funds to create the wealth necessary for secure retirement. It must be taken out of the hands of the politicians so that it can no longer be a political football.

Until this is done, and during the present crisis where the survival of our entire senior citizen population is at issue, the current political leadership of the nation must effect an interim solution, whatever the means or format. Both the integrity and conscience of the nation is involved and no American citizen would have it otherwise.

HIDDEN TAXES:

While the forgoing visible taxes are in themselves a crushing enough burden for the taxpayer, there is still another vast range of hidden taxes which are a major contributor to our high cost of living and inflation.

These taxes are levied on every single product, service and activity in our society and they are limited only by the creative imagination of our legislators who impose them. For the average person, such taxes now take in excess of 20% of his or her total income.

There are, for example, some 47 hidden taxes in each loaf of bread we buy, hidden taxes on every telephone call and utility bill we pay. Every bottle of liquor, gallon of gasoline, package of cigarettes, etc. contains a huge percentage of taxes in their selling price. There are import taxes, transportation taxes, excise taxes, etc., etc.—all of which are ultimately passed on to the consumer, dramatically raising his cost of living. In combination, such taxes now take in excess of 20% of the average persons total income.

In all of this, we have not even touched upon the endless array of license fees and permits now required for virtually every conceivable activity, which is merely taxation under another name.

Suffice it to say that this almost endless array of hidden taxes constitutes yet another spike in the cross to which we are all collectively nailed.

And even as this book goes to press, Congress has just passed the largest peacetime tax increase in U.S. history—a record 99 Billion dollars in new and higher levies on business and consumer items. In spite of public opinion polls showing nearly 70% of the public adamantly opposed to any further increase in the already crushing tax burden—the bill was shepherded through Congress by Senator Robert Dole over fierce conservative opposition.

Coming in the midst of one of the country's worst recessions, this dramatic increase in taxation will help to cancel the benefits of last years tax cut and could well abort any meaningful recovery of the nations economy. But with or without a recovery, a still larger share of the nations productivity—and that of the individual—will now be going to the government in even higher taxes.

Since combined taxes—income, real estate, sales, Social Security and hidden levies—now constitute one of the major threats to the individual's personal survival, one of the prime objectives of our battle plan will be the avoidance and reduction of this tax-load to the greatest possible extent.

THE MARKET ECONOMY VS. THE HOUSEHOLD ECONOMY

The final economic reality that the reader must understand is that in the past several decades, the United States has changed dramatically from a traditional household economy to an almost total market economy.

For the first 150 years of our existence—until roughly about the time of W.W.I.—we were essentially an agrarian, household economy. From the colonial frontier days on through the westward development of the nation, the major economic activity centered around the independent, self-contained family household. Each individual family produced themselves most of what they consumed. They built their own houses, grew their own food, made their clothing and provided for their own transportation. The need for money was minimal and then only to buy tools and luxury items which the family could not produce themselves.

While life under this household economy was simpler and the working hours longer—there was far greater independence and families were not subject to or affected by the pressures of inflation, taxation, and regulation as they are today. There was no welfare, unemployment insurance, social security or consumer credit. But there was also far less unemployment, crime and financial instability. Each family took care of its older members and private organizations and churches took care of the sick and infirm. Regardless of industrial slumps, banking failures and foreign wars—the average family was little affected and survived quite nicely.

Most important of all—the enormous wealth of the nation was

40

centered primarily in the hands of these individual households —and beyond the reach of the politicians. It would have been quite impossible for the government to confiscate and redistribute this hard-earned wealth. The enormous transfer of wealth from the producers to the non-producers being effected by our current political leadership could never have taken place in this home-centered economy.

In the brief period from the turn of the century to W.W. II, however, the United States went through a radical change from a rural, household economy to that of a market economy. The tremendous growth of industry, machine technology and mass production techniques transformed the country into an industrial giant.

In a vast exodus, millions of people left their self-sufficient households in the country for the factories and offices of the rapidly growing urban centers. By the beginning of W. W. II only a third of the population remained in the rural areas. Today, that has dwindled to less than 3%. The economic impact upon the individual brought about by the abandonment of our earlier way of life was far reaching and permanent.

Where he had previously used his labor to produce his own goods and the things he needed—the individual now exchanges his labor for money. Since he no longer produces any of his own living necessities—he must now use money to acquire every-thing—housing, food, clothing, transportation, etc., etc. In brief, the average American today has been transformed from a formerly self-sufficient producer into a total consumer—and this massive new consumption of industrially produced goods forms the basis of the market economy in which we all now live.

Briefly defined, a market economy is one based upon a continuous cycle of the production and consumption of goods and services.

In the first part of the cycle—the production phase—the individual, along with millions of other fellow citizens, goes to work in the factories and offices of the nation. Here they collectively produce a vast array of goods and services for sale in the marketplace. In exchange for his or her labor in helping to produce these goods and services—the individual is paid a certain amount of currency (paper money).

In the second phase of the cycle, the goods previously produced by the industries are now placed on sale through still another extensive network of stores and shops. The individual, with the money received from his production labor—now assumes a second vital role. He becomes a consumer, purchasing the goods and returning the money to circulation—where it is sent back to the factories for the production of still more goods.

The business cycle of the market economy is thus complete. The individual fulfills two vital roles—producer and consumer and money is the lubricating oil that keeps the system running. As long as there is full consumption of all the goods produced and as long as the money supply is uninterrupted—production will continue, the individual will remain employed and the cycle will work successfully.

According to the conventional wisdom, this new market economy has led us out of a primitive existence and into the Garden of Eden. In this sophisticated new society, it is no longer necessary for the individual to toil from dawn to dusk to produce his own food, shelter and other necessities.

Instead, he will, along with his fellow citizens, man the factories and offices which, because of their efficient technology, can produce goods cheaper and faster than he could ever hope to do himself. Huge, mechanized farms, in addition, produce a super abundance of food with far less effort than he could hope to do. For his greatly shortened work week, he receives an excellent payment of money—with which he can purchase the super abundance created by this massive industrial and business structure. He not only helps to produce the goods for the marketplace—he also consumes them—and in the process, everyone enjoys the good life on a scale never before possible.

On the surface, it is a splendid picture and no one would deny that in the last several decades, the average American has reached an unprecedented standard of living.

But there are very dangerous pitfalls in our market economy which the conventional wisdom does not teach us and of which the average American is only vaguely aware. It is vital, however, for the individual to understand these negative factors if he or she is to survive and prosper in the coming decades.

Because of the profound economic impact on our everyday existence, the reader should carefully review and consider the following negative aspects resulting from our changeover to the current market economy:

(1) The Illusion of Cheaper Abundance.

Much has been made of the idea that the American public has been the happy beneficiary of the abundance of low-cost goods and services produced through the efficiency of our advanced technology and sophisticated equipment. Certainly shoes, automobiles, appliances, clothing, etc. can be produced abundantly and cheaply through mass production industrial techniques. Theoretically, the consumer benefits by being able to purchase inexpensive, quality goods. He is thus better off than when he had to produce these goods himself.

Unfortunately, this much-publicized concept of cheaper abundance is largely a myth. The sad fact of the matter is that while such goods are produced inexpensively, the consumers—which is everyone of us—benefits very little from our production miracles. The tremendous savings created by this industrial revolution have not been passed on to us as consumers. Instead, they have quietly been taken away by an army of middlemen, tax collectors and assorted regulators.

The incredible fact is that for virtually any item we currently purchase—the actual production cost, including labor, is only 20% of the price we pay! The remaining 80%—tacked on by forces unrelated to the actual cost—represents the savings we should have gotten and didn't.

The bottom line is that as the ultimate consumer—you pay for all of these hidden costs. Not only does the individual not benefit from the savings of the mass-production society—he pays a very high price for each item and must thus exchange a disproportionately high number of his precious hours of labor for the money with which to buy it.

(2) The Consumer Trap And The Business Cycle.

Consumerism is the indispensable foundation upon which the entire market economy is founded. As the profusion of goods pours forth from the network of plants and factories—there must be a continuous consumption of these goods for the system to survive.

During the earlier stages of our conversion from a household economy, the new system worked quite well. By the end of W.W.II, after two decades of depression and wartime shortages, there existed a huge, pent-up demand for housing, transportation, clothing and other basic necessities.

Under these conditions, the new market economy worked like a charm. Consumer demand exceeded production, there was full employment, and for the next several decades, through the 1950's and '60's, there was an explosive growth throughout the nation. Highways, cities and industry expanded at an incredible pace and the standard of living for the individual rose to an unprecedented level.

To the vast majority of our citizens, it appeared that we had entered a golden age of prosperity that would last forever. Surrounded by such seemingly unlimited affluence, huge segments of our society and especially the young, came to believe that a life of abundance was their inalienable right.

In the midst of this general state of euphoria, however, several major developments began to disrupt the system.

First of all, the political leadership, to pay for the escalating cost of a vast range of social welfare programs they had introduced—began to exact increasingly heavier taxes from workers and industry. This dealt a double blow to the worker by reducing his purchasing power and at the same time causing him to pay higher prices for the consumer goods he needed (since the manufacturers simply passed on their additional taxes by increasing the prices).

The net result was a forced drop in consumption by many workers because of reduced purchasing power.

The second major development, as we entered the 1960's, was the realization that the market for the goods we were producing was becoming saturated and that consumption was dropping. The hangover demand from W.W. II had largely been satisfied and the ability of the consumers of the nation to absorb an ever-increasing quantity and range of goods was diminishing.

Caught between these twin pressures of tax-reduced purchasing power and overproduction—our market economy had begun to falter. Put simply, we had begun to reach the limit of our ability to consume and pay for an ever-increasing production of goods and services.

The political and business leadership of the nation understood full well that we were facing a disaster of epic proportions. If consumption declined sharply, the cutback in production would result in factory layoffs and rising unemployment. This in turn would bring a sharp drop in the taxes collected, making less money available for the new social welfare programs at a time when growing numbers of people were becoming more and more dependent upon them.

If consumption continued to decline, not only would there be distrubing financial losses in the business sector—but the political implications were explosive. We were no longer a rural society that could weather such a major contraction of the business cycle—instead we were now an urban society with millions of people jammed into sprawling cities and totally dependent for existence on a continuous flow of money—whether they were employed or not. Any prolonged interruption of the money flow to these masses of people who had no other means of securing their basic necessities, could well ignite massive civil upheavals and violence in our cities.

In the earlier enthusiasm for the new market economy, none of its supporters had anticipated the far-reaching and dangerous side-effects which this transformation of the economy had brought to our society—namely, that by luring the individual off the land and into the crowded depersonalized cities, we had stripped him of his self-sufficiency and made him completely dependent upon a fluctuating monetary system for his survival. The overwhelming majority of our citizens, now living in compact urban centers had literally been made hostage to an economic system which they little understood and over which they had little or no control.

Obviously, the system had to continue no matter what the cost and by whatever means necessary. The consequences of a collapse or serious interruption would be catastrophic—and it could not be allowed to happen.

Since consumption was the key to the survival of the system —a massive and comprehensive campaign was mounted to insure that consumption would not only continue—but that it would even increase. In company boardrooms across the nation —war was declared. The long-range objective was to convert the citizens of the nation into insatiable consumers under any and all circumstances.

Never has there been a more unequal battle.

On one side were assembled the combined talents of the most creative and ablest minds in the country—psychologists, social scientists, advertising executives, bankers, economists and assorted politicians. On the other side, slightly dazed—and totally unaware that he was even in a battle—stood Mr. John Q. Public.

When the assault came—it was relentless and total.

Working from one approach, motivational research teams began to explore every nook and cranny of the human mind— not to better the well being of the individual—but to discover the psychological "hot buttons" that would induce the individual to buy. It was discovered, for instance, that because of childhood training, many people felt guilty about not brushing their teeth after every meal. Using this psychological insight, a toothpaste manufacturer increased its sales by over 300% by simply advertising that their product was for people "who were unable to brush their teeth after every meal"! Thus consumption was increased—not because there was a greater need—but because it assuaged the buyers feelings of guilt. In a similar manner, the entire range of human emotions and drives—fear, sex, love, guilt, anxiety, etc., etc.—was carefully explored and then exploited as a motivation for increased consumption.

Close on the heels of the new motivational research, came an awesome tidal wave of sophisticated marketing and advertising techniques. Supermarkets and shopping centers became emporiums of pleasure, with soft lighting and relaxing music—subtly suggesting to the individual that shopping was a pleasant and rewarding way to spend ones time and money. Simultaneously, through every channel of the communication media—T.V., radio, newspapers—he was constantly bombarded by imaginative commercials and subtle persuasions to purchase the things that made up the "good life".

Slowly and subtly, a growing number began to feel somehow deprived and unfulfilled when they did not possess these obvious symbols of success and happiness. Accordingly, they began to buy compulsively a growing range of baubles, bangles and widgets, which had nothing to do with their basic needs.

Just how successful this massive assault has been is evidenced by the fact that children today go around singing commercials instead of nursery rhymes and in a recent survey it was shown that the majority of adult Americans today regard shopping as a rewarding recreational activity that constitutes one of their major pleasures!

As the final coup de grace, the industrial and business sector now devised the ingenious new concept of "built-in-obsolescence"—a technique that would guarantee a high rate of consumption forever.

When the market economy was just beginning, the workmanship and quality of the products created by industry were superb. Automobiles, appliances, furniture, etc. were finely crafted from top-grade materials and had tremendous durability. Some of the early autos and refrigerators, built more than 30 years ago, are, in fact, still being used and with care—could probably continue to be used for years to come.

With the realization that the products they were building would last for many years—the moguls of industry were filled with a sense of horror. Once an individual had purchased a product—he would be lost as a consumer for years and the market would quickly become saturated.

Such a situation was obviously intolerable—and thus was born the concept of "built-in-obsolescence". Very simply, the previous practice of building rugged, durable products was to be abandoned immediately. Instead, it became an industry-wide policy to purposely build all products so that they would become obsolete, worn-out or even self-destruct within a very short time. To accomplish this objective, cheaper and less durable materials were used, less workmanship was invested and—to thwart home repair—increasingly complex design and structure were added.

In this manner, industry insured for itself that consumption would continue forever, since the individual would be forced to purchase the same product over and over again. No sooner had he finished paying for a product, than it would be worn-out or obsolete—and he would have to purchase another one. The cycles would continue endlessly, and once on the treadmill—the individual could not get off. In a recent survey, for example, it was shown that 80% of adult Americans are constantly indebted for monthly payments because of the need to continuously replace such basic items as appliances, automobiles, furniture, etc.

Quite aside from the economic bondage forced upon the individual, the unnecessary plunder of our precious and limited resources resulting from the introduction of this concept—will adversely affect future generations who will have to cope with greatly depleted supplies of virtually everything. And the growing mountains of rusting metals, non-biodegradable junk and rubbish created through the throw-away mentality of this concept are grim monuments to the folly of the entire system.

The combined strategies of motivational research, seductive advertising and built-in-obsolescence have won the war for the prophets and leaders of the new market economy. The consumer trap has been tightly closed and Americans have been converted into links of a gigantic cycle of production and consumption. They have become the victims, and not the beneficiaries, of the market economy—and they must continue to consume if they are to survive. It matters little whether or not they can afford the consumption—or even if they need it. If they do not have the money, the banks will loan it to them—in return for committing the next 5–20 years of their productivity. If they do not have a job—the government will put money into their hands by transferring it from those who do have it. Whatever his or her status, the system has thus insured that the individual will be regarded as a consumer above all other considerations.

As we enter the decade of the 1980's, our market economy has led us to a new and even more threatening plateau:

The average American family today has already committed or mortgaged 5–20 years of future income to pay for today's consumption. They are literally only 3 months away from bankruptcy should there be an interruption of income due to job loss or prolonged illness.

In a single decade, we have moved from a simply bad situation where the individual spent all of his current income for current consumption to where he is now hocking his future income to pay for his present standard of living. With his future income already spent—just what he will do for his future survival needs is an unanswered question—but it has frightening implications.

One of the major keys to individual survival in the coming decades will be to return to the old household economy to the greatest extent possible.

No one would seriously suggest that we all pack up our bags and move back to the farm or head into the hills—although a growing number of Americans are successfully doing just that. It would be impossible to turn back the clock to earlier times even if we wanted to. We are today an almost totally urbanized society, created by, and dependent upon, the market economy cycle and the continuous flow of money. The average American, comfortable in his modern home and apartment, and with the convenience of 20th Century gadgetry—has largely lost the survival skills demanded of our frontier predecessors. To completely produce all of his own physical necessities, to grow all of his food—the way his grandparents did—would not be possible and it would be unrealistic to expect this to happen.

But while we may not be able to return completely to the financial stability of yesterday—we can individually return to some of the basic economic principles that made the citizens of our previous household economy so much more stable and independent than we are today.

First of all—we can reject the economic bondage thrust upon us by the consumer trap. The closets, backrooms and garages of the average American today are filled with baubles, gadgets and widgets—many of which are unused and most of which are totally unnecessary to his basic needs and happiness. Persuaded by motivational researchers, advertisers and peer group pressures, that these things are vital to his well-being, he has traded his precious time and labor for this unnecessary accumulation. If he understands just how ruthlessly he is being manipulated—he will begin to dramatically reduce this unnecessary consumption and the amount of time he must work to purchase these items.

Secondly, we can stop the "throw-away" mentality cultivated by the barons of our market economy. The individual can greatly increase his productivity by learning how to repair, recycle or somehow reuse almost every item. By extending the useful life of every product or material, he not only lessens his own need for consumption—thus further escaping the consumer trap—but he will also help lessen the unconscionable plunder of our dwindling resources currently being perpetrated to the detriment of our children and grandchildren, who will be forced to ration the increasing scarcity of everything.

Finally, the individual can reap enormous rewards by consciously investing his time and money into his own household economy—and learning to run it more like the business it actually is. By investing time and money to increase the productivity of one's individual household—rather than buying the inflation ravaged goods of the market economy—we will realize a far greater return.

To give just one small example of such returns, let us examine one of the staples of our everyday life—a loaf of bread—of which the average family of four consumes slightly more than one a day. The difference in price between the natural wheat at $.10 per lb. and the loaf of bread purchased in the store at $.79 per one pound loaf—is $.69 per lb.!

If this family were to invest $150–170.00 for a high grade electric flour mill and bake their own bread, they would annually save about $303.00! That's a return of 178% on their original investment of $170.00 for the grinder!

Where in todays economy can one obtain such a return? In contrast to this extraordinary return, the same family would have had to have invested over $3000.00 in the stock market or in bank certificates @ 10% average return to earn $303.00. Or to earn this much by working, the family would have had to earn $450–600.00 before taxes.

Yet another example is the investment in a household vegetable garden. An expenditure of $40.00 in seed will produce approximately $750.00 in vegetables. And again, the individual realizes the same extraordinary economic gains. The same powerful case can be made for almost all of the basic necessities we require—food, housing, clothing, transportation, etc.

By turning inward and concentrating once again on our own households—increasing their productivity and thus lessening our consumption of outside goods of the market economy—we can escape some of the major damage being inflicted upon us.

In the final analysis—only the household economy can legitimately avoid distribution costs, inflation and taxation.

AN ECONOMIC OVERVIEW

In this first section of our manual we have briefly defined the major economic concepts—capital, money, inflation, productivity, taxation, the market and household economies—which the individual <u>must</u> understand if he or she is to successfully devise a survival strategy for the coming decade.

It should by now be quite clear that our national economic crisis and the worsening plight of the average individual can be traced directly to the political violations of the Constitution by our former leadership. First, through the Sixteenth Amendment, which unconstitutionally levied a tax on income and imposed upon the American people a major Marxist concept—the graduated income tax. The result has been the most massive confiscation and redistribution of individual wealth in history. As the average individual is forced to surrender a growing percentage of earnings—a correspondingly greater portion of the nation's wealth is thus concentrated in the hands of the Federal government—which, in turn, is spending this wealth on a growing non-productive bureaucracy and an endless range of socialistic experiments.

The second violation of the Constitution—the debasement of our national currency—has allowed the political leadership to inflate the money supply without restriction—thus further impoverishing the producers of the nation by reducing the value of the dollars left in their hands. In reality, this is nothing more than a subtle and deceptive further form of taxation.

Thus, while both of these factors are now solidly entrenched and sanctioned by the courts and political leadership—they remain complete violations of the Constitution and the principal causes of our present economic crisis.

While the picture presented is hardly pleasant, and certainly not what the conventional wisdom would have us believe—they are nonetheless the harsh economic realities with which all of us today are faced. Understanding them is the first and most important step in creating effective countermeasures for survival. Again, you cannot effect solutions until you first understand what the problems are.

Having defined our major economic problems, in the following section we shall now examine some very effective techniques and methods for solving these problems. Finally, in Part III, the reader will be shown how to devise an individual "battle plan" for his or her own successful survival strategy.

PART II

ECONOMIC SURVIVAL TECHNIQUES

ECONOMIC SURVIVAL TECHNIQUES

In this section, we will outline specific survival secrets in all major areas (housing, food, clothing, etc.) that you may use in your own individual plan later on.

While specific survival strategies will vary somewhat from one person to another, depending on the individual needs, wants and abilities, the most successful strategies will always follow three basic principles. So important are these principles that we should here briefly review them before examining specific techniques.

Memorize these following three points and keep them in mind as you begin to develop your own survival strategy:

(1) AIM FOR SELF-SUFFICIENCY.

The less dependent you are on outside forces, the higher your survival level will be. This nation was built on rugged self-reliance and individualism and it is still the most productive philosophy. Wherever possible, produce your own housing, food, clothing, etc. This is less difficult than you think and we shall explore this in detail later on.

Above all else, try to avoid asking the government for anything. It should by now be obvious that there are no "free benefits" and that Uncle Sam is us. For every "free benefit" we obtain from the government, we automatically create another bureaucracy and with the additional taxes we will have to pay to support it—the "free benefit" will cost us four times as much as if we just went out and got it ourselves without involving the

57

government. There is no greater cause of inflation than this excessive government spending. The quicker we get government off our backs and out of our pockets, the lower will be the inflation rate and the better off we all will be.

While circumstances may make it impractical or even impossible for some individuals to be completely self-sufficient, each individual should strive to be self-reliant in as many areas and to the greatest degree possible. For the individual, becoming more self-sufficient brings a truly satisfying sense of accomplishment and collectively, the more of us that are successful in reaching a high level of self-sufficiency, the better will be the economic health of the nation as a whole.

(2) AVOID THE USE OF MONEY.

Since money (paper currency) is the principal instrument through which inflation is forced upon you and since it is also the medium through which the tax collector is able to siphon off a large portion of wealth produced by your labor—you are twice victimized as long as you continue to use money in exchange for the necessities of your existence.

For example, let us say that you earn $5.00 per hour and you need a product or service that costs $40.00. If you use money —that is, if you pay for the product in dollars—you must actually work 12–16 hours in order to obtain that specific item. Because taxes generally will take 30–50% of the total number of dollars paid for your labor—you will need to earn $60–80.00 in order to have $40.00 left for the purchase of the product. And since the dollars themselves have far less real value than their face value (because of the inflated paper money supply) the $40.00 being asked is a highly inflated price far beyond the actual value of the item.

You therefore are going to exchange 12–16 hours of your precious time and labor—which does have a real and constant value—for a product or service that probably has an actual value worth no more than 2–3 hours of your time and labor. This is

a terrible price to pay for that item and is an excellent illustration of the grim reality of being caught between the twin horrors
of taxation and inflation.

But if you do <u>not</u> use money to pay for the product or service
—if instead, you exchange your labor <u>directly</u> for the item—you
will get a much fairer return and beat the inflation trap by
avoiding it altogether.

There are two ways of exchanging your labor for goods and
services:

(A) Using your time and labor to produce the goods or service
yourself. If you are able to do so—you will completely avoid
both taxes and inflation.

(B) If you are not able to produce the goods or service yourself
—you may be able to barter—exchange your labor in return for
the goods or service from the other party.

In either instance, <u>2–3 hours</u> of your labor will probably be
adequate—a far better arrangement than having to labor <u>12–16
hours</u> when dealing with a money transaction.

While the I.R.S. has ruled that barter is subject to the same
tax rules as using cash—if you only "barter" or exchange
say <u>4 hours</u> of your labor rather than the original <u>16 hours</u>
needed for a cash transaction—your taxes will be <u>75% less</u>! You
still come out a winner.

Again, while there are a number of instances where the use of
money is unavoidable—you will be amazed at how many of your
needs and services can be obtained <u>without</u> the use of money.
The more you can avoid the cash economy, the fuller your life
and the higher your standard of living will be.

(3) <u>INCREASE YOUR PRODUCTIVITY.</u>

Regardless of your age, sex or occupation—give top priority
to improving your productivity as an individual. There is no

quicker or better way to beat inflation than by increasing the value and quantity of goods and services produced by each hour of your labor.

It makes no difference what the activity or service you perform —if you can do it better and faster, you will quickly and dramatically raise your income and keep yourself well ahead of inflation. Whatever your skill or speciality—improve upon it. If you do not have a particular skill—learn one; it will be the best investment of time you will ever make.

The major factors in increasing one's productivity are knowledge and tools. If, for example, a mechanic using certain tools can repair an automobile in half the time it would normally take without these tools—then his investment in the tools will double his productivity and increase his income.

If a gardner, through careful observation, discovers that by using a different planting arrangement, he will get four bushels of tomatoes instead of three from the same garden plot—he has increased his productivity through knowledge and he will thus have more to eat or sell from the same amount of time and labor invested.

These two examples are very simple illustrations of increased productivity.

Because of the impact on the individual's standard of living, we shall explore this principle of increased productivity in greater detail as we proceed further into the development of our inflation survival strategy.

In general, the most successful and productive survival strategy—regardless of your individual circumstances—is based upon these three forgoing principles:

(1) Self-sufficiency
(2) Avoidance of money
(3) Increased productivity.

Follow these three principles and you will not only survive the ravages of inflation, but you will also learn how to prosper in the midst of it. The basic reason for the success of these principles is that through them you receive the maximum value for your time and labor—which is the only real wealth that exists—and you avoid the exploitation which the current system thrusts upon all of us.

Let us now examine specific methods for beating the ravages of inflation and taxes. Each of these techniques has proven highly effective and will definitely cut your costs and increase the amount of money that stays in your pocket. Collectively, these combined techniques give the individual a fighting advantage he or she has probably not previously enjoyed.

Carefully review each of the suggested techniques in all of the major areas and start making a list of those that you feel you will be able to use. While some may not be applicable to your individual situation—the more that you can later work into your "battle plan"—the more you will benefit.

Conservation

with taxes and inflation, a penny saved is ten cents
rned!

CONSERVATION

The whole concept of conservation runs counter to our present culture. Over the last 50 years, the market economy—with its concepts of "built-in-obsolescence" and "disposable" products —has developed in the American people a wasteful and destructive "throw-away" mentality. Not only is this a shameful waste of precious and limited resources—but we face the threat in coming years of perishing ignobly under a tidal wave of garbage. Future historians may well calculate the vanished wealth of our 20th century society by measuring the mountains of junk on the sites of our former cities.

For the individual struggling to cope with the ravages of inflation—this passion for discarding things carries a very high price tag in the annual battle for survival. It has been conservatively estimated that with disciplined conservation, the cost of living could be reduced by at least 20%! Since the average family spends approximately $7–8,000 per year on goods and services, that works out to about $1500 in cost of living savings—a very considerable sum of money.

And even that, I am convinced, is a very low rate of savings. In the case of my own family—all of whom are dedicated conservationists—I have calculated that regularly practiced conservation has reduced our cost of living by more than 40% over the years, without reducing our standard of living. I know of a number of others who have done even better.

For example, national statistics show that each American produces nearly ¾ of a ton, or 1500 pounds of garbage a year. For my family of ten, that would mean almost 8 tons a year. However, since we rarely throw <u>anything</u> away, and so completely do we recycle or reuse virtually everything—that we ultimately cancelled the weekly garbage service because there was never anything for them to pick up.

We routinely separated all items into five categories: bottles, cans or containers, metal, paper goods and actual garbage. The garbage we placed in a large compost bin which later provided superb fertilizer for our vegetable garden. The bottles, containers and metals, if we could find no further productive use for them (and we discovered many)—we sold to commercial recyclers. The paper goods had a wide vareity of other uses from insulation to packing to fuel.

Each year, as our accumulation of useful and reusable items increased through conservation—our outside purchases and cost of living steadily declined until we reached a point of nearly complete self-sufficiency in most of the normal household necessities.

There is no magic to reaping the definite economic benefits of conservation—which includes a more productive use of our society's resources and a lowering of the individual's cost of living—it is simply a matter of developing a more disciplined system of conservation in our consumption habits.

To create a system of <u>productive</u> conservation, there are three specific habits which the individual should develop:

(1) <u>EXPAND THE USES OF ITEMS OF MARGINAL UTILITY</u>

A huge number of items produced by our market economy have only a <u>marginal utility</u>—meaning that they have only a single or limited use—and are thrown away when they have served this purpose. Such things as bread wrappers, plastic milk jugs, styrofoam packing, etc. are good examples of items of marginal utility. Once used, they are discarded into the garbage can and used no further.

But while these items may have limited use—they are nonetheless expensive to produce and since they are added to the cost of the product, they raise the cost of your consumption quite substantially.

For example, when you buy a gallon of milk, the $.10 cost of that nice plastic container (and it may even be more now)—represents approximately 5% of the price you pay at the checkout counter. Even the lowly paper bag, at $.06–.08 a piece probably raises the overall cost of your groceries by about 1% since it must be included in the store's cost of doing business.

But if you expand the use of these materials beyond the marginal utility for which they were created—you increase your own economic well being. You've already paid for the product, so instead of discarding it—make it serve you further at no additional cost.

If for example, you cut the plastic milk jug in two—the bottom part makes a great planter and will save you the cost of a $2.00 flower pot. The top part makes a super funnel and will save you another $.98 at the hardware store. These jugs make excellent covers for new plants, storage for water, grains, bolts, nails, etc. One summer, my sons and I used some 80 of these jugs to build a four-man pontoon raft and a paddle water bike which gave us endless hours of enjoyment.

The number of items of normally marginal utility is endless. However, if you retain these items and put them to further use —it will save you substantial sums of money by not having to buy many household items you've been accustomed to buying.

The following partial list of some of these items that can be reused and save you money will give you a good idea of the concept. As you develop the habit, you'll come up with many more.

Reusable items:

(a) Aluminum foil. Can be used as an insulator, reflector, moisture barrier, etc.

(b) Zippers from worn out clothing. New Ones cost from $.80–$1.30.

(c) Nuts, bolts, springs, hinges, etc. from broken down or worn-out appliances. Remove them and save them. New ones are very expensive.

(d) Plastic bags, bread wrappers and sheets of plastic. All have an infinite variety of uses and will save you the cost of buying high-priced sandwich bags, food containers, etc.

(e) Coffee cans make fine containers for almost everything from food to nuts and bolts. Covering them with cloth or contact paper can even make them decorator items.

(f) Glass jars can be reused for storage or canning. Purchasing new ones can be quite expensive.

(g) Newspapers make excellent insulation, under carpets or in the walls. Rolled into paper logs, they are good fuel for the fireplace or woodstove.

(h) Plastic containers, butter dishes, and dish soap bottles can be put to a variety of other household uses.

(i) Metal cans and bottles. If you can't find a use for them, they'll bring a good price from salvage and recycling companies.

In general, almost all so-called "disposable" items can be reused again for something, so don't throw anything away until you're certain you can find no other use for it. You'll be surprised at how much this habit will save you over a period of time.

(2) EXTEND THE LIFE OF ALL APPLIANCES, TOOLS AND EQUIPMENT.

No matter what the item, if it breaks down, try to repair it instead of discarding it and buying a new one. As a general practice, if you can get a few more years of use out of every item —you'll save an unbelievable amount of money. A recent illustration of such repairs will give you a rough idea of just how incredible these savings can actually be.

Several months ago, within the space of a few weeks time, I

repaired three small appliances—a toaster, a coffee-maker and a plastic wind-up clock. The clock, retail price of $11.95, at one-year old, had reached its maximum life span since, with the stress of daily winding, the plastic stem had become stripped, so that the clock was no longer functional. This was its "built-in-obsolescence" factor. Since the clock could no longer be wound, it could not function and the normal reaction would be to go out and buy another clock—at a cost of another $11.95.

Instead, I removed the casing, and discovering the internal works to be sound, I replaced the plastic wind-up stem with a homemade metal one. I estimate the clock will now function effectively for at least three more years—saving me $35.85 over this future period!

With the five year old coffee-maker, now retailing at $23.99, I removed and replaced the corroded electrical wires on the underside with new ones at a cost of less than $.20 and it works as well as it did when new. We will get at least another three years of usage, for another savings of $23.99 over that time.

On the four-year old toaster—now retailing at $34.00—I replaced a burned out element with one I had on hand, saving still another $34.00.

On all three repairs, I spent less than one hour—for a total savings of $93.84 over the next three years. Moreover, this $93.84 was after-tax savings. If I had to go out and earn enough money to buy these three new appliances, I would have had to earn $187.68 before taxes! So actually my real savings was $187.68!! Not bad for a mere hour of conservation repair!

To carry this illustration just a bit further, if I were to spend only 10 hours a year making such repairs—and I normally spend far more than that—it is obvious that I would save the astounding total of $1876.80 for these few hours of labor!! Such conservation really pays. It's tax-free and it's money in your pocket.

There is a very simple formula to help you calculate the real value of such conservation repairs and which will quickly show you how much you are saving by making the effort:

First, take the current retail price of the item (which is what you will have to pay if you buy a new one). Let us say that you have a small 5 year old appliance which has just broken down and the current price for a new one is $20.00. In all probability, you paid only $10–12.00 five years ago when you bought your present one—so you are now facing an inflation penalty of 50–80% if you buy the new one.

Now take the $20.00 price and double it to $40.00—which is what you will have to earn before taxes in order to have the $20.00 left to buy the new appliance. So $40.00 is actually the amount you will save by repairing the appliance. Use this same formula to calculate the cost of anything you have to go out and buy (and in reverse, the amount you are saving if you repair and extend the life of the item).

This is a very simple economic principle, but many people do not grasp its true significance because they do not understand the real nature of inflation and taxation. However, because such conservation practices score a knockout blow to both inflation and taxation—the individual who systematically develops such habits can save amazing amounts of money. In fact, not practicing conservation—following instead the wasteful spending habits taught by our market economy culture makes the individual the victim of inflation and taxation and accounts for his or her high cost of living.

There is virtually no item or product which cannot be repaired and its useful life extended. Engines can be overhauled, elements in appliances replaced, broken tools mended, furniture rebuilt, pots and pans rehandled etc., etc. Even a hole in a plastic pail can be resealed and torn rubber boots easily revulcanized. If you don't know how to do it—there is someone else around who does and there is a growing volume of books, magazines and articles to assist you in becoming an expert "fixer-upper."

Aside from helping you to win the battle against inflation and taxes, the feeling of self-sufficiency that such conservation brings is truly exhilarating. So begin to practice such conservation. The benefits it will bring to your life cannot be exaggerated.

(3) PRACTICE PERSONAL ENERGY CONSERVATION.

While it may not be apparent to other than a student of economics—your energy and time have a definite and real value, and the effectiveness with which you use them has a decided impact on your economic well-being.

For example, if it takes you twice as much time and energy to complete a task as it should—then your <u>productivity</u> has been cut in half and you have definitely suffered an economic loss— to say nothing of the negative psychological impact. Such cumulative inefficiency will lead to a general lack of accomplishment and a negative self-image. In our frantic and competitive society, the complexities of just mere existence are often so overwhelming that much of the individual's precious time and energy is wasted on compulsory trivialities.

The way to beat the game is to conserve your personal time and energy through organization. Set up energy saving systems and before you rush in furiously to do something—spend a few minutes in planning. Don't, for example, rush out to the grocery store every time you discover you're out of a specific item. Instead, write the item down on a "needed" list on a kitchen bulletin board. When you have a number of items—make just <u>one</u> trip instead of five or six. If you have a number of errands, don't run back and forth on each one individually—set up an itinerary and do them all on one swing.

Over the years, I have created little energy-saving systems for most of the tasks confronting me. In cutting the back lawn, for instance, getting into the corners and under the bushes was a time-consuming and frustrating task. So I created attractive rock gardens in all the corners and around each bush. I was then able to cut the lawn in continuous circle sweeps in half the time and with far less energy.

I mark up a large wall calendar with future things that need to be done, noting specifics and actions necessary. Each morning at breakfast I glance at the current date and thus rarely forget or neglect anything of importance. I keep a "To Do" list on my desk and once a week, I sit down and do them all at once —thus minimizing the time and conserving my energy through the rest of the week for other things I wish to do.

By "grouping" activities and setting aside specific times for specific things—I have tremendously increased my efficiency and productivity and minimized the energy in so doing. At the same time, I have also greatly increased my leisure and recreational time—a treasured prize even if there were no economic gains. So for further conservation gains—give consideration to the idea of saving your time and energy through better organization.

In the final analysis, this systematic conservation has been one of the real secrets of our family's successful economic survival and prosperity. We never throw away anything and we make everything last five times longer than it was meant to. We repair, rebuild, refurbish and reuse, and we buy less from the outside economy. In the process, we have learned carpentry, plumbing, electronics, mechanics, a dozen crafts and we have all become expert survivalists. I truly believe that we could survive successfully no matter what the outside rate of inflation or taxation, since we have largely withdrawn from its clutches. On the basis of our experience, I would strongly urge the reader to begin a practiced conservation at the earliest possible time.

SUMMARY OF THE ECONOMIC BENEFITS OF CONSERVATION

TECHNIQUES	NET SAVINGS
3 CONSERVATION METHODS	20–60%

Barter

—you did make a good swap for this cow, Mr. Fields. But surely you must relize that we're entitled to our share of all barter transactions.

BARTER

Barter, which is the direct exchange of goods and services without the use of money, is an ancient and honored practice as old as civilization itself.

In our current society, bartering—precisely because it avoids the use of money—is a super technique for reducing the impact of taxes and inflation and even of avoiding them altogether. There are no complicated rules, no gimmicks and it is completely legal. As a result, bartering today is enjoying an explosive growth throughout the nation.

As the movement grows, dozens of barter clubs, swap sheets, trading magazines and other less formal avenues of exchange are beginning to provide an almost unlimited range of goods and services for barter. With a little effort and practice, it is now possible to obtain virtually all of the economic necessities through barter—real estate, food, clothing, transportation, services, etc. The individual thus has the option through barter of reducing his or her costs of taxes and inflation by 20%, 50% or even in some instances by 100%.

For the individual, there are essentially two major approaches to the benefits of bartering:

(1) JOIN A BARTER CLUB.

Barter clubs were created to facilitate the exchange of goods and services among the members of the club. Most clubs charge an initial membership fee and each member has an open account of "credits" or "points" which are used instead of money. Credits are added to the members account for the goods and/or services he or she contributes and credits are subtracted for the goods and services used. Such a system allows for greater flexibility and a greater range of barter opportunities than would a simple or direct exchange of goods and services between two parties mutually seeking the other's services.

For example, let us say a dentist who needs an addition on his home is willing to barter his dental services in return for the construction services. Under a direct barter or swap, however, he must find a carpenter who needs his teeth fixed in order to effect such an arrangement. This may or may not be difficult.

Under the club credit system, however, the dentist will simply fix any club member's teeth—for which he gains so many plus credits that can then be used to "buy" the construction services of a club member carpenter who in turn may use his credits so gained to "buy" any other services or goods offered by the club. Members may thus avail themselves of the entire range of goods and services of the club without ever directly bartering or swapping with each other. In brief, you have the same range and level of economic exchange of goods and services that normally takes place in our modern society except that club "points" or "credits" are used as a medium of exchange instead of money.

Officially, the I.R.S.—which understandably is less than ecstatic over this dynamic growth of bartering—has ruled that "the receipt of such services by club members constitutes taxable income to the extent of their fair market value."

This means, for example, that if the club dentist and carpenter would each have received say $1,000 for their work had they charged cash—that they must declare that amount as taxable income when they file their annual income tax return.

This ruling, it should be pointed out—affects only services exchanged. If goods of equal value are traded at cost—then there is no capital gain—hence no tax, because there is no basis for it. If, for example, you trade a kitchen table and chair set, for which you paid, say $250, for a $250 lawnmower, then you have had an even exchange, and there is no tax liability.

Concerned about the growing volume of this exchange of

services, the I.R.S. has begun to compel barter clubs to turn over their membership lists so that they can determine if the members are properly declaring there bartered services for tax purposes. Considering the sheer volume and increasing number of people involved, the I.R.S., already short on manpower, may well find this to be a task of monumental proportions.

But even assuming the possibility of a meticulous monitoring of every barter club member and an exact payment of taxes on the fair market value of all services—a barter club member still comes out a real winner in the economic battle. The economic gains are still quite real and the savings most impressive:

(A) Even with the payment of taxes on the "fair market value" of bartered services, the average individual still realizes a net savings of 20%–50% on the services he receives!

For example, let's go back to the case of the dentist who received the $1,000 worth of carpentry services from his club. We shall assume that he is in the 50% tax bracket, so that he will have to pay an additional $500 in income taxes, so that his total cost of the services he received comes to $1500.

However, if instead of obtaining these services through the barter club, he had gone out in the marketplace to buy them for cash—it would have cost him $2290:

(1) Since the $1,000 is *after tax* money, @ 50% income tax rate, he would first have to earn $2,000
(2) As a self-employed person, he would also have had to pay Social Security taxes @ 11%, an additional 220
(3) On the purchase of $1,000 of services in the marketplace, an additional 7% sales tax 70

Total Earnings Necessary if Cash is Used $2,290

Therefore, at a $1500 cost through the barter club, the dentist paid $790 less—or a net savings of 34.5% over the cash cost!

If we use the same analysis on an individual in a low income level and at the very bottom of the tax system—14% instead of 50%—the savings would still be $154 or 13.5% gain over the use of cash on $1000 worth of services.

Therefore, even though you are obligated to pay income taxes on the fair market value of your service exchanges, belonging to a barter club can still save you a lot of money and reduce your cost of living substantially.

(B) Tight money or lack of cash in our market economy often poses a serious threat to small businessmen and professionals who often require a substantial flow of capital to remain in operation. Not only does a lack of operating capital threaten their continued existence—but even if they are able to secure the necessary funds, the exhorbitant rates of interest may well destroy their decreasing margins of profit.

Barter through a club or trade exchange can often mitigate these evils of the cash economy, permitting a free exchange of goods and services in addition to the substantial savings on taxes and bank interest. In times of economic crisis—such as now exists—it could well make the difference between success or failure.

(C) Surplus or unwanted goods can easily be traded through a club or exchange for goods or services that are more appropriate to the individual's specific wants or needs, thus reducing or eliminating additional expenditures and helping to lower the overall cost of living.

The average family normally has a substantial number of items which they no longer use or need. By trading or bartering such goods for items which they do need—they are upgrading their standard of living by simply rearranging the wealth they already possess.

For the average person, membership in a barter club can bring savings of 20–50% on the goods and services which are exchanged. Most cities today have at least one or more barter clubs or exchanges and a quick look through your telephone book will tell you what's available locally.

If your local area does not have a barter club, try writing to:

International Association of Trade Exchanges
5001 Seminary Road, Suite 310
Alexandria, Virginia 22311

This association represents some 200 barter organizations throughout the United States and you might ask them for a list of their membership or the names of those clubs closest to the place where you live.

(2) BARTER DIRECTLY ON YOUR OWN.

Informal barter has always been a strong element in both our social and economic culture. The early settlers and pioneers depended heavily upon each other for an infinite range of goods and services. In a developing society where cash was scarce or often non-existent—bartering was essential. Exchanges of labor and materials for home-building, food production and household necessities were the rule rather than the exception.

In contrast to our society of today, which too frequently evaluates the worth of individuals by the size of their bank accounts and financial statements, our former more primitive—but far more vital society—placed as much value on human needs and concerns as it did on commodities. Because such a barter or exchange of services required an active, personal involvement with others, and because each one's service was essential to the survival of the entire community—each person developed a strong sense of personal self-worth as an individual—something often denied to many in our present impersonal, materialistic culture.

Instead, our cities today are filled with scores of people who feel isolated and unwanted. Because there is no demand for their services, they have a minimum of interpersonal relationships with others and there is difficulty in establishing a sense

of self-worth and value as an individual. This is particularly true
of the elderly, the teenagers and the unemployed whose valuable services and time go unused, representing a loss to themselves and the entire community.

So quite aside from filling the economic needs of our former
society, bartering—because it required a direct and active in-
teraction between people and because it made productive use
of everyone's services—provided a profound social and psychological benefit to the individual. Our emphasis today upon a
cash economy has done far more than to increase the flow of
merchandise—it has also done much to destroy the involvement
of the individual in the surrounding society. And in the final
analysis it is involvement which mainly determines the qualify of
one's life.

I personally believe that for the average person, barter is the
way to economic freedom. It is inflation-proof because the value
of services exchanged does not fluctuate no matter what the
outside economy does. If you babysit your neighbors children
in return for his mowing your lawn, the value of these services
remains constant—regardless of whether there is inflation, de-
flation, banking failures, depression or prosperity. The vast majority of human needs are not dependent upon money—whether
it be dollars or doughnuts—and bartering is a marvelous way to
satisfy most of them. Moreover, bartering in itself marks a return
to the simpler, more direct way of life of our former household
economy—which ultimately is the only solution to the growing
chaos and instability of our current market economy.

It has been recently estimated that some 35–40 million Americans are now involved informally in direct bartering to some
degree. This ranges from a simple swapping of household services such as babysitting, lawn maintenance, etc. to the exchange of services and equipment at a high level of business
activity.

The I.R.S. has ruled that the bartering or swapping of simple,
"in kind" services between relatives and friends is not subject
to taxation and does not have to be reported. However, beyond
this level, the exchange of goods and services represents taxable

income "at fair market level" and should be reported. It's up to the individual to keep track of his or her transactions.

While bartering through a club brings very substantial savings in goods and services, bartering informally and directly will bring the individual just as great—and often greater—reductions in the cost of living. Savings can range from 20–80%, and with a little ingenuity, as high as 100% in some instances.

To become involved in direct barter, there are several major points for the beginner to consider:

(A) Locating the goods or services you are seeking or trading partner for the things you wish to barter is the first and principal step. First, check to see if there is a local swap group—not a club —but an informal group who barter and trade groups and services in your area. There are many such groups that have formed in recent years and can be most helpful in getting you started.

Next, find out if there are any local barter publications, swap sheets, etc. Again, many such publications have also sprung up recently in response to the growing trend toward barter. Also, placing a small ad in the local Pennysaver, or a notice on laundromat bulletin boards, etc. announcing your desire to barter will bring quick response from others who are interested. Local bartering partners are, of course, the easiest and most convenient with which to deal.

Thirdly, you may wish to subscribe to one or more bartering magazines who bring people together from around the nation with a vast range of goods and services available. These are not clubs and you deal directly with other persons who wish to barter. The magazines simply tell you who they are and what they have to offer.

Two such recent bartering magazines that you may wish to write to are:

Barter News
P.O. Box 3024
Mission Viejo, CA 92690

The Traders Journal
P.O. Box 1127
Dover, N.J. 07801

Both will send you information on their magazines which can get you started in bartering with others all across the nation.

(B) <u>Properly structuring the exchange</u> is the second major point. Determining the proper value for each of the goods or services being traded is very important and must be negotiated by the two parties who are bartering. In general, there are several guidelines that can be followed in arriving at an agreement:

(1) In the exchange of services, it is normally best to consider all skills as being equal. For example, my skill as a mechanic is equal to yours as a plumber, so that we do not need to make fine distinctions in that area in our exchange of services. While it can be argued that the skill of say a dentist is higher than that of a mechanic—the main point is that each is supplying the other with a needed service and both are avoiding the use of money and the impact of higher taxes and inflation.

A better basis for a fair exchange then is the amount of time involved in the rendering of each one's service. If the amount of time is relatively equal—then an even swap is a good exchange. If the amount of time is very unequal, then the adjustments can be made in the exchange.

(2) In the exchange of goods, much wider differences will exist. With each item, the age, condition, scarcity or availability, current replacement cost, etc. must all be considered. However, these factors can all be easily evaluated and a barter arrangement reached if both parties are reasonable and objective.

(3) If <u>material costs are going to be</u> involved in a barter agreement then these costs should be paid up-front by the party receiving that specific service. Full understanding and agreement should be made at the beginning of the exchange so that there will be no further difficulties.

As the crisis of our current market economy worsens—barter is a splendid and proven way out of dependence on a money system with its creeping confiscation of personal wealth and productivity. In the end, it may be the only means of survival in our present society. Development of your bartering skills will not only dramatically reduce your present cost of living—it will also provide you with an indispensable survival tool no matter what the nature of our future economic upheavals.

Finally, and most important of all—bartering will bring you a more active and fulfilling lifestyle through your involvement with an enormous range of other people.

So get involved in bartering—the benefits are too extensive not to.

SUMMARY OF BARTER TECHNIQUES

TECHNIQUES	NET SAVINGS
(1) JOIN A BARTER CLUB	20–50%
(2) BARTER DIRECTLY ON YOUR OWN	20–80%
TOTAL POSSIBLE SAVINGS	20–80%

Housing

—recent surveys indicate that Americans are opting for smaller and less expensive housing.

HOUSING

The first major concern of the individual is that of housing—which must either be rented or purchased.

For Americans particularly, home ownership has not only been one of the most cherished of objectives, but one of the major factors of stability in our society. Some 70% of American families own their own home—a record unmatched by any other nation and this widespread ownership has had a profound economic and psychological impact upon the development of our culture.

From the economic view, this historical drive for ever-expanding home ownership has created a huge construction industry which directly and through dozens of supporting supplier industries, employs millions of workers. The banking, insurance and real estate activities catering to the buying and selling of homes constitute still further related economic enterprises. Collectively, housing construction and its related industries account for a significant share of our total national economy, providing jobs and business profits for millions of our citizens.

Psychologically, it would be difficult to overemphasize the impact of home ownership on the individual and the community. For the individual, such ownership is often a life-long ambition. Not only is a home a sound investment—possibly the only secure one he or she will ever make—but it is a refuge, an island of stability in a world of change, a repository of the fruits of years of toil and sweat. It is a place of pride. Man has a deep inner need to feel that there is a specific place or niche that belongs to him and having his own home brings him a great sense of security. Americans historically have been willing to make great sacrifices to achieve this ownership and as home owners their interest in the surrounding communities has produced an active civic-minded society of great stability. The right to home ownership has become a solidly entrenched part of the American dream.

We may, however, be witnessing the passing of an era in American history.

Today, inflation, scarcity of money and prohibitively high interest rates have all but excluded the vast majority of Americans —particularly young couples seeking their first home—from achieving home ownership. In desperation, many young couples are entering into agreements that can only end in disaster.

For example, a former student of mine wrote to me not long ago from a city in the midwest. After four years of penny-pinching struggle, she and her husband had managed to save $10,000 which they used as a down-payment on a $72,000 home, a modest 3-bedroom ranch home. Elated at being homeowners, they happily glossed over the enormous and potentially destructive obligation they had undertaken.

Given the term and interest rate of their mortgage, I calculated that they would ultimately pay more than $250,000 for their home! Moreover, with a combined annual income of $25,-000, the monthly payments of $734.00 per month (plus taxes) will take 40% of their total income. Should either of them become ill or lose their job—they will possibly forfeit the house and all of their investment.

In a similar situation, still another young couple in a nearby town—and with even less income—have committed themselves to monthly payments of over $800.00 per month, roughly 50% of their income!

Such purchases are almost certain prescriptions for disaster.

Suffice it to say that these examples are becoming all too prevalent and they serve to illustrate at once both the desperate desire for home ownership and the tragedy of our current economic situation which is rapidly destroying one of the most cherished of American dreams.

The rental market is just as ominous. Bedeviled by the same high interest rates and ever more crushing real estate taxes, investors are ceasing to build new rental units. For the hardy few still in the game, they must today rent their new units for $550–650.00 per month in order to cover costs and a return on investment. Such prices exclude the vast majority of citizens seeking to rent. There is today a dwindling supply of rental units across the country and as the shortage grows there will be a strong upward rise of rental costs for everyone.

In the midst of this depressing picture, however, there are positive and productive approachs that will solve or alleviate the problem. Carefully review each of the following for application to your own specific housing situation.

(1) PREPAY YOUR MORTGAGE.

Very few people understand the awesome impact of compound interest in a finance contract and just how much money it actually generates over a long period of time.

For example, under the compound interest principle, if you were to loan someone $1,000 at 17% interest over a 30 year period—you would get back the incredible sum of $5,132.5— 5 times the amount loaned or a return on your money of over 500%! This is the financial magic of compound interest and it is a veritable goldmine for banks, finance companies and anyone else involved in the consumer credit game.

One of the interesting anecdotes from our American Revolution is an incident in which George Washington quartered his horse in a local stable and ordered that it be groomed and fed. Short of money, he signed a voucher due and payable by the Continental Congress for the bill of approximately $100.00. The unpaid voucher—just recently discovered— was currently calculated to have a compound interest due of over $4,000,000!!

This same compound interest principle is currently applied to the financing of houses, automobiles, appliances and the entire range of consumer purchases. To illustrate the mind-numbing obligation this creates for the individual currently buying a house, let us examine a specific mortgage:

Let us say that John and Mary are buying a home for $50,000. They have made a downpayment of $20,000 and the local bank has agreed to give them a 20 year mortgage of $30,000 at 17%, the current interest rate.

John is a little concerned when he discovers that the monthly payments on a 20 year mortgage for $30,000 will run a hefty $440.05 per month—plus taxes and insurance. His friendly local banker, however, helpfully points out to him that if he takes a 30 year mortgage instead of the 20 year one—that his payments will be only $427.71 per month.

John has more reason to be concerned than he realizes, and a quick glance at the sums involved will show that he is hardly getting a bargain on either one of these mortgages:

$30,000 @ 17%	MONTHLY PAYMENT	TOTAL AMT. PAID
(1) 20 year mortgage	$440.05	$105,612.00
(2) 30 year mortgage	$427.71	$153,975.61

If John takes the 20 year mortgage—he will have to pay back $105,612.00—3½ times what he borrowed!! If he takes the 30 year mortgage, he will pay back $153,975.61—5 times the original amount!!!!

While either of these dizzying sums is alone enough to give one instant spasms, the payment differential between the two mortgages is a further heart-stopper:

If John is naive enough to take the 30 year mortgage at $427.71—saving a pitiful $12.34 per month over the other mortgage payment—he will pay an additional $48,363 for his foolishness!!

The better part of wisdom would of course be to flee the bank with all due haste and find another alternative. But if you have no other option, or if you are already paying a mortgage—there is an excellent way of reversing the compound interest burden and dramtically reduce the amount you pay back to the bank. By prepaying your mortgage, you can easily reduce the amount you repay by 50–70%!!

Anyone can use this method and save themselves incredible amounts of money on their mortgages. Virtually all mortgages have a "prepayment without penalty" clause—meaning that you can repay all or part of the principal amount ahead of schedule without being penalized by the bank. If you are just now nego- tiating a mortgage—absolutely insist that this clause be included in your contract.

Applying the method is quite simple. First, ask the bank for an amortization schedule—which will look something like the schedule below. For purposes of illustration, we will use a 30 year mortgage of $30,000 @ 17%, such as that described in the previous example.

AMORTIZATION SCHEDULE FOR FIRST 24 MONTHLY PAYMENTS
ON A 30 YEAR (360 PAYMENTS),
$30,000 MORTGAGE @ 17%.

MONTHLY PAYMENT	INTEREST	PRINCIPAL	LOAN BALANCE
(1) $427.71	$ 425.00	$ 2.71	$29,997.29
(2) 427.71	424.96	2.75	29,994.54
(3) 427.71	424.92	2.79	29,991.75
(4) 427.71	424.88	2.83	29,988.92
(5) 427.71	424.84	2.87	29,986.05
(6) 427.71	424.80	2.91	29,983.14
(7) 427.71	424.76	2.95	29,980.19
(8) 427.71	424.72	2.99	29,977.20
(9) 427.71	424.68	3.04	29,974.16
(10) 427.71	424.63	3.08	29,971.08
(11) 427.71	424.59	3.12	29,967.96
(12) 427.71	424.55	3.16	29,964.80
1st. Yr. $5,132.52 Total	$5,097.32	$35.20	$29,964.80

(13) 427.71	424.50	$ 3.20	$29,961.60
(14) 427.71	424.46	3.25.	29,958.35
(15) 427.71	424.41	3.30.	29,955.05
(16) 427.71	424.36	3.35.	29,951.70
(17) 427.71	424.31	3.40.	29,948.30
(18) 427.71	424.26	3.45.	29,944.85
(19) 427.71	424.21	3.50.	29,941.35
(20) 427.71	424.16	3.55.	29,937.80
(21) 427.71	424.11	3.60.	29,934.20
(22) 427.71	424.06	3.65.	29,929.55
(23) 427.71	424.01	3.70.	29,925.85
(24) 427.71	423.96	3.75.	29,922.10
2nd Yr. $5,132.52.	$5,090.82	$41.70	$29,922.10
Total			

You will note that at the end of the first year of the mortgage, out of a total of $5,132.52 paid to the bank, only $38.20 has been applied to principal—the rest is interest! In the second year, only $41.70 is applied to principal. During the first five years, in which you will pay a total of $25,662.60 in payments —only $241.50 will come off of the principal. The remainder— $25,421.10—will be kept by the bank as interest!

In general, for the first 20 years of a 30 year mortgage— virtually all of the payments go for interest and very little comes off the principal amount owed. This is something the average person does not understand and which the banks are less than enthusiastic about publicizing.

However, by setting up a simple prepayment approach—you can dramatically reverse the situation and beat the bank at their own game. Begin immediately to do one or both of the following:
(A) From the amortization schedule, it is obvious that during the first 5 years of payment—you will only pay $241.50 on principal ($35.20 1st yr., $41.70 2nd yr., $48.20 3rd yr., $54.70 4th yr., $61.20 5th yr.—$241.50 total). If you can scrape up the $241.50 send it along with one of your early regular payments of $427.71—advising the bank that you wish this to be applied as a prepayment of your principal for the first 60 payments (5 yr.).

By so doing—and for this measly $241.50—you will knock 5 years off your mortgage and save $25,421.10 in interest!!!!!
If you can scrounge together $750.00 extra—you could reduce your mortgage by 10 years and save $50,842.20 in interest, etc. etc.

In general, whatever extra money you get from time-to-time such as tax refunds, overtime pay, bonuses, etc.—refer to your amortization schedule, see how many principal payments it will cover and send it along with your next regular payments. For each small principal payment you thus prepay—you eliminate one month from your mortgage and literally save hundreds of dollars in interest.

(B) Set up a systematic prepayment with each of your regular payments. For example:

From the amortization schedule shown, your regular payment is $427.71, which includes your interest and principal. When you send in your first payment of $427.71, however, also add principal payment #2 of $2.75 (from the amortization schedule). When you send in your second payment of $427.71, add principal #4 ($2.83), on third payment, add #6 ($2.91), etc.

By thus adding the next principal amount to your regular amount—you are making a double principal payment in advance. If you do this regularly—you will pay off your mortgage in 15 years instead of 30 and you will save 50% of the interest you normally would have paid. For the miniscule sum of $2.75, for example you will save a full payment of $427.71!

You may, of course, pay more than one extra payment, which will even more rapidly accelerate the payoff of the mortgage. For example, with your first payment of $427.71, you may wish to add principal payments #2 ($2.75), #3 ($2.79), and #4 ($2.83) or a total of $8.37 extra—which would be 3 months reduction.
Whichever approach you decide upon—keep an accurate record of the payments you make. Be sure to advise the bank what you are doing and send a notation along with your payments as

to which principal payments you are prepaying. A good idea is to send two checks—one for the regular payment and the other for the amount of the principal prepayments—noting such on the face of the check. If you do not have an amortization schedule, your bank should be willing to make one up for you, although you may have to pay a charge of $5–10.00 for the service. If you are already paying on a mortgage—begin prepaying on the balance at whatever monthly payment you're at.

Having seen the incredible effect that compound interest has upon the price you ultimately pay for a mortgage—bear in mind that the same principle applies to all consumer credit whether it be for products you buy or money that you borrow. While the impact on a shorter term contract—such as that for an automobile, household goods, etc.—is not as devastating as that of a long term mortgage—it still adds a very substantial amount to the final price you pay. If you must use consumer credit—try to apply the prepayment principle whenever and wherever you can.

(2) KEEP YOUR HOUSING COST WITHIN BOUNDS.

Whether you buy or rent, your cost should not exceed 25% of your net income (take-home pay after tax deductions). The rule-of-thumb used to be 25% of your gross or total income— but taxes today take a large portion of your income and your real purchasing power is only the number of dollars you have left.

If you are paying more than 25% of your net income for housing—you actually cannot afford it and you will sacrifice other vital needs such as food, clothing, medical care, etc. in order to pay the bill. It is an unsound living strategy and you should take definite measures to bring this expenditure into line.

If you are already renting or buying and exceed this 25% limit, consider the following:

(a) Rent some of your space to another person or persons. Many homes and apartments have a spare room or area that would accommodate a student or a working adult. You'd be helping them and the additional income would help to reduce your monthly cost.

(b) If you are renting, you might also approach the landlord and check the possibility of lowering your rent in return for your doing some building maintenance or acting as guardian or care-taker.

(c) Consider the possibility of becoming involved in an outside sales or service business—real estate, Avon, insurance, etc.— even on a part-time or second-job basis. Part of your housing could then be designated as an "office" or working area, thus providing substantial tax deductions for a percentage of the rent, utilities, etc.

(d) If you now own your own home, are paying in excess of 25% of your income for mortgages and taxes and find none of the forgoing feasible—you may wish to consider still another possi-bility: sell your present house and get out from under the pre-carious burden you are now carrying. Take the proceeds from the sale and secure another home using one of the alternatives further listed in this section.

If you do not presently own a home and are out looking for one—be extremely cautious:

(a) If you must take on a mortgage of more than 10–12% inter-est—avoid the purchase altogether. In general, a mortgage rate above 10% makes the purchase prohibitively expensive—both in the ultimate total price and in the incredible monthly pay-ments necessary. And be equally wary of the new "variable rate" mortgages, which rise and fall with the fluctuations of the money market. The argument is made that your interest rate may drop in a good economy. Wonderful. But what if the rate soars to 20% or higher—a definite possibility. You could be wiped out —and lending institutions are not known for their charity and empathy when you cannot pay the bill. Even in prosperous times, you could find yourself on a financial yo-yo—with your payments fluctuating wildly.

(b) You will normally fare much better by avoiding the lending institutions and seek out a home seller willing to carry his own mortgage. In today's market there are many home owners who wish to sell their properties and are having much difficulty disposing of them for the same reasons you are having difficulty buying—high prices and lack of reasonable mortgage financing.

You will almost always strike a better bargain with such a home seller than by going through a lending institution. Not only will you probably get a lower price and a reasonable mortgage rate—but if you later run into financial difficulties, you will usually find it easier to work out your problems with an individual than you would with a lending institution holding your mortgage.

Again, when dealing with the individual, the situation is much more flexible and there are many more options available. For example, a number of years ago when my children were quite young, I found myself in immediate need of larger than average living quarters. Because of many children—no one would rent to me and I was forced to buy a home.

The only problem was that I had no money and little prospect of securing enough for a down payment. Through the grapevine, I learned of a large, solid old house for sale in a nearby village—which, as it turned out, was ideal for my family and had a sale price of $7500.

After talking with the owner, an elderly gentleman, I discovered that he wanted $3000 down and was willing to carry a mortgage for $4500, which would give him a monthly income.

I advised him that we wanted the house, the price was fair, the terms agreeable, but that I had no money. I suggested, however, that if he were willing to carry a second mortgage for $4500 rather than a first—that we could effect the purchase. He could obtain a first mortgage for $3000, which the local bank agreed to give without hesitation—thus giving him his cash in hand. I would assume this first mortgage and its payment and also give him a second mortgage, thereby giving him the monthly income he was seeking.

It was an excellent agreement. The buyer received the cash he was seeking and a regular monthly income from the second mortgage payment. I, in turn, acquired a home I badly needed with no money of my own needed for a down payment. True, I had to make payments on two mortgages, but through a small part-time second job I was able to pay off the first mortgage at the bank in a relatively short time. When we moved some years later, I sold the home at a substantial profit.

Through the years I have used the above technique a number of times with great success and it is still a sound approach to buying if you have little or no money. In today's market, there are many sellers who might be willing to consider accepting a second mortgage as a down payment if it were presented to them. Don't be afraid to ask.

As a general principle then—whatever your present or anticipated housing status—try to hold the cost at no more than 25% of your net income for a sound survival strategy.

(3) BUILD YOUR OWN HOME.

There is absolutely no better inflation survival strategy than building your own home. It is a super technique that involves all three basic principles outlined earlier in this section:

—increased self-sufficiency
—avoidance of money
—increased productivity

Any economic approach that embraces all of these principles is a sure winner, and this particular one is especially productive. Not only will it provide the individual with the desired housing —but it will further produce extraordinary economic gain beyond this initial objective. The case of a young couple whom I counseled several years ago will illustrate just how productive this approach to housing can be.

The husband, Fred, was employed at $15,000 as a technician

by a local company and his wife Claire was an office manager at an annual salary of $12,000. From their combined $27,000 yearly income, they had managed to save about $10,000 and were shopping for their first home.

After looking at dozens of homes and after much debate, they had narrowed their search down to two possible choices and it was at this point that they asked me for my opinion. They liked both of the houses and were elated at the prospect of having their own home. They had carefully calculated that with very tight budgeting that they would just be able to handle the high monthly payments that either of the houses would require.

I advised them to buy neither of the houses. Instead, I suggested that Fred leave his job for a year and build his own home.

They were both aghast at my suggestion until I pointed out to them several startling calculations which I had made:

(A) From their joint income of $27,000, combined taxes, social security, state and federal income taxes—took nearly $9,000. Fred's cost of going to work—auto transportation, lunches, union dues, etc.—took another $3,000, for a total of $12,000—so that their actual net income and purchasing power was really only $15,000 annually, and not $27,000. The biggest benefactor from Fred's employment was actually the tax collector.

If they dropped back to Claire's single income of $12,000, there would be a dramatic drop in the tax level—leaving them about $10,000 in net income and an elimination of Fred's $3,-000 work costs. Therefore, their net income would drop only $5,000 per year—not $15,000 as it would first appear to be if Fred left his job.

Put still another way—Fred was really earning only $5,000 a year for his labor! Using the same analysis and reversing the situation—that is if Fred were to keep his job and Claire leave hers—it developed that Claire had actually been earning even less than that for her labor as long as the two of them were working.

This is one of the grimmer realities of today's economic scene

—that in the many two-income families, one of them is usually just working for the tax collectors and given the additional costs of transportation, baby-sitters, lunches, etc., the second income-earner in the family may actually be <u>losing</u> money just by going to work.

In Fred's case, he was shocked to realize how little actual return they were getting for their combined labor. Keeping this in mind, I then suggested that if he were to spend the following year building his own home, he would enjoy far greater compensation for his labor then the low return he was now getting.

(B)   Traditionally, total housing costs have followed a fairly steady pattern—land cost 5–10%, materials 60–65% and labor 25–30%.

Today, however, the pattern has altered dramatically because of taxes and inflation and the cost distribution now is—land 10–25%, materials 25–35% and labor 45–50%.

Because of this altered pattern and the much higher percentage of labor cost in the final price—the person who builds his own home will automatically cut the cost by 50% or more—and that adds up to an enormous sum of money.

There are other exciting rewards that are not immediately obvious, but which are enormously significant:

(1) Solid, tangible wealth is created by the individual's labor in building a house.

(2) The individual gets a far greater return per hour for his labor then he normally will receive from employment—and unlike a salary—this return cannot be taxed unless and until he later decides to sell the home—and then it will be at a much lower capital gains rate. If he waits until after age 55, he may not have to pay any tax at all, because he is allowed a one-time tax-free sale of up to $150,000 on property.

(3) The individual avoids the horror of a large mortgage and the economic slavery of bone-crushing payments.

(4) The completed home is superb collateral for future borrowing if necessary.
(5) Nothing can compare with the personal satisfaction of having built one's own home.

After carefully considering all of the points we had examined, Fred and Claire made the decision to try the suggested plan.

Obtaining a one-year leave of absence from his job, Fred commenced the building of his own home some two months later. In addition to his $10,000 starting capital, he borrowed another $8,000 from relatives to cover his basic material costs. Since land costs in our area are still fairly reasonable, he was able to secure a large, pleasant building lot for $3500. The remainder of his capital he used to purchase materials.

Although Fred had never before built a house, he was quite handy with tools and he was able to get excellent advice and some assistance with the more difficult phases such as the plumbing and electrical wiring.

Working an average of 10 hours a day—which was roughly what he had previously spent working on his job and commuting —and about half of his weekends, he completed an attractive 3-bedroom home within the allocated year. Shortly thereafter, their new home was appraised at $54,000.

Several months after Fred had returned to his job and he and Claire were settled, we did a final analysis.

The total cost of the home had come to $22,000, of which they still owed $12,000. They calculated that because of the rent they would now be saving that they would be able to pay this back completely in 2–3 years.

Beyond the thrill of being in their own home, however, the economic gains they had made were astounding:

(1) In a single year, they had created and owned—except for the $12,000 outside debt—real tangible wealth of $54,000! To have accomplished this feat through working, Fred and Claire would have had to jointly earn $120,000 that year!

(2) Subtracting the $22,000 cost from the appraised value of $54,000—Fred had actually earned $32,000 for his years labor—a far cry from his normal earnings. Considering tax deductions normally taken from his salary—he had literally received a rate of return on his labor 3 times greater than he normally received working! Moreover, the entire $32,000 gain stayed in his pocket until such time in the future as he might decide to sell the home.

(3) The impact of not having a mortgage and $500–600 per month payments was profound. In 2–3 years, after the borrowed $12,000 had been repaid, they would be able to live forever without the burden of rent or mortgage payments and the money thus saved would bring a dramatic rise in their standard of living—some $5–6,000 a year in additional disposable income.

Viewed still another way, that's a return on their $54,000 of over 11% annually—and it's non-taxable!

There is no other way that Fred could have accumulated such wealth so quickly. To realize a net of $32,000 through working, he would have had to earn at least $55–60,000 before taxes. If he had gone into a business of his own, to net $32,000 would have probably required a six-figure initial investment—which he certainly did not have—and he would have had to have a gross sales volume probably in excess of $300,000—a feat seldom achieved ones first year in business.

Not only did Fred and Claire keep pace with the inflation monster—they beat the daylights out of it! So enthralled was Fred at the economic success of his accomplishment that he and Claire have purchased another building lot and Fred has begun construction of a rental duplex on evenings and week-ends as a second job. He feels that even if it takes him 3–4 years to complete the project that he has discovered a key to economic prosperity.

Again, the reason for Fred's success was the three basic principles:

—he achieved a high measure of self-sufficiency by doing the work himself and avoiding reliance on outside forces.

—except for purchase of basic materials, he avoided the use of money. No institutional financing or mortgage or committment for after tax income—which would have cost him double the number of working hours.

—increased productivity. By using his previous hours of labor to directly produce what he needed—rather than trading them for money (salary) he received a return 3 times higher for each hour of his labor.

To prosper economically, whatever the individual needs or wants, whether it be housing, food, clothing—or anything—he or she should always first ask themselves:

—can I produce or make it myself?
—to what degree can I avoid the use of money in acquiring the item?
—can I increase my productivity in obtaining or making the item?

To the extent that you can follow these principles, the rewards can be enormous.

TEN INFLATION BEATING TECHNIQUES IN HOUSE BUILDING

If you have decided to build your own home, there are a number of approaches that can help to further reduce your costs:

(A) Use "rough-cut" lumber as much as possible. Rough-cut is lumber just as it comes from the saw-mill and is much cheaper than the smooth, kiln-dried lumber you later buy at the local lumber yard. It is excellent for all parts of the house frame that are not seen when the house is completed—such as the 2 × 4's and 2 × 6's etc. that are used for the wall studding, floor joists, roof rafters, etc. Many people have even used rough-cut boards as outside house sheathing and interior walls to beautiful effect. The use of rough-cut lumber can produce substantial savings in material costs and with a little checking, you can probably locate a saw-mill within a reasonable distance.

(B) Check Out Used Building Materials. There is a growing trade in the sale of good used building materials, such as lumber, windows, doors, etc. salvaged from buildings being demolished or those partly destroyed by fire, floods, etc. These can often be purchased at far less than the cost of buying new ones. Many communities now have one or more companies dealing in such salvaged materials and you can quickly locate these in your telephone book. Still another good source of used materials are local "swap sheets" and classifieds in the evening newspapers. Using salvaged materials can literally cut thousands of dollars off your building costs and it will pay you to investigate this possibility.

(C) Avoid State Sales Tax By Buying Materials In Another State. State sales tax, usually ranging from 7–9% are levied on all goods and services purchased within the state by their own citizens. Residents of other states are usually not subject to the sales tax for goods purchased because technically such taxes furnish no services or benefits to out-of-state residents. While policy may vary from one state to another—if you are going to spend $15–20,000 for materials purchases—you may well be able to save a substantial amount of money by buying in another state. It will pay you to investigate your surrounding area.

(D) Try Bartering For Necessary Materials and/or Services. You may well be able to obtain all or part of the materials and services you need by trading your own goods or services. On a local level an inexpensive advertisement placed in the classifieds will usually bring good results since the practice is growing and more and more people are beginning to barter. I have personally used the local classifieds successfully quite often.

In the last section, we explored the specifics of bartering and referred the reader to several organizations which can assist them in bartering with others nationwide.

(E) Seriously Consider Non-Traditional Types of Construction.
The average American usually thinks of house construction in terms of the traditional "stick and frame" wood house. However, there is today a growing resurgence of older, often more durable types of housing than the modern ones being constructed.

For example, log or stackwood, field stone, tamped earth (used by the ancient Romans) adobe and even underground houses are not only architecturally pleasing and more energy-efficient—they are usually much cheaper to build than most of our modern houses. While the use of these materials may require somewhat more labor on the part of the builder, they are abundantly available locally in almost every part of the country.

As an example, our local barber recently built a magnificent 4-bedroom, 2 bath log home appraised at over $60,000. He obtained all of the logs from the nearby state forest lands and had them cut and trimmed by a saw mill and then delivered to his building site. His total cost for the logs, cutting and trimming and delivery was only $3,850! When completed, with the additional interior expense of wiring, plumbing, etc.—his total investment was slightly over $11,000—and he had a home anyone would be proud to live in!

Similarly, field stone and rock abound in many parts of the country and the major cost is the labor expended in collecting the rock. It is not as difficult to build a stonehouse as most people think and there is nothing more beautiful or durable. For value—it equals or usually exceeds that of a traditional wood house. Tamped earth buildings were a favorite of the Romans, and once set—they will outlast concrete. Underground or bermed houses, because of their heat conservation qualities, are becoming ever more popular.

All of the above, in addition to the lower cost of building materials are more energy-efficient than traditional housing because of their greater insulation factors—which affords even greater economies in energy costs for heating and cooling.

(F) Investigate The Possibility of Co-op Building. There are many other people in your community who would also like to acquire their own house or apartment. You might be able to find another individual or several who would be willing to work together collectively to help each other build. This could take one of two directions:

(1) You and the other person would assist each other in each building his own home on his own lot. This could be cooperative assistance on the entire building or just partial help on the more difficult tasks. Mutual agreement could be reached as to the number of hours and the degree of assistance rendered by each.

(2) You and another individual might agree to build a duplex together with each owning and inhabiting one of the apartments, or four individuals might agree to co-build and own a quadruplex (4 apts.) under the same arrangement. There are definite advantages in both building and cost savings in such situations and proper legal agreements as to ownership, maintenance, etc. can be drawn up without difficulty. It would be quite similar to acquiring a condominium except that it would cost far less because you would be doing the building yourself and participating in the economic gains just as if you were building a single home.

Co-op building is nothing new to Americans. In frontier days, collective "barn-raising" and "house raising" by community neighbors accounted for a large portion of the building during our westward movement. There is a long tradition of such cooperative building and it is still an excellent idea to consider.

(G) <u>Pay Close Attention To Insulation and Other Energy Conservation Features.</u> One of the biggest contributors to inflation is the high and rising cost of energy in heating and cooling your home. The use of extra insulation, thermalpane or storm windows, large southside windows for passive solar energy, etc., will cut your energy bills dramatically. It has been estimated that the use of storm windows alone will cut the heating bill for the average home from $500–800 per year at current energy costs.

In general, the additional costs for such energy-saving applications will be returned in 3–5 years by the money saved in energy usage. Thereafter, in the face of constantly rising energy costs—the homeowner may well enjoy a savings bonus that could range as high as <u>$1500–2000</u> per year!

(H) <u>Consider Enrolling In A School For "Do-It-Yourself" Home Builders.</u> For a nominal tuition fee of $200–350, you can enroll in one of a number of excellent new schools specifically created to teach amateurs how to build their own houses. In practical, "hands-on" seminars normally lasting 4–6 weeks, students are taken through all aspects of home building. The classes, consisting diversely of people from all levels and professions—housewives, bankers, doctors, retirees and even family groups—are shown how to use power tools, read blueprints, and work on the actual construction of a house. In addition, they are also taught the basic economics of material selection and purchasing and cover the electrical, plumbing and heating systems.

For the individual who wants to build his or her own home—but is detered by lack of experience—the time and nominal cost involved in such a seminar could be one of the most worthwhile investments that could be made. Full details of these training seminars can be obtained by writing to any of the excellent schools listed below:

    (1)   Cornerstones
           54 Cumberland St.
           Brunswick, Maine 04011

(2)   The Owner-Builder Center
      1824 Fourth St.
      Berkeley, California 94710

(3)   Heartwood Owner-Builder School
      Johnson Rd.
      Washington, Mass. 01235

(4)   Northern Owner-Builder Center
      Plainfield, VT 05667

(5)   Shelter Institute
      Bath, Maine 04530

(6)   Owner-Builder Center
      2615 6th St.
      South Minneapolis, Minn. 55454

(I) Act As Your Own Contractor If You Are Unable To Build
Your Own Home. If, for one reason or another, you are unable
to physically build your own home—then at least be your own
contractor. Take each phase of the house construction and shop
around for a sub-contractor to complete that specific phase.

For example, get bids from several contractors for digging
and construction of the basement. Check to make certain that
they are competent and properly insured and get an agreement
in writing of the terms and conditions before you award the
contract. Then follow the same procedure for each of the remaining phases—construction of the frame, electrical, plumbing
and heating systems, etc. In addition, you may be able to effect
further substantial savings by buying your own materials and
simply pay the sub-contractor for his time and labor.
    While the overall savings will not be as great as if you were
able to build the home yourself, by the above procedure, you
will save the profits normally made by a building contractor on
the construction materials and the erection charges. This will
substantially reduce the overall cost of your home and the sav-

ings are well worth the investment of your time in acting as your own contractor.

(J) <u>Build Your House In Stages</u>. If you do not have enough money to tackle the complete construction of a house—do it in stages over a longer period of time.

I have always been impressed by the rugged ingenuity of the residents of our local community. We live in the foothills of the Alleghanies, just north of the Pennsylvania border—a truly beautiful area of rolling hills, pine forests and idyllic valleys. But it is also one of the poorest counties in the entire nation—with median annual income of only $5900 for a family of four—well below the national poverty level of $8300.

In spite of this, an extraordinarily high percentage of the population own their own homes—attractive, well-constructed dwellings—and almost all are owner-built. Because of the lack of capital, many of the houses are built gradually over a number of years.

After acquiring a lot or building site—which, in itself, may take a family several years to accomplish—the first phase of construction is the excavation and building of the basement. Since this frequently consumes all of the capital available, a temporary roof is put on the basement and the family moves in and uses this underground structure as their dwelling. This has a number of distinct advantages: Since it is primarily under-ground, the structure benefits from the thermal effect of the ground itself, keeping the cost of winter heating to a minimum. Secondly, the family saves the cost of rent—which it is then able to invest in construction materials for the rest of the building. These basement homes are quite comfortable and the rudimentary sinks and plumbing fixtures which will later become part of the laundry and game room areas of the completed house serve nicely on a temporary basis as the kitchen and bathroom.

In the next phase of construction, as the family is financially able to—the upper exterior structure and roof are completed. In the third phase, plumbing and electrical wiring are installed and finally, the upper interior is completed. The process may take 5–6 years or even longer to complete. One family with six children took 8 years to complete their home and it was a continuous project involving all of the members. But when completed —it was a spacious and handsome home. And it was completely paid for—without the burden of a long-term mortgage.

With many of these homes so built, after the initial basement stage—most of the capital required for the building of the rest of the home comes from the rentals saved over the years.

For the individual with little capital to start, building a home in stages is worth considering. Even if it takes a number of years to complete the project, it is probably one of the most practical ways of acquiring a home.

SUMMARY OF ECONOMIC SURVIVAL TECHNIQUES FOR HOUSING

TECHNIQUES	NET SAVINGS
(1) PREPAY YOUR MORTGAGE	20–80%
(2) KEEP YOUR HOUSING COST WITHIN BOUNDS	10–25%
(3) BUILD YOUR OWN HOUSE	40–60%
(4) TEN INFLATION-BEATING TECHNIQUES IN HOUSE BUILDING	20–30%
TOTAL POSSIBLE SAVINGS	10–80%

The acquisition of a home, in addition to satisfying one of the most basic of needs—still represents the largest economic project in which the majority of people will be involved during their lifetimes. It also provides the single greatest opportunity for the individual to accumulate a large amount of economic wealth— even though there is minimal capital with which to start.

As a method of beating inflation, taxation and the consumer trap—nothing is more successful or rewarding than investing ones time and labor directly in the production of housing.

Food

—Americans at all levels are finding ways to keep their food expenses within bounds.

FOOD

In the average family budget today, one of the largest single expenditures is for the purchase of food. For those in the lower income levels—it is often the greatest of all expenses.

In the overall variety and supply of foodstuffs, Americans enjoy a greater abundance than any other nation in the world. In the other industrialized nations of the western world, the purchase of food takes 35–40% of the average family income and in the lesser developed countries it ranges as high as 70%.

By comparison, food purchases take only 20% of a typical American family's budget. Even further, this superabundance, which feeds not only our own citizens, but which is exported in vast quantitites, is produced by a farming community of only 3% of the total population—an astounding record unmatched by any other nation in the world.

But here again, we have the same destructive principles of the market economy operating to the detriment of the producer (the farmer) and the consumer. In spite of the incredible miracles of food production created by our superb technology—we do not benefit from the savings thus created. The farmer—the heroic producer of this phenomenal abundance and to whom we should erect a national monument—gets a pretty shabby return for his enormous productivity. The typical dairy farmer, for example, with an investment of $300,000–500,000 in land, livestock and equipment, and a seven-day, 80 hr. work week— is lucky to have an income of $15,000–18,000 a year. For a gallon of milk, he receives about $.30—the same gallon for which we pay upwards of $2.00 in the supermarket— and he exists on the edge of financial disaster.

In a similar manner, the entire farming community—upon which we all depend for one of the most vital and basic of our needs—receives a minimal return on its productivity. At the other end of the system, the consumer pays a price 5–6 times the cost of each item as it leaves the farm. The unit of food for which the farmer receives only $.20 ultimately costs the individual $1.00–1.20 at the checkout counter. Again, this enormous difference in cost to the consumer—representing billions of dollars on a national scale—is created by the middleman forces of the market economy (including the tax collectors). While no one questions the basic transportation costs of moving these volumes of food from the farm to the marketplace—by far the largest portion of the steep prices charged the consumer is due to the costs of the seductive packaging, processing, advertising, and other persuasions which constitute the basic elements of the consumer trap.

As in all the other areas of the present market economy—the end result is that we are all poorer and the cost of the food we consume is pushed to a far higher level than it should be.

Understanding these hidden forces of the market economy is, of course, the first step in devising countermeasures for an effective survival strategy.

Just as with housing, the individual can—with planning and discipline—effect dramatic savings in the cost of the food he consumes.

But before we begin the counterattack against the exhorbitant prices at the check-out counter—we must first consider an even more dangerous aspect of the food situation created by the market economy—the very real threat to our actual physical survival!

Very few Americans today realize just how complex and precarious the food delivery system of the nation actually is—and the vast majority are totally unprepared to cope with any interruption of the system. With most of our basic necessities, there is a wide margin of compromise. If we do not have a house or apartment—we can find some temporary shelter. If our clothes are not the best—we can still wear them a little longer. And if we do not have transportation, we can always walk. But we cannot do without food for more than a few days. Of all survival necessities—food is the one indispensable need.

In the face of this compelling need, however, our market economy has placed the survival of our citizens in serious jeopardy. The industrial northeast, for example, produces locally only 20% of the food it consumes daily. It is self-sufficient only in the production of milk. The south and west have somewhat higher levels of self-sufficiency, but even here, the bulk of food consumed is also transported over great distances from other parts of the nation and from abroad. When a New Yorker sits down at the table to eat, his vegetables are from California or Florida, his meat and bread from the Mid-West, his coffee from Brazil and the sugar he puts in the coffee from Louisiana beets. On the Californians table is cereal from Kansas, bacon from Iowa and dairy products from Wisconsin.

In between the production and consumption of this bountiful abundance is an incredibly complex chain of processors, wholesalers, warehousers, salesmen, agents, merchandisers, financiers and a vast transportation system of trucks, railroads and even airplanes. The failure of any single link in this endless chain can precipitate a massive breakdown of the entire delivery system. The financial failure of a wholesaler, a trucker's strike, a sudden blizzard—or any of a dozen other potential hazards can bring a sudden and catastrophic halt to a delivery system upon which our very lives depend.

So delicate and vulnerable is the system that no American city today could survive longer than 2 weeks should there be an interruption in its delivery of food. And long before that—there would be panic and violence in the streets.

The blizzard of 1977 that hit the city of Buffalo, New York is an excellent illustration of just how suddenly such an interruption can occur. Long accustomed to very cold winters and heavy snowfall, the city was well equipped to handle the burdens of a normal winter. Snow removal procedures and traffic control in and out of the city were excellent. The daily routine of life had a high degree of normalcy even in the midst of the harsh winter weather.

But the city was hardly prepared when, in late January, a sudden shift in the prevailing wind pattern brought a full-fledged Arctic blizzard raging down upon the city from the polar regions. During three days of unrelenting fury, the storm buried houses up to the rooftops, brought all traffic to a standstill and stranded thousands in offices, bars and public buildings. When the storm subsided, it took another four days to open emergency supply arteries and restore vital services.

While the overwhelming majority of the citizens responded to the crisis with exemplary behavior and some with heroism—braving the terror of the storm in snowmobiles and on snowshoes to rescue trapped motorists and to carry supplies to the hospitals—there were ominous signs of panic and beginning ugliness. During the early storm warnings and in the early hours of the actual blizzard, there was a wave of panic-buying, which cleaned out the supplies of bread, milk and other staples in food stores throughout the suburbs and many areas of the city. During the storm and the later cleanup, with the police force largely tied up in emergency duties—there was a growing incidence of vandalism and looting—particularly of the foodstores. Had the cutoff of the city lasted another week, the plight of many of its citizens would indeed have been truly grim.

Make no mistake—in our society of today, the most dangerous threat to our existence is the potential cutoff of our supply of food. It is bad enough that we have been made almost hopelessly dependent upon a paper money system for securing our vital food necessities—but we have been placed in double jeopardy by a further dependence upon a fragile and delicately balanced delivery system. If there is no food on the shelves of your local grocery store—even a trunkful of hundred dollar bills will not buy your survival.

Given the vital importance of a continuing food supply and the precarious nature of our current delivery system, our first consideration then should be to insure that we do not become victims of some future interruption.

(1) CREATE A SURVIVAL STORE OF FOOD.

There are in the United States today, a growing number of "survivalists" who, believing that the nation faces imminent disintegration through nuclear attack, civil rebellion, government breakdown or a host of other disorders—are laying in elaborate stores of food, guns and other supplies prior to the final breakdown. Accordingly, there is a growing variety of survival foodstuffs being prepared by a number of companies catering to this market. For the family affluent enough to afford these foods, both the variety and quality is excellent.

However, while any or all of the above catastrophes are certainly possibilities—I do not personally believe that any of them will actually happen. This nation of ours—despite the current economic woes and political tensions—is far too solidly based and our traditions too deeply entrenched, for the society not to survive. Far more likely over the next decade is a continued political and economic turbulence, high inflation and increasing pressure on the individual from taxation and regulation. Prosperity and survival for the individual will depend increasingly on the degree to which he or she can become more self-sufficient.

In creating a survival store of food, the major concern should be those of nutrition, durability and ease of storage. While the systematic stockpiling of all types and quantities of food is a habit that every individual should begin to develop as part of an overall strategy, current finances, storage room, etc. must be taken into consideration. While a well-balanced nutritious diet of specifically prepared survival foods are available at a cost of $750–1500 per person for a one year supply, for many individuals such an initial outlay might well be prohibitive in the current economic situation.

Begin instead by laying in an emergency store of basic cereals and grains. Not only are they highly nutritious and easily stored —they are quite inexpensive, and well within the reach of even those with the lowest income. Wheat, oats, rice, barley, rye, cornmeal, beans and lentils have adequately nourished mankind since the earliest days of civilization—and they are still among the best foods we have.

During the depression of the 1930's, I and my brothers were virtually raised on oats and cornmeal. For breakfast we had hot oatmeal porridge or cornmeal mush. The remaining porridge or mush was then poured into a flat pan and after cooling, was cut into strips and fried in lard for our lunch. Supper was a bowl of potato or onion soup with a generous hunk of oatmeal or corn-meal bread. While such a diet would hardly excite the gourmet and we often yearned for a change of menu—we were all healthy and robust throughout our childhood. In the days of the Roman Empire, the major staple of the foot soldiers diet was wheat and the galley slaves chained to the oars of their ships were kept alive as long as 20 years on nothing but lentils and lentil soup.

For about $200.00, a "bare-bones" emergency survival store, sufficient to feed a family of four for 3–4 months can quickly be created by assembling the following:

100 lbs. —Oats
100 lbs. —Rice
100 lbs. —Cornmeal
100 lbs. —Assorted Flours (Buckwheat, Rye & Wholewheat)
100 lbs. —A combination of Beans, Split Green Peas and Lentils
100 lbs. —Soybeans
5–6   —Large containers of boullion bases & assorted dehydrated vegetables.

For an additional $150.00—and especially if there are children involved—you can add either powdered milk or 100 gallons of Meadowfresh, an excellent new milk alternative, made from a milk base, but more nutritious and costing 25% less than whole milk. In powdered form—it has a shelf-life of <u>4 years</u> without refrigeration.

From this basic store, which contains an adequate level of proteins, vitamins and carbohydrates—a nourishing diet of soups, breads and porridges can easily be prepared. All of these foodstuffs, if kept dry, will last for years without refrigeration. An excellent method of storage is to place them in plastic bags and then put the bags in sealed 20 or 30 gallon galvanized garbage cans which in turn, can be stored in a convenient, out-of-the way place. Using the galvanized cans will also protect the stores from insects and rodents.

All of the forgoing grains and cereals can be purchased in bulk from a local feed mill, food co-operative or health food store.

Begin immediately to create such a rock bottom emergency survival store. If you cannot immediately make the minimal investment suggested above—start with whatever you can and add to it as you are financially able to do so.

(2) BEGIN A SYSTEMATIC "FOOD INVESTMENT" PROGRAM.

A systematic investment in food is one of the smartest moves you can make—and it is something that everyone can do successfully.

As an inflation fighter—it certainly beats the stock market, bank certificates and many of the other highly touted investment vehicles.

In each of the past several years, most of the common items of food have increased in price from 15–35%. Food costs overall have been rising more than 20% annually—well above the general inflation rate—and they will continue to do so in the future. You can be certain that for each $10.00 you spend this year for food—next year you will spend $12.00 (or more).

Given this economic situation, investing your money in food will bring you a far higher return than putting it in the bank. Let us say, for example, that a year ago, you were spending an average of $50.00 per week—or $2500.00 annually—for food. If at that time, you had had an available $2500 and gone out and bought a full years supply of food in advance—you would have saved $500.00 over the same supply of food today, which would now cost about $3000.00.

Put in a different way—you would have received a 20% return on your investment.

In using this inflation beating approach, you should aim for a full years advance stockpile of food:

(A) If you are able to purchase this supply at one time, all the better. If not, systematically add to it each week or month as you are able to. Of course, whatever vegetables, fruit or other foods you grow or can yourselves can be added to your stockpile. In that case—use your money to purchase the staples.

(B) Build up your stockpile from the emergency survival store you have already created. After this emergency store is completed, the next level of foods to purchase and store should be dried or canned fruits, vegetables, peanut butter, powdered eggs, various pastas, coffee, tea, cooking oil and shortening, canned meats that do not require refrigeration (such as corned beef and spam), canned fish (tuna, sardines), seasoning, condiments and sweetners such as honey and fructose. Most canned foods, either commercial or domestic, have a shelf-life of at least 1–2 years and you are better off with a stockpile that does not require refrigeration in case of an electricity shortage or black-out.

In the third level of food purchases, add the "goodies" or luxury foods such as jams, jellies, hot chocolate and packaged desserts (puddings, jello, etc.).

(C) Once you have acquired a full years advance stockpile of food, start rotating these supplies in storage. Start using this food and as you withdraw the various items—replace each item with one you buy today. By such continuous rotation, you will keep your stockpile in excellent condition.

By investing in such a one year supply of food and keeping this stockpile in good condition—you will reap several very substantial advantages:

(A) You will save at least 20% on your annual food costs.

(B) You will insure yourself and your family against a sudden or catastrophic interruption of the food delivery system—for whatever the reason.

(C) Should you suffer a personal loss of income due to unemployment or financial reverses, one of your major pressures will be relieved because you can "coast" on your food supply for some time.

(D) Finally, in the event of a national financial collapse—you can happily eat your investment. Try doing that with a stock certificate or a bankbook! Further, if such an event should occur —food itself will be a highly prized form of money—with which you will readily be able to barter for other necessities you need.

In brief, you cannot lose by investing in food, and the sooner you start, the better.

(3) BUY FOOD "SEASONALLY" WHENEVER POSSIBLE.

Very substantial savings can be realized by buying foods "in season"—or at harvest time. For most parts of the country, that's late summer or early fall. Fruits and vegetables are then in abundant supply and can be purchased for only 30–50% of what they will cost the following winter and spring.

Buy as much of this produce as you are able to at that time and either can or freeze them for later use. Many of these fruits and vegetables will keep as long as 4–6 months if kept in a cool, dry "root cellar" outside in the ground or in your basement. In March and April, for example, we are often still eating apples, potatoes, carrots, etc. from our basement root cellar that were put there the previous September. Care must be taken however, that the root cellar is well sealed against mice and other rodents. Other variations of this approach are:

(A) To buy such produce at wholesale terminals where goods are brought into the city for relay to the food stores around the community. Costs here are substantially lower than they are later in the food stores—although you may have to buy larger quantities.

(B) Try the rural farmers markets for real bargains. They usually are open one day a week and almost every rural county has at least one such market. There are usually several of such markets within easy driving distances of every large city—and the savings are well worth the time and effort. We have one about 15 miles from our town and it is open every Wednesday from 10:00 AM–4:00 PM. Farmers bring their produce here from around the county and one can buy cheeses, meat, vegetables, etc., etc. at savings of 20–30% over the costs in local food stores and supermarkets. To save on transportation—we usually go once a month and load up on everything.

(C) Buy "returned" bread and bakery goods at return outlets. There is usually one in every metropolitan area. They are just as good as the "fresh" goods and they cost 40–50% less. My wife buys large quantities and puts them in the freezer for future use. We calculated several years ago that on just bread alone that we were saving $320.00 a year!

Practical use of just this technique alone can shave 25–30% off your annual food bill—which for the average family would mean a savings of about $1500!

(4) BUY "INSTITUTIONAL" FOOD AT WHOLESALERS.

Restaurants, hotels, hospitals and other "institutions", because they consume large volumes of food—buy their supplies from wholesalers or discount houses at substantially lower prices than you pay at the supermarket. Canned foods are usually in the larger #10 cans, dressings in the gallon size, etc. and you may have to buy in case lots. But if you are able to purchase from these outlets, you will realize savings of 10–30% on what you buy.

(5) GROW YOUR OWN FOOD.

If you have the time and a small piece of land—putting in a vegetable garden is a great inflation-beater as well as being a source of pleasure and personal satisfaction. Almost every suburban backyard and many inside the cities are large enough to produce a substantial portion of the families annual vegetable consumption. $50.00 worth of seed will yield about $1000 worth of produce—roughly 20–25% of the annual food bill for a family of four. In the cooler northern parts of the country, where the growing season is relatively short—the yield can be increased by sprouting the seeds in inside window boxes and then transplatning the seedlings when the weather permits.

There are a number of excellent magazines available that will assist the beginner with highly expert advice on the subject. (See Index at the back of the book).

(6) SQUEEZE YOUR FOOD DOLLARS TO THE LIMIT.

Americans throw away or waste vast amounts of food. Even in economically difficult times, the majority of our citizens spend far more of their money for food than they should. Here again, the market economy—relentlessly pushing the individual to ever greater consumption and spending of his available dollars —has subtly seduced the general public into a wide range of wasteful and expensive food buying habits. Tops among these "dollar-eaters" are:

(A) Fast food establishments. An almost endless and still growing variety of "fast food" centers, touted by the promoters for their "convenience" and "gastronomic delights"—now take $2.00 out of every $5.00 spent on food in the United States! It is estimated that by 1985—they will take $3.00 out of every $5.00 spent! Many individuals and even some families now eat regularly in these establishments and some spend the greater part of their food budgets for such consumption.

While such statistics may fill the merchandisers with unbounded joy—the consumer is hardly getting a bargain. Not only is there a real question of the nutritional value of some of these products—but the consumer pays a very high price for such food—despite the continual bombardment of advertising portraying them as an inexpensive alternative to the drudgery of home eating.

The fact is that the purchase of fast foods costs the consumer at least twice as much as the same food would cost him if prepared and eaten at home. Moreover, while food traditionally has always been regarded as one of the sacred items exempt from taxes—our ingenious collection officials have devised a strategy to overcome this prohibition by taxing the "service" on top of the price of the food you buy.

You thus save 55–60% in food cost when you eat at your own table rather than a fast food outlet.

(B) Processed and Convenience Foods. The desire for convenience is a natural human trait and in the food industry, capitalizing on this foible has almost reached the level of an art. A growing proportion of food items now appearing on the shelves of the supermarket have already gone through one or more stages of expensive pre-preparation or processing. There are T.V. dinners that merely have to be heated, pre-cooked sauces, instant mashed potatoes and an endless range of other pre-prepared "convenience" foods designed to spare the modern consumer from the terrible pain of preparation and cooking.

Creatively packaged and with sophisticated design graphics, some of these products have reached the point of ridiculousness. My favorites in this hit parade of absurdities are frozen waffles and canned, precooked potatoes.

For this "convenience"—the consumer pays a terrible price. The actual food he gets in the package accounts for only a small portion of the price on the label. A large part of the cost is for the preparation and the costly packaging. You can effect very substantial savings on the purchase of food by skipping these "convenience" foods altogether and doing your own preparation at home.

As a general rule, savings of 20–50% on annual food costs can be realized by stretching your food dollars in the following manner:

(1) Reduce your visits to the fast food establishments.

(2) Avoid the purchase of "convenience" foods and do your own processing and preparing.

(3) Use inexpensive and nutritious "extenders" to increase the quantity and lower the cost of meals. For example, adding soybean or oatmeal to hamburger, rice to casseroles etc.

(4) Save the liquids from canned vegetables for use in soups and gravies since they add flavor and valuable nutrition.

(5) Use bones from meat and poultry to make tasty and nutritious soup stock.

(6) Make a habit of sprouting seeds (such as soybeans, alfalfa, wheat, etc.). This is a simple, inexpensive process and they make extremely nutritious and tasty additions to salads, soups and even sandwichs. This is especially helpful in winter when fresh vegetables are scarce and expensive.

(7) Use hot grain cereals such as oatmeal, etc. rather than the packaged, processed cereals which are much more expensive and far less nutritious.

(8) If there is an infant in the family, puree your own vegetables and fruit in a blender rather than buying commercial strained baby foods.

(9) Bake your own bread and pastry. Not only can you make them more nutritious through the use of whole grain flours, wheatgerm, etc., but they also taste better. The average family can save $300.00 or more annually on just this item alone.

(10) When preparing foods, cook larger amounts—using a portion immediately and freezing the remainder for future use, thus using your time more efficiently.

(11) Never throw any food away. If it cannot be used for consumption, use it to create a compost pile for your garden.

You will undoubtedly discover further ways to get more from your food dollars. The important point is that you spend your dollars wisely and use what you buy to your maximum benefit.

(7) AVOID THE CONSUMER TRAP THROUGH SHOPPING STRATEGY.

Food shopping today bears a striking resemblence to the ancient art of warfare. Prominent among the historic techniques were psychological ploys designed to confuse and demoralize the enemy. The fierce Scottish Highlanders used eerie bagpipe music to strike terror into the hearts of their opponents, the Plains Indians used flaming arrows and bloodcurdling warhoops and the Chinese in Korea used bugles just before the attack.

None of these, however, could hold a candle to the psychological strategies devised by the generals of the market economy in their ambush of the unsuspecting consumer. When you walk into the supermarket to shop for your supply of food—you're literally walking into a battle zone. At stake in the conflict are billions of dollars—some of them yours—and you are pitted against highly trained professionals. Since you are outgunned and outmaneuvered in these weekly skirmishes—try to even up the odds by devising a strategic battle plan of your own. In brief, learn to shop as if you were going to war:

(A) Be aware of the fact that you are walking into a well designed trap. The pleasant music, the artful decor and even the color combinations of the stores interiors have been carefully researched and created to lull you into a feeling of pleasant complacency. Even the physical arrangement of the products themselves is based upon motivational research:

(1) The basic staples that you always need, such as milk, sugar, potatoes, etc. and will always buy without persuasion —are drably packaged and placed in the lower areas of the counters.

(2) The expensive "convenience" foods that you do not need and must be enticed into buying are always placed at eye level

on the counters. In addition, they are beautifully packaged in attractive colors and graphic designs. They are heavily advertised and abound with further enticements of coupons and sale offers.

(3) Meat, baked goods and "deli" products, which are among the most expensive of all food items—are purposely arranged across the back of the store, at right angles to the aisles. This is so that as you reach the end of the aisles you are confronted again and again with these expensive food products. This is effective psychological conditioning. Human beings, exposed continuously to a given stimulus, ultimately react in the desired manner—which in this case is the compulsion to buy these products.

(4) The "marked down", "reduced" and "sale" displays are another of the effective ploys in getting you to buy items that you do not need and would not buy if not so persuaded. People are always looking for bargains, so such signs trigger the impulse to buy even unnecessary products. A favorite trick is to place such displays just inside the entrance of the store to catch you before you have settled down to the serious shopping for which you originally came. Other strategic locations for such displays are at the ends of the aisles or even in the middle of one—so that you cannot maneuver around the display without looking at it.

Often the signs themselves are part of the subtle deception. "Why Pay More?" is a great favorite. More than what? No comparison is ever made to anything else—but the implication is that you're getting a helluva bargain. I recently saw such a display of a certain product "on sale" for "only $1.39," and there were a dozen shoppers happily filling their carts with this "bargain" purchase. Two aisles further away and on a lower shelf, I later found a similar product of the same size and quality for $.20 less. And the "2 for only—and 3 for only—" sale signs are also booby traps for the unwary. Invariably you will find similar products on other shelves in the same store that cost less than the supposed sale item.

(5) Time was when the size of a package or container was a fairly accurate gauge of price and quantity. A large package logically meant that there was more product inside than that of a smaller one and that one could effect a small savings by buying the larger size. No more. Today, the size of the package has little relationship to the price or the quantity of product contained therein.

As our market economy and the forces of inflation pushed the prices of food to ever higher levels, the food manufacturers, seeking to avoid outraged rebellion by the consumers, resorted instead to an ingenious approach that would mask the explosive growth of food prices: while maintaining the same size packaging and only slowly rising prices—they dramatically reduced the amount of product inside.

The result is that while we still have the same sized package —instead of a pound of product that we formerly got, we now get only 10–12 ounces. In addition to the higher price on this same sized package, we also get more inside packing and a goodly amount of dead air space. It is thus now necessary for the buyer to compare both the price and the inside weight or quantity to determine what he is getting for his money.

(6) The final obstacle in this running skirmish is the checkout counter. Like a well-equipped machine-gun nest, every available inch around the station bristles with a vast array of impulse items for the final assault upon the individuals wallet. Idly trapped in the waiting line for some 5–15 minutes, at least 3 out of every 5 customers passing through impulsively picks up additional items that he or she had not originally intended to buy.

Cumulatively, through these highly organized techniques, the food industry extracts billions of dollars more from the consuming public than they normally need or want to spend. If you are not aware of the multitude of weapons being used against you —you're going to get bushwacked. But if you realize the nature of the battle—you'll be able to keep more of your money in your pocket.

(B) Devise a specific shopping strategy to counteract the psychological forces of persuasion ranged against you:

(1) Never shop for food when you are hungry. The hunger drive itself powerfully stimulates the urge to buy a greater range and quantity of food than you really want. Satisfy your hunger before you shop and you'll keep your purchases within bounds.

(2) Make a shopping list in advance. Put down only those items you have decided to buy and stick to the list once you enter the store. Do not buy anything that is not on the list unless it is something important that you have forgotten.

(3) Try to estimate the total cost of what you will be buying and take just that amount of money with you. This will inhibit any tendency to spend more than you had intended to.

(4) Avoid buying items at eye-level on the counters. These products are usually the expensive and unnecessary food items.

(5) Take advantage of "loss leaders". "Loss leaders" are the super bargains advertised by the stores to lure the customers. Once in, the customers usually buy many other products, compensating the store for the bargains used as bait. Plan meals around these loss leaders and then go into the store and buy just those specific items. Also watch for sale specials on staples—the foods you really need—and buy as much of these items as the sale permits.

(6) Buy paper goods in a discount store. They are usually less expensive than if you had bought them in the supermarket. You can further reduce the money you spend by using dish cloths rather than paper towels.

(7) Reduce your trips to the store as much as possible. The more often you go into the store—the greater your exposure and the more likely you are to spend extra money.

Research has shown that those who do their food shopping just once a month save substantial amounts of money on their food bills. Most of the money spent is for the staples and necessities and very little on the expensive, unnecessary items the store would rather have you buy.

If once a month is not feasible or possible—try to go no more than once a week. Since most of the extra trips one makes to the store are for items such as bread and milk—stock up on these items so that you have at least a weeks supply, and will not have to make those additional visits. By reducing your trips to a minimum, you will substantially reduce your expenditures. You will also save on the extra time and transportation costs incurred through frequent trips to the supermarket.

Avoiding the consumer trap through the planned shopping strategy outlined above will save you a minimum of 20–30% off your annual food bill—an accomplishment well worth the time and effort.

SUMMARY OF ECONOMIC SURVIVAL TECHNIQUES FOR FOOD

TECHNIQUES	NET SAVINGS
(1) CREATE A SURVIVAL STORE OF FOOD	
(2) BEGIN A SYSTEMATIC "FOOD INVESTMENT" PROGRAM	20–30%
(3) BUY FOOD "SEASONALLY" WHENEVER POSSIBLE	30–50%
(4) BUY INSTITUTIONAL FOOD AT WHOLESALERS	10–30%
(5) GROW YOUR OWN FOOD	20–25%
(6) SQUEEZE YOUR FOOD DOLLARS TO THE LIMIT	20–50%
(7) AVOID THE CONSUMER TRAP THROUGH SHOPPING STRATEGY	20–30%
TOTAL POSSIBLE SAVINGS	10–50%

You can definitely win at the food game. Using a combination of the techniques above—or all of them—you can save up to 50% of your current food costs!

Transportation

The new, more fuel-efficient models will bring the American motorist greater economy during the coming decade.

TRANSPORTATION

One of the most prominent features of the American culture is the love of and devotion to the automobile. Not only do we have the highest per capita ownership of any nation in the world—but the manufacture and maintenance of our 120,000,000 vehicles is one of the mainstays of the economy. Because of the incredible mobility it has brought to the entire nation, the average American has developed a lasting love affair with the automobile. It is at once a necessity, a status symbol, a second home and one of the most prized of possessions.

It is also one of the most expensive—and it represents an increasingly heavier financial strain upon the individual.

Prior to the last decade—before the meteoric rise in taxation, the Arab oil embargo, double-digit inflation and lofty interest rates—automobile transportation took a distant third place in the family budget, well behind the cost of housing and food.

In the past five years, however, the situation has changed dramatically.

Today, the cost of owning and operating an automobile now rivals the cost of food and housing. For many families, it now exceeds these costs. For example, the average family of four now spends approximately $4,000 annually on food and about $5,000 on housing.

But if they own a new automobile, it is costing them $5500–6000 annually!

Because the concept of "built-in-obsolescence" is an inherent feature of today's automobile—when the family finishes its four-year payment plan—they will have to buy another automobile and begin the cycle all over again. Thus the overwhelming majority of the nation's consumers are in a permanent state of indebtedness for an automobile. Over a ten-year period, they will spend an amount equal to the purchase of a new home.

Unlike a house, however, which will continue to shelter them —and which represents an accumulated investment of real value —all they will have to show is a cancelled payment book and a worn-out vehicle for the junkyard.

In spite of the fact that the automobile has become an almost inseparable part of our everyday life—given the current economic state of our society, it is obvious that for many individuals the financial burden of owning and operating an automobile will become increasingly difficult, if not impossible.

We are thus faced with a truly critical dilemma: That while the widespread dispersal of factories, shopping centers and housing has made the individual almost totally dependent upon the automobile for his everyday existence—he is also faced with the grim fact that he can no longer afford to own one. To continue to do so may well force him to cut back on other vital necessiites such as food, housing, clothing, etc.

In the face of this harsh reality, however, there are definite strategies to hold down and even beat back the rapidly escalating costs of automobile ownership.

(1) MAKE YOUR PRESENT AUTOMOBILE LAST AS LONG AS POSSIBLE.

The longer you can drive an automobile the less it will cost you for each mile of your transportation. The average individual in the United States today drives approximately 15,000 miles per year at a cost of $.22 per mile or a total cost of $3300 per year . This includes the original cost of the automobile, insurance, tires, repairs, etc. Since only about 10% of the 110–120,000,000 automobiles operating on the highways each year are new automobiles bought that year—the $.22 per mile operating cost is based upon older automobiles—which are much less expensive than new ones to operate.

But even $.22 per mile—which translates into an average of $64.00 per week—is a pretty hefty bite out of the weekly paycheck.

No matter what the age or condition of your present automobile, if you coax it along for another 15,000 miles—or roughly another years worth of driving—you can effect very substantial savings. Whether your auto is 3 or 4 or even 10 years old—you have several definite economic advantages if you can continue to drive it:

(A) Your investment in the auto has already been made, so you can avoid another "up front" layout of capital for another year —or for as long as you can continue to drive it.

(B) Without the burden of new car payments, interest, etc.— those next 15,000 miles or more will be the cheapest auto transportation you can find—costing you only for fuel, which actually is only a modest portion of today's auto expense—even if you have a gas-guzzler, getting only 13–15 miles per gallon.

In the 1950's and early '60's during my own private economic depression supporting a family of eight children—I raised this technique to a highly elevated form of art. Despite the fact that in those days the cost of driving a new automobile was an incredibly low $.16 per mile—even that modest cost was quite beyond my financial capacity.

Since I had to drive nearly 20,000 miles a year to my teaching position in a central high school, I devised a year-to-year strategy to find older, used automobiles from which I felt I could wring out another 20,000 miles of life before they expired. Reviewing the classified ads in the evening newspaper from a large nearby city, I would circle all the automobiles listed for $100.00 or less. There were usually at least a dozen or more.

Armed with this listing, I went into the city and carefully examined each of the offerings until I found one that suited my purpose. I discovered to my surprise, that the majority of automobiles that people discard are still road-worthy and with minor repairs can be driven for another year or two.

For more than a dozen years, I followed this strategy religiously, getting at least 20,000 miles of driving from each of the automobiles. I followed an iron-clad rule of never spending money for a major repair. If such a necessity arose—I would simply dispose of the vehicle and get another one. Simple maintenance I took care of myself. I changed my own sparkplugs, fanbelts and oil. I repaired holes in the mufflers when they developed and I picked up good used tires from the local gas stations for just a few dollars. When an auto finally gave out and would go no further, I hauled it to a back field on our farm and made another pilgrimage to the city to buy another one.

In all those years, I never paid more than $100.00 per year for an automobile and the average was $80.00. One incredible old Dodge sedan I bought for only $65.00 and I drove it another 60,000 miles before it finally died.

As a result of this approach—which provided me and my family with perfectly acceptable transportation, my average cost over those thirteen years was only $.038 per mile—77% less than the normal cost of automobile transportation at that time!!!!

While specific costs today are different—the economic principles remain the same. If you can push your automobile another 15,000 miles, another year of driving—your cost for next years transportation will be only about $.12 a mile—45% below the national average and a savings of approximately $1500 on your next years budget!!!

$1500 more in your hand will buy a lot of extra groceries, pay your utilities, or make a nice cash reserve for emergencies. So nurse your old car along for another year if you can.

(2) REBUILD AN OLDER CAR INSTEAD OF BUYING A NEW ONE.

The cost of a new automobile in the United States today is breathtaking. With an average base sticker price of $10,800, the added costs of financing, insurance, and operational expense over a four-year period comes to a grand total of $22,800—or $5700 per year!! That averages out to about $.38 per mile— prohibitively expensive for a growing number of Americans and as in the housing industry, the resultant catastrophic drop in the sale of new units has placed the giant automobile industry in serious danger of collapse.

For the individual who cannot afford this heady cost of owning and operating a new vehicle, an excellent and money saving alternative is to completely rebuild an older automobile.

One of the great economic myths currently being perpetrated by the minions of the market economy is that the high price of gasoline is the major culprit in the lofty cost of automobile transportation today. As a result, there has been a massive rush by the consumer to buy the small, compact cars with higher mileage per gallon under the illusion that by saving on gas consumption—that in the long run, they will be overcoming the current higher costs of a new automobile.

In fact, this widely held belief is directly contrary to the actual economic reality.

Of the $.38 per mile cost of a new automobile—even for a big gas-guzzler getting 13–15 mpg—the cost of the gasoline is only $.09 per mile!! For the smaller compact getting 25 mpg, the cost is only $.056 per mile, and at 30 mpg—only $.03 per mile!

By far the greatest portion of the cost of new car transportation is not the gasoline—but the car itself, the finance charges, insurance, etc. And like the shrunken candy bar inside the big wrapper and the 12 ounces of produce in the big 16 ounce package—the consumer is now getting less automobile for a higher price. The market economy rides again!

Since the cost of gasoline—even though it has doubled in price in the last few years—is not really the major cause of the high cost of auto transportation today, the rebuilding of a big old gas-guzzler will bring you dramatic savings in transportation costs. A recent example will serve to illustrate how effective an inflation beater this approach can be.

About six months ago, my son Kurt purchased an 8-year-old

Plymouth Sattelite for $650. A big, 8-cylinder vehicle, it was getting only 14–15 mpg and had already been driven over 95,-000 miles. The shock absorbers and springs were weak and the transmission was beginning to slip.

However, the car was roomy and comfortable and structurally sound. For a further investment of approximately $2,000.00, he had the automobile completely refurbished—with a rebuilt engine, rebuilt transmission, new shocks and springs, radial tires and body repainted. With a cleanup of the interior and new seat covers, the old Plymouth is a handsome looking vehicle again and is as comfortable and road-worthy as the day it originally left the showroom.

Kurt estimates that conservatively, he will be able to drive the auto at least another 60,000 miles, and with proper maintenance —it may well go another 90,000 miles. Best of all, with a total investment of only $2,650.00—and even at only 15 miles per gallon—he is driving his rebuilt automobile at a cost of only $.16 per mile—which is 27% below the national average cost.

By thus rebuilding an older car, he is enjoying an annual savings of $875 over the average cost and $3,275 less cost than if he were driving a new car. Moreover, as inflation pushes the costs even higher, his savings over the next few years will become even more dramatic.

There are millions of solid older automobiles in the nation today that can be purchased quite inexpensively. If you can rebuilt one for $3,000 or under—it's a great way to lower your transportation cost and beat the inflation trap.

(3) GET MAXIMUM MILEAGE OUT OF YOUR GASOLINE.

The internal combustion engine used in our automobiles is grossly inefficient. At least 70% of the gasoline run through the engine is not utilized but rather is expelled through the exhaust system as incompletely burned carbons and other polluting emissions. The result is an expensive and shameful waste of a dwindling energy resource. Simultaneously the consumer gets a minimal return for the ever-increasing prices he must pay at the pump.

If the full energy potential in gasoline were used by completely combusting it—since only the vapors and not the liquid, are used to fire the engine—the average automobile could easily be driven from 80–100 miles on a gallon of gasoline!!! Moreover, with complete combustion—there would be an incredible and immediate decrease in the pollution and smog currently poisoning the atmosphere in which we live. It has been estimated that 40–50% of the current air pollution in the United States is due to the emissions from automobiles.

Our automobile industry, with its massive brain trust of engineering skills, has long possessed the capability of producing a carburetion system that would deliver such a complete combustion and high mileage. Over the years, rumors have continued to surface that, in fact, such systems have been devised and then quickly buried by forces of the market economy which will not tolerate such a challenge to the established economic structure. Thus the waste of energy and the consumers money continues unabated.

There are however, a number of ways in which the consumer can fight back. For each one mile more of mileage that you are able to gain from a gallon of gasoline in your automobile— you will effect an annual savings of $70.00!! Thus, 4–5 miles more per gallon means $300–350 in your pocket. The following techniques, if utilized, will give you this extra mileage and savings:

(A) INFLATE YOUR TIRES TO 32 LBS. PRESSURE.

Most automobiles today carry only 26–28 lbs. of pressure. By increasing the air pressure to a full 32 lbs., you will get a slightly harder ride, but your mileage will increase substantially. If you have radial tires, be careful not to overinflate, i.e., more than 32 lbs., which would be destructive to such tires. However, if you are getting, say 15 mpg currently, by inflating your tires to 32 lbs., you will gain an extra 2–3 mpg. That translates into a tidy $250 savings for the year.

(B) USE HIGH TEST GASOLINE.

Engine performance and mileage depend upon the octane rating of the gasoline used. Whereas we formerly had gasoline of up to 94–96 octaine ratings, we currently have regular low-leaded gas of 87 octane rating and regular unleaded gas of 89 octane rating—both of which give a much poorer performance than our former fuels and which do nothing to enhance the long range health of your engine. A third available fuel—high test or "premium" unleaded gas still has an octane rating of only 91–92, but even at $.10–12 more per gallon—is still actually the most economical fuel to use.

My current automobile is a 1979 Chevrolet Impala which gets 18 mpg on unleaded gasoline with an octane rating of only 89. I long ago switched over to burning premium unleaded gas at $.10 per gallon more. However, I now get 22 mpg because of the higher octane rating, for an annual net savings of $180.00 . Further, because the higher octane gas causes less wear and tear on the engine (increasing the life of the engine and reducing repairs) I am saving at least one engine tune-up annually for another $75.00 savings, so that my total annual gain is about $255.00 or 8% off my annual transportation cost.

A "do-it-yourself" approach to raising the octane of the gasoline you use is to add commercial octane boosters or additives to your gas tank whenever you fill up. You can buy these items in automotive and discount stores. Try to buy the larger containers rather than the small can sizes which are more expensive. If you live near an airport or any location where you can obtain aviation fuel—which has an octane of 100–110, you can create an excellent auto fuel by mixing one gallon of aviation fuel to every four gallons of automobile gasoline. This will give you an overall 91–93 octane for your fuel. Not only will you have a better running automobile—but it will be less expensive to drive.

(C) USE A WATER-INJECTION SYSTEM ON AN OLDER CAR.

If you are driving an older vehicle that uses regular leaded gas —it will pay you to install a water-injection system. A small amount of water injected into the carburetor in the correct ratio to gasoline (5% water to 95% gasoline)—will not only give you better performance and more power—it will also give you a 20–30% increase in gas mileage (about 3–5 mpg more).

The water entering the carburetor does not burn—but it does produce a number of benefits to the engines performance. First of all, by cooling the gas-air mixture, it creates a greater expansion pressure (which is what drives the pistons of your engine). As the water is vaporized into steam it creates even greater pressure and finally, the conversion process of water to steam in itself absorbs heat from the combustion, thereby lowering the running temperature of the engine for better and more economical performance.

There are a number of commercial water injections systems currently available at from $70–150.00. If you are mechanically inclined, you can probably put one together yourself for under $30.00. The system requires a water reservoir (a 5-gallon plastic jug) in the trunk of the car, plastic feed lines to the carburetor and several metal nozzles inserted into the mouth of the carburetor. I've used such a water injection system on several of my older cars—and properly installed, they're a real winner. Savings on gasoline costs will average $250–300 per year or about 8–9% of your annual transportation costs.

(D) REDUCE THE BARRELS ON A FOUR-BARREL CARBURETOR.

If you do a lot of highway driving, it would pay you to consider eliminating the two back-barrels of your four-barrel carburetor. Most of the older, larger automobiles—and some of the newer ones—are equipped with a large, four-barrel carburetor. Under normal, straight driving, only the two front barrels feed gasoline into the carburetor. The two back barrels give the car a quick, forward thrust of power and speed when you suddenly press down on the accelerator.

While a driver may revel in the luxury and power of his vehicle —each time his two back barrels "kick-in", he is literally burning up gobs of money and gasoline, and his overall miles per gallon will be dramatically lower over the course of the year.

My son and I once experimented with this approach on a 1961 Pontiac Bonneville that I had acquired on one of my annual trips to the city. It was one of the most comfortable and desireable of the vehicles I had driven during those hard-pressed years— but it was getting only 12 mpg. We disconnected the linkage and removed the nozzles for the two back barrels of the carburetor and took the car out for a test run. We discovered that we had sacrificed the fast bursts of passing power and the vehicle climbed hills a bit more slowly than it had before, but on straight highway driving, it ran like a charm with no appreciable difference in the comfort of normal driving.

Checking the mileage at the end of a two-week period, I discovered that I was now getting an incredible 21 mpg! Over the next year, I saved many hundreds of dollars in gasoline costs and since then, dozens of friends to whom I described this approach, have used it with equal success.

For anyone considering the use of this technique, bear in mind that it will have little impact on mileage where city driving is concerned since such driving rarely calls for the bursts of power and speed which bring the back barrels into play. Also, it is a mistake to change the four-barrel carburetor and substitute a two-barrel carburetor, as one of my friends once did. The two front barrels of the four-barrel are specifically engineered to the performance of the large engine and if a basic two-barrel carburetor is substituted, it simply sucks in more gas than it was originally intended to do. The net result is that you do not get the economy of gas consumption that you do if you simply disconnect the back barrels of the original four-barrel carburetor.

(E) TUNE UP YOUR ENGINE AT LEAST TWICE A YEAR.

To get the peak gasoline mileage out of your automobile, get an engine tune-up at least twice a year. This will cost an average of about $75.00 per tune-up, or about $40.00 for parts, such as spark plugs, points and condenser, if you are able to do it yourself. If you cannot afford a tune-up, at least take out the spark plugs and clean them thoroughly.

While tuning up your engine will not generally increase your gasoline mileage—not keeping the engine properly tuned will cause a decrease in your gasoline mileage of 4–6 mpg—costing you far more for additional fuel than would the cost of the tuneups. If you burn high test gasoline, as suggested earlier, you can probably get away with only one tune-up for the year, since the higher octane will keep your engine running at greater efficiency and with less carbon buildup.

So keeping your engine running at peak performance is good economic practice since it brings longer engine life, fewer repairs and the highest mileage from your fuel. It is also good practice to get a wheel alignment at least once a year. If the front end of your car is out of alignment, you will have abnormal wear on the tires and decrease in gas mileage. The $20–25.00 cost of an alignment is good insurance for maximum mileage.

(F) AVOID THE USE OF YOUR AIR-CONDITIONER.

While summer heat and humidity often necessitate the use of your automobile air-conditioner—particularly in some of the southern regions of the country—whenever possible, avoid using your air-conditioner, since it lowers your gas mileage by as much as 3–4 mpg, making it a fairly expensive convenience.

You should also be aware of the fact that driving with your windows open causes an extraordinary wind drag on your vehicle, causing a drop in your gas mileage of 2–4 mpg.

(4) ADDITTIONAL WAYS OF REDUCING YOUR TRANSPORTATION COSTS.

There are a number of further methods by which you can effect considerable savings in your cost of transportation.

(A) AVOID USING YOUR CAR AT ALL ON SHORT TRIPS.

Many people automatically use their automobile for all trips, no matter how short a distance. I have known many who will drive as little as one or two blocks to the deli or drug store. Surveys show that roughly 6% of the average drivers total mileage is for short trips of one mile or less. Further, fuel efficiency is reduced by 70% if you use your auto for trips of one mile or less and the engine isn't allowed to warm up.

Based on these statistics, the average driver is wasting $462.00 each year on short little trips that he or she could easily have walked to!

The moral of the story is that if you have a short trip to make —leave your automobile at home and walk. You'll save a whopping 14% of your annual automobile cost!

(B) LEARN TO USE SELF-SERVICE GASOLINE PUMPS.

Instructions are usually on the pump and the procedure is quite simple. At $.05–.10 per gallon differential over full service, you will save $50–100 per year, some 2–5% of your fuel costs.

(C) REDUCE YOUR AUTOMOBILE TRIPS THROUGH PLANNING.

At least 20% of all automobile travel is due to random, unnecessary trips that could have been eliminated with a little planning and organization. That amounts to an annual $660.00 needlessly spent by the average driver.

Set up a weekly schedule of your activities and necessary errands and try to consolidate two or more into a single trip. For example, try to do all of your grocery shopping just once a month or at the most just once a week. Car-pool with others whenever possible.

Try to eliminate whimsical, "spur-of-the-moment" jaunts. If

the trip is not really necessary at that moment—don't make it. It'll keep a lot more of your money in your pocket.

(D) ON LONG DISTANCE TRIPS—TAKE A FEW EXTRA PASSENGERS.

On long distance trips, automobile transportation is reasonable only when there are at least 3–4 people in the vehicle. For a single person to drive an automobile over a long distance— the cost is astronomical.

For example, a trip from New York to San Francisco—a distance of slightly over 3000 miles, if made in a new automobile at $.38 per mile, will cost $1,140! If made in an older car at only $.22 per mile—it still will cost $660!

The same trip by airplane can be made anywhere from $100 on a night excursion flight to about $250–300 on a regularly scheduled run. If you're going to travel alone—take the airplane! Most people, when looking at the cost of an automobile trip, calculate only the cost of the fuel—without stopping to realize that the total cost of the automobile transportation is actually much higher than they have calculated.

However, if 3–4 people are being transported, the cost to each of them is quite reasonable.

On a recent roundtrip to Washington, D.C.—a total of 700 miles—I and three friends jointly shared the expense of the transportation, which happened to be in a brand new automobile. At $.38 per mile, the total cost came to $266.00, of which we each paid one-fourth, or $66.50, which was very reasonable and just about half of what a roundtrip air flight would have cost.

Whenever you're planning to go on a long distance trip alone —drop an ad in the local classifieds for "share-the-expense" passengers. You'll be amazed at the response you get. It's a good deal for you and it's a good travel bargain for the passengers you take with you. And not the least of the benefits are the people you'll meet. I've been doing this for years and have formed splendid and lasting friendships with people from all over the country.

(E) <u>USE OTHER TRANSPORTATION WHENEVER POSSIBLE</u>.

For individuals living in cities where public transportation exists—using an automobile is a terrible waste of money.

The city of Buffalo, NY, for example, is approximately 13 miles across from the downtown harbor to the northern and eastern suburbs. A complete roundtrip from either location can be made on a municipal bus for a total of $1.00. To drive the same 26 mile roundtrip in an automobile—as thousands do each day—is economic madness. In a new automobile, the cost of the daily trip is $9.88! In an older automobile, $5.72! And if the individual stops in the downtown area for work or shopping, he must add another $2.00 for parking.

The same situation exists in almost every large city in the nation. City and urban dwellers, while they might prize the convenience and privacy of their private automobiles, could shave a whopping 60–70% off their daily automobile expense by using the public transportation systems. That's about $4,000 on annual new car expenses and $2,300 on older cars. Such savings are certainly worth the sacrifice.

Where municipal public transportation is neither available nor convenient, by all means use car-pooling if possible. Here again, massive savings are possible for all those involved in a car pool.

SUMMARY OF ECONOMIC SURVIVAL TECHNIQUES IN TRANSPORTATION

TECHNIQUES	NET SAVINGS
(1) MAKE YOUR PRESENT AUTOMOBILE LAST AS LONG AS POSSIBLE	40–50%
(2) REBUILD AN OLDER CAR INSTEAD OF BUYING A NEW ONE	25–58%
(3) GET MAXIMUM MILEAGE OUT OF YOUR GASOLINE	10–30%
(4) ADDITIONAL WAYS OF REDUCING TRANSPORTATION COSTS	15–70%
TOTAL POSSIBLE SAVINGS	10–70%

The simple economic fact is that the cost of automobile transportation has now become so exhorbitant that the average person can no longer really afford it—no matter how deeply ingrained the tradition or the necessity. But the above techniques, if carefully followed—will give the individual a fighting chance against the rising financial burden of automobile ownership.

Utilities

—in spite of the rising cost of energy, Americans everywhere are making splendid individual adjustments.

UTILITIES

For the average American family today, the combined cost of utilities—electric, gas, oil, water and telephone—is approximately $2,000.00 a year. This represents 10–13% of their annual budget. For the poor and the elderly living on a fixed budget—it accounts for a crushing 20–25% of their total annual income.

Compounding these already grim statistics is the further bad news that within the next five years—it is estimated that these costs will be double their present level!!!

The primary blame for this national economic crisis again rests with the powerful forces of the market economy which over the last 30–40 years have:

(1) effected a conversion of our industrial and residential energy usage from our former domestic energy self-sufficiency to a major dependence upon foreign oil. We have thus been made hostage to foreign oil producers who are plundering our national wealth and weakening the value of our currency by the exhorbitant prices—which have increased 1000% in the last ten years alone!!

(2) In the interest of increased and continued consumption, the market economy has further created and encouraged a policy of incredible energy wastage on the part of the American public: gas-guzzling automobiles, energy-wasting appliances, poorly insulated houses, etc., etc. The net result is an appalling waste of energy by the average American.

151

The fact is that there is really no shortage of domestic energy resources and we can return to energy self-sufficiency and freedom from dependence upon foreign sources. For example, there is enough coal in the United States to run the country for the next 300 years at its present energy consumption level. Enough bio-degradable material—such as manure—which, if instead of being thrown away, were converted to methane gas —could furnish 40% of our annual energy needs. And the replenishable resources such as our forests—if properly managed —could also furnish a major portion of our energy requirements. If, for example, 1.5 Billion tons of wood annually were converted to alcohol—we could run every engine in the country on pure alcohol, eliminating entirely the need for gasoline. In 1980 alone, over 800 Million tons of wood rotted away in our forests for lack of harvesting. And these are just a few of the incredible resources this nation possesses.

But while we have both the resources and technology to effect a return to energy self-sufficiency, the conversion will be long and painful in coming, and the situation will get much worse before the turn around can be completed.

During the energy transition of the next decade, the individual will be forced to fight the rapidly escalating cost by both desciplined energy conservation and adoption of alternative energy methods. The following techniques should be extremely helpful in reducing your current utility bills.

(1) STOP WASTING ENERGY.

The first and most immediate way of saving on utility bills is to stop using unnecessary energy. Because of the prior abundance of cheap energy sources that have existed in this country —wood, coal, gas, oil and hydroelectric power—Americans have developed a wasteful and often thoughtless usage of energy. With the rising costs and declining availability, however, we must now reverse these long-held habits. Just eliminating the waste can reduce your costs by as much as 30–50%!

The following procedures will cost you nothing but the effort and collectively will cut your utility bills substantially. Try as many of the following as possible:

(A) Your hot water heater is one of the greatest energy wasters. It keeps water hot for 24 hours a day despite the fact that we only use the hot water for relatively short periods of time. First, cut the water temperature to no more than 120°F. It is not necessary to have your water any higher temperature. Second, try to arrange your hot water activities—showering, washing, etc.—during specific periods of time, say several hours in the morning and several in the evening. Shut your heater off during the rest of the time. You will reduce your hot water cost by 60–70% without sacrificing any of your comfort.

This savings could amount to up to $200.00 or more per year, or about 10% of your whole utility budget!

(B) Lower the thermostat on your heating unit. For each degree lower, you save 3% of your heating bill. If you can lower the temperature by an average of 5 degrees, that's a savings of 15–20% or about $200.00 less for your heating bills.

There are two simple ways of accomplishing this:

(1) Lower the temperature 10 degrees at night while you are sleeping, from 68° to 58°. A few extra blankets will eliminate any discomfort. If you're going to be away at work all day— do the same thing.
(2) Increase the humidity. Water in the air retains heat and you will be comfortable at a lower temperature if the humidity is high. Most winter heating units produce extremely dry air, so raise the humidity either by setting pans of water around or by using a commercial humidifier. It'll really pay off—since you can drop the temperature by 5–8 degrees without feeling uncomfortable.

(C) <u>Get the maximum mileage out of the energy you use.</u> There are dozens of little daily habits that will conserve energy and reduce your total energy bills:

—Use a pressure cooker whenever possible. It cooks the food with less energy.

—Cook entire meals in the oven, since it is the most energy efficient. Allow a space between pans and the sides of the oven.

—Cut everything into small pieces, use covered pans and as little water as possible for fast cooking results.

—If you have a gas range, turn off the pilot lights, since they consume 25–30% of your cooking fuel when not in use. <u>Warning:</u> don't just blow them out—turn off the valves. Hand-lighting will save you a considerable amount of money over the year.

—Use the lowest setting on your cooking range that will do the job. Turn it off a short time before the cooking is completed and let the residual heat finish the task.

—Try cooking enough for several meals at once. Store and refrigerate the extra portions for later use. This conserves both energy and your time.

—Do not use a small pan on a large burner. This wastes the heat escaping around the pan into the air.

—Always wipe out the oven immediately after using. By keeping it clean it will operate at maximum efficiency and uses less energy.

—Heat only the amount of water you need for coffee or other uses.

—Thaw frozen foods before cooking.

—Whenever possible, use small appliances in preference to large ones.

—If you keep reflectors under burners clean they will speed up the cooking because of the reflected heat.

—Keep the seals on your oven door airtight to prevent loss of heat. Replace it if it's defective.

—If you have a freezer, keep it full or you're wasting money on electricity. If you have just a few things in the freezer, you're better off to pull the plug and make other temporary arrangements for the food.

—If you have a dishwasher, run it only when it's full. If you keep usage to just once a day, you'll save $50–60.00 per year.

—Do not allow excessive frost to build up in freezers and refrigerators. They are less efficient and run more.

—Use hand mixers, can openers, etc. instead of electric variety.

—Keep all liquids in the refrigerator covered to prevent escape of moisture which causes the compressor to work overtime.

—Keep your freezer and refrigerator in an area away from heaters and stoves.

—Open the refrigerator and freezer doors as infrequently as possible.

—Whenever possible use fluorescent lights instead of incandescent. They use 75% less electricity and last 8–10 times longer. Also turn off the lights when you leave a room.

—When doing your wash, do not overload—which uses more power—but wash full loads. Try to use cold water rinses as much as possible.

—When using your dryer, run it only as long as necessary and do not overload it. Do all your clothes at once in consecutive loads. Once you've heated it up, you'll use less energy with succeeding loads.

—In the winter time, vent your dryer heat indoors through a filter, which will help reduce your overall heating needs as well as adding humidity to your inside air.

—Close off unused rooms in the winter time to save heat.

—In the wintertime, use only one exterior door to minimize incoming drafts and heat loss.

—Take showers instead of baths and use one of the newer fine spray nozzles which uses less water. Both of these will reduce your hot water costs.

—If you have a micro-wave oven, use it to do as much of your cooking as possible, since it is the most efficient of all cooking devices. It uses 75% less electricity and does the job in a fraction of the time.

By developing the forgoing energy habits, you will save at least 10–20% on your annual utility bills. That's roughly $200–400 and is certainly worth the effort.

(2) DEVELOP MORE EFFICIENCY IN YOUR ENERGY USAGE.

Developing more efficient approachs to the use of energy can bring eye-opening reductions in your annual utility costs of as high as 50% with no decrease in your standard of living.

(A) Get an energy audit on your home. Such an audit can pinpoint precisely where you are losing valuable heat and cooling energy. There are a number of techniques for conducting such audits—some of them using infrared heat sensors—and your local utility companies will be happy to conduct one for you, either free of charge or for a very nominal fee.

If your home isn't weathertight—and millions of American homes are not—you could be wasting up to 40% of the dollars spent on heating and cooling because of escaping energy. That's about $400–600.00 a year of needless expense. Just plugging up the leaks will often save you as much or more money than an expensive insulation job.(1) Install storm windows and storm doors. At least 25–30% of heat loss is through the glass in your windows. If you don't have outside storm windows or thermopanes—and even if you do—try putting up inexpensive, plastic storm windows inside. They're very effective in reducing your heat loss.(2) Plug up all the leaks and cracks. Weatherstrip around the edges of windows and doors, and use insulating gaskets around electrical outlets on exterior walls. Plug up any holes or cracks with caulking and put insulation around any heating ducts or pipes that run through unheated spaces, such as under the floor.(3) Try to insulate your attic, walk and floors. Start with the attic, which is most important in retaining the heat within the house. You can save substantially by installing your own attic and floor insualtion, but you may have to hire a contractor to insulate the walls, a much more difficult job. At current costs, proper insulation can cut heating and cooling costs by at least 30% and that figure will rapidly rise as the cost of energy escalates.

(B) <u>Introduce energy efficient appliances and methods into your home.</u> Most older appliances and heating and cooling systems are real energy "hogs."(1) As you replace your appliances, such as refrigerators, water heaters, air conditioners, etc. shop around for the most energy efficient new models you can find. All new appliances must now carry a label giving the energy consumption level of the device so that you can calculate its future operational cost. Spend a little time making these calculations—it could save you a lot of bucks in the future.(2) <u>If you have an older furnace</u>—consider changing it. Most older furnaces have a far greater capacity than is required and therefore switch on frequently for short heating bursts. This is grossly inefficient and could be running up your heating bills as much as <u>30% higher than necessary!</u> First, you might try "underfiring" the furnace by installing a smaller fuel nozzle which restricts the flow and makes the furnace run longer (and therefore more efficiently) each time it comes on. This will cost you about $20.00 and could reduce your fuel bill by about <u>12–15%</u>. Secondly, you may wish to consider just replacing the furnace with a smaller, more efficient model. The cost of such a replacement should be returned over a 3–4 year period by the 25–30% fuel savings you will realize.(3) <u>Install an inexpensive air-circulation system.</u> Because of air stratification, the temperature in a room can vary as much as <u>10–20</u> degrees difference between the floor and ceiling. By breaking up this stratification—that is, by circulating the air, we create a more even temperature distribution throughout the room. Most important of all—we reduce the heating energy necessary by as much as <u>30–35%</u>!

A relatively simple system can be constructed consisting of a verticle duct against a wall, with an open space between the top of the duct and the ceiling and a small fan at the base of the duct and a short distance from the floor. The fan literally pulls the warmer air from the ceiling and down through the duct where it blows it out across the cooler floor area.

In the summertime, if there is a basement in the house, the same principle can be used to exchange the cooler air from the basement for the warmer air upstairs, thus reducing or eliminating the need for air-conditioning.

Look into air circulation—it's worth a lot of money!

(4) Consider switching to a "demand-use" hot water heater. Rather than using energy to keep a 30–40 gallon tank filled with hot water 24 hours a day as the standard systems now do, you can save $100–150 a year by converting to a new type of hot water heater that simply heats and furnishes hot water "on demand." They have no large tanks of water to keep constantly heated, but can heat and deliver water quickly when it is needed.

Further, the units are small and can be located close to the point of usage, so they further eliminate the "line loss" of heat in water that normally has to be piped a long distance from the hot water heater.

Smaller units range in cost from $100–200 and larger units from $500–600, but they use far less energy and over a period of a few years, more than pay for themselves in energy savings.

(5) Use practical solar energy when possible. Solar hot water heaters and home heating units requiring electrical and mechanical equipment are still not cost effective and require many years for a payback of investment.

Passive solar heating, however, is much less expensive and can effect substantial savings. In the simplest form of usage, in the wintertime, open the drapes and window shades completely to let in the sunlight. Close them at night to keep the heat from the sunlight trapped inside.

If you're in the process of building or altering your house— put a large concentration of windows on the south side of the building to capture the sunlights warmth. Still another approach is to build a small greenhouse "lean-to" against the south wall. In addition to its use as a greenhouse—it will capture a tremendous amount of solar heat which can be transferred into the house for heating purposes. Use of this greenhouse approach can effect a dramatic reduction of up to 40% of the heating cost of the home!(6) Fix all leaks in your water system. A single, small leak in your water lines or faucets can waste as much as 5–6000 gallons of water a month! Not only is this a terrible waste of a precious resource—it drives up your water and heating bills. Those leaks could be costing you upwards of $100.

(C) Investigate the possibility of wood heat.

Of all the heating fuels, wood is by far the least expensive. During the Arab oil embargo in 1973, the cost of heating our nine-room farm house with a propane gas furnace tripled to over $1,800 per year!!!

We shut down the central heating system, installed two air-tight wood space heaters and cut old-fashioned air registers in the ceilings so that warm air could flow into the upstairs bed-rooms. The following winter, we cut the cost of our winter heating to only $380.00 and the house was warm and comforta-ble. In later years, we replaced the gas furnace in the basement with an efficient wood furnace which made use of the original heating ducts throughout the house. It had to be loaded only once a day and our winter heating costs were approximately 25–30% of that of our neighbors using other fuels. We saved well in excess of $1,000.00 a year by using wood heat.

In addition to reducing the base cost of heating through the burning of wood, still a further clever reduction is possible:By routing water lines from the hot water tank through the wood stove or furnace, a continuous supply of hot water can be made available free. By locating the water tank above the heating unit —for example, if the furnace is in the basement, place the tank on the first floor—the natural force of convection will carry the hot water upward from the furnace to the tank and effect a continuous flow throughout the system. This can additionally save hundreds of dollars in water heating costs using the heat used for the house.

While the use of wood is a splendid alternative to the use of other energy forms, there are major drawbacks to its use by large segments of the population: First of all, you must have access to a plentiful supply at reasonable prices. In the rural areas and small towns, wood is usually available from nearby forests and wood lots and relatively inexpensive. In the cities, however, the cost of transporting and delivering of wood dramatically increases the cost to the consumer. Further, in space restrictions of the urban areas and apartment buildings, there is a critical shortage of storage space for an adequate supply of wood.

Secondly, the user of wood must observe very strict safety precautions. The chimney used must be of solid construction and cleaned regularly to avoid the buildup of tars and creosote which are highly inflammable and pose the threat of fires within the chimney if not properly guarded against. Also, the wood burned should have been seasoned for at least six months—and ideally for a year. Burning of green wood, i.e., wood just recently cut, gives off 50% less heat, since half of the energy created by the burning is used just to dry out the wood. Moreover, as green wood burns, it drives out the tars and creosote which heavily coat the lining of the chimney, creating a dangerous fire hazard. Properly seasoning the wood beforehand eliminates these problems and gives the user double the heat in his stove or furnace.

But if the use of wood is at all possible or feasible, you can cut your heating bills 50–70% by converting to this excellent fuel.

SUMMARY OF ECONOMIC SURVIVAL TECHNIQUES IN UTILITIES

TECHNIQUES	NET SAVINGS
(1) STOP WASTING ENERGY	30–50%
(2) DEVELOP MORE EFFICIENCY IN YOUR ENERGY USAGE	12–70%
TOTAL POSSIBLE SAVINGS	12–70%

In the coming years, rapidly rising utility costs will become one of the heaviest of our living expenses. Beginning immediately, a disciplined use of energy and a close attention to the appliances and equipment which use these precious resources will pay enormous dividends in your survival strategy. The forgoing approachs will give you a productive direction in combatting the rising costs.

Clothing

—Next years fashions will feature a back-to-basics trend.

CLOTHING

The average American family spends at least 10% of their annual income for clothing. If there are a number of children in the family, particularly teenagers or young adults, the percentage is much higher because of the high discard rate due to simply the outgrowing of clothes and the peer group pressure for all of the latest "fads", which are expensive.

It has been estimated that 30–40% of all the clothing purchased is very little used or not even worn at all because they were either ill-considered impulse buys or purchases of inappropriate styles or color patterns. This amounts to a hefty $800.00 annual waste due to poor purchasing habits!

More than any other segment of the market economy, the clothing industry caters to and ruthlessly exploits the individual's desire for recognition and individuality. The constant change of fashions, "designer" clothes and prestige "labels" are the industry's techniques for capitalizing on these basic psychological motivations of the consumer. The exhorbitant prices thus extracted have nothing to do with the durability or quality of the clothing itself—but rather it is the price charged for creating the illusion that the wearing of specific labels or styles by the consumer will automatically elevate his or her status and prestige as an individual. Those individuals who have fallen prey to this consumer trap will indeed be quickly parted from their money—and unless they recognize the nature of the game—they will pass their naivete on to their children, further compounding the hemorrage of the family income.

In general, if the individual is overly concerned with keeping up with all the changes in fashion, designer clothes and labels —he or she can forget about saving money on clothing. Given this outlook on the part of the individual, the major emphasis is not on clothing anyway, but rather the satisfaction of ego and it will take an unlimited bank account to accomplish this.

But if the individual can turn aside the persuasions of the marketplace he or she can be well dressed and comfortable for a far smaller portion of the annual budget than is currently being expended. The following approachs are very effective cost cutters in the annual clothing battle. In practice, they can reduce your expenditures by 10–80% or an annual savings of $200–$1,600!!

(1) ALWAYS BUY CLOTHING OFF SEASON OR ON SALES.

Begin a practice of buying new clothing after the normal season is over. Before a specific season or occasion, prices for all goods are at their highest because of peak buying demand. After the season, the demand is virtually nil and merchants, anxious to get rid of left-over merchandise, dramatically drop the prices and use any excuse to hold a sale. That's the time for the thrifty shopper to buy.

(A) Immediately after Christmas and New Years, buy clothing (and other items) for next Christmas. There are usually a wide variety of clothing items left over from the pre-Christmas merchandising and price reductions range from 40–70%.

(B) In late January and early February, with winters end approaching, over-stocks of winter clothing, boots, men and womens winter suits, blankets, etc. are put on sale to get rid of these items in time for the spring merchandise. Savings of 20–50% are common. Merchants frequently use Washington's and Lincoln's birthdays as the occasion for these clearance sales, although what these worthy gentlemen have to do with the situation has yet to be discovered.

(C) In April, use after-Easter sales for purchases of spring clothing. The major spring sales period has passed and again, such clothing is now marked down substantially.

(D) During the summer, take advantage of Memorial Day, Mother's Day, Father's Day and Fourth-of-July sales and the after holiday sales on clothing. Again savings will range from 20–40%. In late August, there are terrific reductions on summer clothing. Buy them then for next summer.

(E) Do not buy school clothing for children until late September, when the buying rush has passed and prices have dropped to sales bargain levels. There are many clearance sales offered at this time.

By following such a disciplined approach to buying off-season and on sales only, you can literally cut your annual clothing bill by as much as 70% or up to $1,400 annually! Moreover, since most of the buying you do through this approach is for next years clothing, you are also beating the 10–20% inflationary price rise that will occur over the next year—so that your savings are actually even greater than would appear.

(2) BUY FROM FACTORY OUTLETS AND DISCOUNT CENTERS.

Very substantial savings can be realized by purchasing from factory outlets and discount centers. Many manufacturers maintain local outlets either at the factory or nearby where consumers can buy merchandise directly at greatly reduced prices. Items with small defects, known as "seconds" can also be purchased very cheaply. This is common practice in the textile areas such as New England and the Southeast, and covers a variety of items from suits to linens and towels.

For example, for years, while driving south to visit relatives in Florida, we purchased all of our towels and linens from factory outlets in North Carolina at about a 40% discount off the regular retail price. Each time we drove down for a visit we stocked up a large supply of these items and saved many dollars in the process. In a nearby town, a manufacturer of children's clothing maintains a small outlet for "seconds" which are discounted as much as 75–80% in price. Needless to say, the outlet does a thriving business.

In virtually every metropolitan area there is one or more discount centers that handles factory close-outs, bankrupt inventories and overstocked goods from other stores. Clothing can be purchased in these centers for a fraction of their original costs. More than once at a local center happily called "The Price Cutter", I have purchased "off-the-rack" suits and sportcoats for $15–25.00 that originally were priced in excess of $100.00.

If you've never used such outlets, you'll discover with a few inquiries that there are a surprising number in your local area. It's well worth taking the time and effort to locate them.

(3) BUY CERTAIN GOODS IN QUANTITY.

There are certain items of clothing—such as underwear, shirts and socks and household sheets, linens, etc. that can be purchased at discounts of 25–40% by buying in quantity directly from the manufacturer or from wholesalers.

Buying in large quantities—possibly a several years supply of an item—gives you a twofold advantage, first in the initial discount and secondly by beating the inflationary price rise of the next several years because you don't have to buy that item.

As an example of the effectiveness of this approach, a friend of mine with four sons always buys socks by the gross (144 pair). In addition to saving 40% in cost, one such purchase gives approximately a three year supply. He calculates that between the discount and inflation avoidance, he's saving $80–100.00 a year on socks alone!

Still a further suggestion to the buying of socks in quantity is to buy all one color—such as black. That way, you'll always have pairs, no matter how many get lost or worn out.

If buying in quantity is neither feasible nor financially possible

—team up with friends or relatives to get the discount that quantity purchase brings.

(4) <u>BUY USED CLOTHING</u>.

The purchase of used clothing used to be a practice of only the poor people—but with rising prices and the growing economic squeeze, many people are now discovering that there are terrific bargains in good used clothing. In recent years, there has been a rapid growth in the number of "thrift shops," as they are called and customers using them can remain well-dressed while shaving as much as <u>60–90%</u> off their annual clothing bill!

In general, there are three major types of outlets for the sale of used clothing:

(A) <u>The charity thrift shops</u>. These are shops run by charitable organizations such as the Goodwill, Salvation Army and various religious organizations. The Goodwill alone operates nearly 1,-000 thrift stores throughout the country and the merchandise on sale has been donated by individuals and businesses. A surprising number of the items on sale are actually new unsold merchandise from stores and manufacturers who then take a tax write-off for their donation. Savings on clothing can range from <u>60–90%</u>.

(B) <u>Independent Thrift Shops</u>. Exchange and consignment shops where people bring their used clothing to be sold to others. The proprietor takes a percentage of the sale (usually 20–40%) and gives the balance to the seller. There are a growing number of such shops springing up in all areas of the country under a variety of names. The one in our town is called "The Next To New Shop" and customers can secure a wide range of clothing for <u>20–40%</u> of the original prices. These shops also handle bankrupt stocks and manufacturers close-outs of new merchandise, all of which are drastically marked down in price.

(C) <u>Flea Markets and Garage Sales</u>. Flea markets and garage sales afford some incredible buys in used clothing. These are usually items that the holder of the sale simply wants to get rid of and sells them for virtually anything the consumer offers. While much of this merchandise has little value or appeal, one can often make some really good buys on used suits, sweaters, shoes, etc. Most articles of clothing at such markets or sales can usually be bought for <u>10% or less</u> of their original value.

The purchase of used clothing is a great way to beat inflation and with a little judicious shopping, you can locate clothing in excellent condition. In fact, some of the best-dressed people I know never buy anything but used clothing and they spend but a fraction of the normal cost. If you've never bought used clothing, look into it. You'll be surprised at how much money you can save and still have a good wardrobe.

(5) <u>LEARN TO MAKE YOUR OWN CLOTHES</u>.

On our first wedding anniversary in 1949, I bought my wife a beautiful imported Necchi sewing machine for $250.00. In comparison to my weekly salary of $50.00 this was an enormous sum of money and it took me an entire year to pay for it. Everyone—including my wife—at first thought I was slightly mad, especially since she couldn't even sew.

As it turned out, it was one of the soundest and most productive investments I have ever made. Not only did my wife develop into a creative and highly competent seamstress, but the design and making of clothes became one of the great pleasures of her life. In spite of only a nominal income, she and our daughters were always very stylishly dressed and our sons wore smartly designed suits and jackets made from discarded adult suits of high quality material. At the height of the Nehru jacket craze, I myself had no less than four handsomely tailored originals hanging in my closet.

On balance, our family wardrobe has cost us an average of only <u>20–25%</u> of what it normally would have cost and over the years we have saved many, many thousands of dollars. The Necchi died about six years ago at the ripe old age of twenty-seven and we actually held a family celebration in tribute to the magnificent performance and years of service it had given us. When the party was over, we stored it in the basement for safekeeping as a family heirloom.

The investment in a good sewing machine is a truly sound one and learning to sew is not that difficult. There are Adult Education sewing classes offered in virtually every area of the country and every major pattern company now has an extensive range of easy patterns for beginners. With practice, one can acquire skill in making many articles of clothing, as well as mending and refurbishing worn clothing, thus extending their wearing life.

Finally, in addition to being able to cut the annual family clothing by 50% or more, with the growing popularity and demand for home made clothing and other fabric articles, skill in sewing could well provide the individual with valuable full-time or part-time income. It's a skill well worth pursuing.

(6) GET THE MAXIMUM USE OUT OF ALL CLOTHING.

Getting the maximum use out of all of your clothing can save you from 10–20% of your clothing budget, which factors out to about $200–400 per year. Never simply throw away any article of clothing. Instead, use them in one of the following ways:

(A) Alter or convert the material into other useful clothes. For example, use the materials from unused adult clothing to make clothes for the children.

(B) Exchange or sell unused clothing to a thrift shop or donate it to the Goodwill, Salvation Army or one of the religious organizations.

(C) If the clothing is completely worn out, cut it into squares for homemade quilts. Still another use is to cut any old cloth, including socks, silk stockings, etc. into strips ¼–⅜ inches wide and sew the ends together into a continuous rope-like length.

They can then be braided into beautiful multi-colored rugs for the floors.

One simple but ingenious method of braiding which my grandmother taught the entire family during the 1930's Depression was to drive four finishing nails into the head of an empty thread spool, creating four work posts about ½ inch high. One end of the rag strip rope was then pulled through the spool and a knot tied in it to secure the end of the braid. The rope was then given a single snug loop around each of the four nails and when this was completed, a second wind of the rope was made above the loops on the outside of the nails and without looping it. Then using a nutpick or darning needle, each loop on the bottom was lifted up and over the nail, ensnaring the top loop into a braid. The tail of the braid coming out of the bottom of the spool was then pulled down snug and the process was repeated by continuing to wrap the rag rope around the outside of the nails and pulling the bottom loops that formed each time over the top. The result was a beautiful braid coming out of the bottom of the spool that could then be rolled and sewen into a rug of any size desired.

I remember my brother and I spending long winter evenings helping my grandmother make rag braids and all of our bedrooms and hallways were covered with the beautiful warm thick rugs she made from them. Rugs comparable to these today would cost from $200–300.00—so make rugs out of your old clothes!

By using some or all of the forgoing techniques, you will be able to save from $200–1800 a year on your annual clothing costs and savings of at least $1000 is not at all difficult.

SUMMARY OF ECONOMIC SURVIVAL TECHNIQUES IN CLOTHING

TECHNIQUES	NET SAVINGS
(1) ALWAYS BUY CLOTHING OFF SEASON OR ON SALES	20–70%
(2) BUY FROM FACTORY OUTLETS AND DISCOUNT CENTERS	40–80%
(3) BUY CERTAIN GOODS IN QUANTITY	25–40%
(4) BUY USED CLOTHING	60–90%
(5) LEARN TO MAKE YOUR OWN CLOTHING	50–80%
(6) GET THE MAXIMUM USE OUT OF ALL CLOTHING	10–20%
TOTAL POSSIBLE SAVINGS	10–90%

Medical and Dental

—After years of steadily rising costs, for the average family,
medical and dental expenditures are now showing a steady
decline.

MEDICAL AND DENTAL CARE

The average American family today spends approximately $1500–2000 a year, or about 10–13% of their annual budget for medical and dental care. That's already a healthy bite out of the family income and as the costs of these services continue to soar, the financial strain on each family will become ever greater.

While most families have excellent health insurance plans through their places of employment and a small but growing number are also covered by dental insurance—fully 30–50% of overall costs are not covered by these insurance plans. This means that in addition to the insurance premium paid, the family must pay out another $700–1000 annually out of their own pockets for medical and dental services.

Most of these additional costs are for routine office visits and partial payments for laboratory tests and surgery which are not covered by the insurance plans. In the case of dental care, if there is no insurance, the individual pays for all of the charges.

There are, however, specific strategies which will help to lower the cost of medical and dental care.

(1) REDUCE THE NUMBER OF VISITS TO THE OFFICE.

The average family of four makes a combined total of about 25 visits annually to the doctor's and dentist's offices. These routine visits are not covered by insurance and at an average of $25.00 per visit—this comes to $625.00 and accounts for a large part of the families annual expense. It has been estimated that

177

as much as two-thirds of these visits are unnecessary. This would reduce the costs by over $400.00 or about 20% of the annual costs.

If the individual is seriously ill or has a major dental problem, there should, of course, be no hesitation about going to the office for help or treatment. But the vast majority of visits to the doctor's office are really unnecessary and are for minor difficulties—such as severe colds or flu—about which a doctor can really do very little except to offer words of comfort.

Fear and anxiety caused by lack of knowledge inspires many individuals to immediately run to the doctor's office when confronted with a small injury or a strange, unfamiliar pain or ache. Reduce unnecessary office calls and expense by trying the following procedures:

(A) Use the telephone first and call the doctor. He can quickly allay your fears and in most instances will save you the cost and inconvenience of an office visit.

(B) A large number of common illnesses—colds, flu, chicken pox, measles, mumps, etc.—are caused by viruses and there is literally no medical cure for anything caused by viruses—no matter how sick one may be. The body must cure itself and the only remedy is simply rest and time. The same is true of most simple cuts, bruises and injuries. Simply clean them and allow them to heal by themselves. The human body has amazing self-healing and recuperative powers and except for major injuries and serious disease will mend itself quite well without the services of a doctor. In most such instances, an office call is wasted money.

(C) If you do decide to visit the doctor—see a general practitioner first before going to a specialist. In most cases, he'll be able to handle your situation and the office visit will cost $10–15 less than that of the specialist. If the doctor concludes that your case warrants a specialist—he'll send you to one.

(2) INVESTIGATE THE USE OF CLINICS AND TEACHING SCHOOLS.

(A) In many metropolitan areas, there are a number of neighborhood clinics and university teaching clinics that specialize in dental care, eye, ear, nose and throat illnesses. Work done on patients is top quality and performed by advanced students under close faculty supervision. Savings over normal costs will range as high as 40–60%. In one unusual case where a child was born with no teeth buds, the local university dental school provided successive free dentures into the child's adulthood, saving the parents thousands of dollars in dental care.

(B) For dental care, check out the fast growing dental clinics where savings can range up to 50% or more in dental care. Such clinics can now be found in most large metropolitan areas and even Sears and Montgomery Ward have gotten into the act by opening such clinics in various stores around the country.

(3) AVOID UNNECESSARY TESTS AND SURGERY.

Many doctors schedule a range of tests during routine checkups. If you've been normally healthy and there is no special reason for such tests, they may be an unnecessary expense that can be eliminated. Ask your doctor if they're really necessary.

If you are considering surgery, get a second opinion as to its necessity. It has been estimated that at least 30% of the surgeries performed each year were probably not necessary.

Unnecessary tests and surgery can dramatically increase your medical costs. Make sure that you really need them.

(4) FOR MINOR SURGERY, USE OUTPATIENT CLINICS OR SERVICES.

Many minor surgeries can be handled on an "outpatient" procedure which does not require you to spend an expensive stay in the hospital. Under this arrangement, you enter the hospital or clinic, have your surgery performed in the operating room and leave the same day. You pay only for the surgery and a nominal charge for the operating room. What you save is an expensive stay in the hospital and all of its attendant costs.

For example, I was a mature adult when I needed to have my tonsils removed and my doctor advised that this would require a 2–3 day stay in the hospital. Instead, I went to an excellent nearby clinic one morning where they quickly and competently performed the operation. One hour later, I walked the six blocks to my home and went to bed. While I had to rest for the several days following, I saved 60% of what the total cost would have been had I stayed in a hospital for the operation.

If the need for minor surgery arises, check with your doctor to see if it can't be performed on an outpatient basis.

(5) GET IMMUNIZATION SHOTS FROM YOUR COMMUNITY HEALTH AGENCIES.

Before paying your doctor $8–10.00 for immunization shots for you or your children, check with your community health agencies, where they are often given free under government auspices.

(6) KNOW WHAT YOUR INSURANCE COVERS.

The average person is overwhelmed by an insurance policy and often does not know the extent of the coverage. This unfortunate lack of knowledge can cause loss of benefits to which the insured is entitled.

For example, many hospitalization plans carry additional "Major-Medical" coverage that picks up medical costs where the basic hospital plan ends—particularly where there are major or catastrophic medical emergencies (if you don't have such coverage, you might well consider getting it, since it is relatively inexpensive). There is usually a $100.00 deductible provision, but once you've accumulated that $100.00 in medical bills (including drugs, etc.)—major medical coverage will usually pay 80% of all further doctor and hospital bills, drugs, dental care, etc., etc. In many respects, it is actually better coverage than the basic hospital plan. However, most people do not understand this coverage and as a result, fail to file for many benefits to which they are entitled.

Make a definite point to understand your coverage. Have your agent explain the plan in detail and make your own notes so that you will understand your benefits if the need arises. As high as 25–30% of these benefits go unclaimed because the insured person is not aware of their existence.

(7) DON'T BE AFRAID TO TALK TO YOUR DOCTOR ABOUT MONEY.

One of the strangest aspects of our modern medical scene is the lack of communication between the patient and doctor—particularly about the subject of money. The same individual who couldn't imagine buying an appliance or an automobile without careful consideration and negotiation would never dream of discussing costs and fees with a doctor.

This is a big mistake.

First of all, a frank and open discussion of costs and fees beforehand with your doctor—such as for an upcoming hospital or surgery situation—can be most productive financially. Often the doctor may be able to suggest cost-cutting combinations of tests, procedures, etc. that can save you money. If you feel that costs and fees are unreasonable—tell him so. You'd be amazed at how reasonable and constructive most doctors are when you discuss such a situation with them. Most people don't.

Finally, most doctors are understanding and generous. If you're having financial difficulty, have lost your job or have other extenuating circumstances, many of them will reduce their bills if you explain and discuss the situation with them.

Whatever the situation, don't hesitate to discuss money matters with your doctor. You'll find him receptive and helpful and in most cases quite willing to work things out with you.

SUMMARY OF ECONOMIC SURVIVAL TECHNIQUES
IN MEDICAL AND DENTAL CARE

TECHNIQUES	NET SAVINGS
(1) REDUCE THE NUMBER OF VISITS TO THE OFFICE	15–20%
(2) INVESTIGATE THE USE OF CLINICS AND TEACHING SCHOOLS	40–60%
(3) AVOID UNNECESSARY TESTS AND SURGERY	25–30%
(4) USE OUTPATIENT CLINICS FOR MINOR SURGERY	50–60%
(5) GET IMMUNIZATION SHOTS FROM HEALTH SERVICES	5–10%
(6) KNOW WHAT YOUR INSURANCE COVERS	20–30%
(7) DON'T BE AFRAID TO TALK TO YOUR DOCTOR ABOUT MONEY	10–20%
TOTAL POSSIBLE SAVINGS	5–60%

While the cost of medical and dental care becomes ever more exhorbitant and the margins for economy ever smaller, the forgoing areas still offer the individual cost reducing opportunities that he or she can effectively employ. Each of them is worth investigating.

Taxes

TAXES

Without question, taxes today constitute the major threat to the individual's economic survival. Combined federal, state and local tax levies now constitute the single, greatest expense in the annual cost of living, exceeding the cost of food, housing, transportation and every other item in the family budget.

Within the last five years, taxes at all levels—federal, state and local—have nearly doubled and are rising twice as fast as the average worker's earnings. Collectively, these taxes now take an astounding 51% of the entire annual earnings of the nation! At the current rate of increase, by 1990, taxes will take 60% of the nation's earnings and by the year 2000—70%!

In brief, the tax collectors already take the majority of our earnings and it is strikingly obvious that unless this appalling trend is halted—and even reversed—that our children and grandchildren will spend their working lives in unpaid servitude to the state. This is hardly what our founding forefathers intended for the citizens of this great nation.

The average individual, increasingly hard pressed to provide the basic necessities of living, knows that something is radically wrong—but untutored in the complexities of the economic system and the massive tax structure—he or she does not really grasp the seriousness of the situation.

The following tables will give the reader a graphic illustration of the terrifying confiscation of wealth currently taking place through our system of taxation. Reviewed in the tables are the total taxes paid by single individuals earning $5,000, $15,000 and $25,000—an income range that covers 95% of the nation's population.

Table I reviews just the income and social security taxes taken directly from the individual's earnings.

Table II reviews the extent of hidden taxes taken from the individual as he spends the money left in his hand after the income taxes. These are just as devastating as the income taxes —and in the $5,000–$15,000 income brackets—they exceed the income taxes! The fact that the individual is not aware of them does not lessen their crippling effect. Even if the individual does not consider them taxes because he cannot see them—they dramatically inflate the cost of all goods and services he buys, thus reducing the real purchasing power of the dollars in his hand. In fact, politicians love hidden taxes for the very reason that the individual is not aware he is paying them. But aware or not—they represent just as definite a confiscation of the individual's earnings as do the taxes he sees.

TABLE I—INCOME TAXES

GROSS EARNINGS	$5,000	%	$15,000	%	$25,000	%
FEDERAL INCOME TAXES	$ 251	5%	$ 2,322	15.5%	$ 5,502	22%
SOCIAL SECURITY TAXES	345	6.9%	1,035	6.9%	1,725	6.9%
*STATE INCOME TAXES	58	1.2%	680	4.5%	1,780	7.1%
TOTAL INCOME TAXES	$ 654	13%	$ 4,037	27%	$ 9,007	36%
NET EARNINGS AFTER INCOME TAXES	$ 4,346		$10,963		$15,993	

*BASED ON NEW YORK STATE, THIS WILL VARY WITH OTHER STATES.

Table I provides some very revealing insights:
(1) Even at the lowest income of $5,000—which is a bare survival level—combined income taxes still take 13% of the individuals earnings!

(2) The progressive steepness of taxation even at these lower income levels is stupefying. For example, let us suppose that an individual, through hard work and good fortune is able to raise his income first from $5,000 to $15,000 and then finally to $25,000. By all reasonable measure, he should be enjoying increased prosperity and success. In fact, just the opposite is true —for the more he earns—the less proportionately he will get to keep.

	TAXES TAKEN	%	LEFT TO INDIVIDUAL	%
(a) First $5,000 of Earnings–	$ 654	13%	$4,346	87%
(b) *NEXT* $10,000 Earned (From $5,000–$15,000)–	3,383	34%	6,617	66%
(c) *NEXT* $10,000 Earned (From $15,000–$25,000)–	4,970	50%	5,030	50%

Obviously, success is punished by confiscation and the more income the individual produces, the more he works for the tax collector and not for himself and his family. Even at the modest income level of $15,000, income taxes alone take 30% of the individual's earnings and at $25,000, they will take 40%!!!

Bear in mind that we have thus far reviewed only income taxes. Let us now proceed to Table II and the further carnage of hidden taxes.

TABLE II

Hidden taxes, which are the least understood by the individual taxpayer, are nonetheless among the most rapacious in the seizure of individual earnings. They include an almost unlimited range of sales taxes, excise taxes, manufacturers taxes, utility taxes, transportation taxes, etc., etc. All are carefully tucked away in the final price the individual pays for the goods and services he must buy. Every single one of these levies are passed on down to the consuming wage-earner and out of every dollar he spends for goods and services, $.28–.30 is for these hidden taxes.

TABLE II

GROSS INCOME	$5,000	%	$15,000	%	$25,000	%
SALES & OTHER HIDDEN TAXES	1,216	24%	3,070	21%	4,480	18%
TOTAL TAXES—INCOME & HIDDEN	1,870	37%	7,107	47%	13,487	54%
REAL PURCHASING POWER AFTER TAXES	$3,131		$7,893		$11,513	

From Table II, it is most obvious that hidden taxes are equally as punishing as the income taxes. At the lowest level of income —they are double the amount of income taxes, and fall most harshly upon the person least able to afford them.

It is also clear that for those in the $15,000 to $25,000 income brackets—those 80% of the nation's wage-earners that constitute the middle class of the nation—that combined income and hidden taxes now take a full 50% of all their earnings!!

Real estate taxes, which make up still a further levy, were not included in the forgoing tables since their payment can be used as a deduction to partially offset income taxes paid. However, even these constitute not only a further burden, but a growing threat to the whole concept of private ownership of property.

While the recently enacted federal tax cuts would seem to hold the promise of badly needed relief for the overburdened taxpayer—the rejoicing may well be premature. There is already a rapidly growing pressure from influential Congressmen to cancel the scheduled 10% income tax cut of 1983 and to eliminate altogether the 1985 tax-indexing provision which would have halted the annual rise in income taxes due to inflation. Moreover, even if taxes at the federal level are temporarily slowed—state and local taxes are rising at an incredible rate and the overall outlook for the next decade is for <u>more</u> taxes—not less.

In the headlong race by all levels of government to confiscate the productive wealth of the individual, the lower class pays only a small portion of this runaway taxation and the wealthy have devised a sophisticated structure of tax shelters to protect themselves from the worst effects of the increasing plunder.

But the working middle class—the blue collar and the white collar worker in the $12,000 to $25,000 income bracket—have nowhere to run, and they are literally being destroyed financially through taxation. To borrow from the great Ben Franklin:

"The common man among tax collectors is like a fish in the company of cats."

In view of this worsening plight of the average citizen—the hypocrisy of our current Congress is absolutely appalling. In a recent late-night session—in which the individual votes were not even recorded—Congress voted <u>themselves</u> the biggest tax break in U.S. history! Giving its members an exclusive tax package that will allow up to <u>$40,500</u> in unchallengable tax deductions for each Congressman—it is quite possible that many will never again have to pay a cent in Federal taxes.

The following are just a few of the "goodies" contained in the package:

(1) While Congress is in session—which is most of the year—each member gets a "working" tax deduction of <u>$75.00</u> per day —or actual expenses if they're higher. This provision alone is worth <u>$20–22,000</u> per year. No other citizen gets that kind of tax break.

(2) Each Congressman's home in Washington, D.C. is <u>completely</u> tax-deductible. How would you like to be able to deduct that on <u>your</u> 1040 form each April?

(3) Every trip back home is deductible. Since they're already

getting a tax-free reimbursement of these expenses—this constitutes a <u>double</u> tax deduction. If you did this on <u>your</u> annual tax report—you'd go to jail for tax fraud.

(4) All of the deductions in the package are <u>retroactive</u> to last year. That means a <u>doubling</u> of the deductions and a real bonanza since they can go back and reclaim taxes that might have been paid out last year.

This incredible self-serving tax package is in addition to the fact that these legislators are already getting discounted meals and haircuts, free travel around the world, free postage, free parking, free office space, etc., etc., etc. Few people realize that it already costs the suffering taxpayer over <u>one billion dollars</u> a year to maintain this small body of legislators in the style to which we would all like to be accustomed to living.

Few rulers in history have ever fared quite so well as the new aristocracy on the Potomac!

These are the same Congressmen who are pompously crying out for a balanced budget and that they are trying to help the average citizen.

Having thus assured their own economic well being by granting themselves exclusive tax privileges, the good Congressmen have now dedicated themselves with zeal to "balancing the budget" for the economic well being of the rest of the citizenry. Rather than cutting spending, however, the plan afoot is to balance the budget by <u>increasing</u> taxes on the average worker.

At the same time as it voted itself a privileged tax status, Congress began drawing up a new gauntlet of horrors for the rest of us. Here are just a few of the new delights we can look forward to:

(1) A delay or outright repeal of the 10% tax cut scheduled for 1983.

(2) A repeal of the 1985 tax indexing provision.

(3) Limits on personal interest, sales taxes and medical de-

ductions. A cap of possibly $100 for individuals and $200 for couples or families. A cutback on mortgage interest deductions.

(4) New excise taxes on telephones, tobacco, alcohol, jewelry, furs, etc.

(5) An income-tax surcharge on top of what you're already paying.

(6) Elimination of the already enacted 1985 faster depreciation schedule for business investments.

(7) Stronger enforcement of tax laws. Authorization for the hiring of 5,000 new I.R.S. agents, to catch the "cheaters"— which obviously means the rest of us who don't have the tax breaks which Congress voted for itself.

The enactment of these and further measures will completely gut the 1981 Tax Relief Bill and raise the confiscation of individual wealth to a level unprecedented in the history of the nation. Congress, of course, will itself remain untouched by the horrors it is now enacting.

In the face of this ominous situation, are there any effective countermeasures—short of dying—that the individual can take to reduce this crushing burden of taxation?

Surprisingly, there are effective strategies which the average man can employ. In the long run, the only real solution is a determined, two-pronged offensive:

—First, to vote out of office the free-spending politicians who continue to create this destructive taxation and inflation in the first place, and,

—A return to the self-sufficiency principles of our former household economy—producing more of our own housing, food and other needs ourselves—which would put a larger share of the individual's wealth beyond the reach of the tax collector.

In the short run, and during the period when hopefully these two policies can be implemented to save the nation from its present course of self-destruction, there are positive techniques which the individual can use to lighten the burden.

(1) REDUCE YOUR MONEY EARNINGS AS MUCH AS POS-SIBLE.

Since money itself is the principal instrument through which your wealth is confiscated—exchanging your valuable time and labor for money will bring you the lowest possible economic benefit. While the conventional wisdom has taught us to believe that higher earnings will bring increased wealth and prosperity —for the average man or woman today—quite the opposite is true because of our system of taxation. In fact, the higher the earnings, the less you will be able to retain. Therefore, working harder and longer to increase your money income will only benefit the tax collector.

For the forseeable future, by far the most effective strategy is to reduce your money earnings—and thus your taxes.

(A) Spend less of your time working for the tax collector and more for yourself.

At first, it is very difficult for the average individual to understand how it is possible, by reducing money earnings, to actually benefit and gain greater wealth. A simple analysis will quickly illustrate the benefits to be gained:

Let us imagine, for demonstration purposes—that you have just been offered a temporary job for the next four months at a local plant or industry. During this time you are paid $5,000 in wages and at the end of the four months, the job is terminated. You do not expect to be employed for the rest of the year and therefore $5,000 will be your total wages for the year. From our previous Table I, out of the $5,000, you will pay $654.00 in taxes and you will have $4,346.50 left in spendable income.

While trying to decide what you will do with all of your time for the remaining eight months of the year, you suddenly receive a call from the plant advising you that the situation has changed and they would like you to come back for the remaining eight months at the same salary.

You are delighted at the news! You already have $4,346 and here is a chance to earn another $10,000. However, a quick glance at Table I again shows that of the next $10,000—you will only get to keep $6,617.

In other words, you will have to work eight months—twice as long as the first time—and only get 50% more income than you did for your first four months of work!

The proposition is no longer quite so attractive, for you realize that you will be working longer and harder for less and less money.

But supposing that you did not return to work at the plant and instead, spent the remaining eight months working for yourself —producing some of your own housing, food, clothing, etc.

If, for example, you kept your $4,346 on hand just to pay for such items as utility bills and spent your full-time working on growing food, remodeling your apartment, rebuilding an automobile, making your own clothing or a variety of other goods and services which you needed—you would be infinitely better off financially.

First of all, you would totally avoid any further taxes on your valuable labor. You would also save the substantial costs of transportation to and from a place of employment. Secondly, the total wealth created by your eight months of labor belongs to you and not the tax collector. The value of the goods and/or services you produced would far exceed the $6,617 the tax collector would leave you with had you gone back to the plant to work for wages.

Remember the example of Fred (in the Housing section) who left his $15,000 job and spent the entire year building his own house? Out of a gross earnings of $15,000—after paying out $7,000 in taxes and $3,000 for the cost of transportation to his employment—he had only $5,000 of spendable income left for his entire year of labor.

By ceasing to work for wages—and instead devoting his time and labor to producing wealth <u>for himself</u>—he and <u>his wife reduced their taxes by 75%</u> and created a <u>tax-free</u> wealth of <u>$32,000</u> for the year (their equity in the new home).

In a still further example of the benefits of reducing your money earnings and working for yourself instead, a very savvy former salesman friend named Alex has adapted this technique into a highly refined and pleasant style of living.

Until a few years ago, Alex led a frantic, pressure-filled existence, constantly on the road covering his sales territory and seeing his wife and two teenage sons much less frequently than he cared to. His wife also worked and together they had a joint income of $40,000—which was far above the average and would certainly seem to indicate that they should definitely be enjoying the "good life."

But somehow, they seemed always to be short of money and just barely keeping up with their current bills. No matter how hard they tried—they seemed utterly unable to save any money at all.

Then one day, Alex sat down and tried to calculate why, with all their effort and their apparent high income—that they were having so much difficulty. He was shocked at what he discovered:

```
GROSS EARNINGS...........................  $40,000
Federal Income Taxes ...............  $8,410
Social Security Taxes ...............   2,760
State Income Taxes .................   3,520
Total Income Taxes.................  $14,690 (37% of Income)
Net Earnings After Income Taxes.........  $25,310
Cost of Transportation (2 autos) to and from
    employment.....................  $7,087 (18% of Income)
Spendable Income after taxes and transportation
    to employment .................        $18,223
Total Cost of Being Employed (Taxes & Transportation) .....  $21,777
                                            (55% of Income)
```

It stunned Alex to realize that out of their joint income of

$40,000—income taxes alone took nearly $15,000—37%! Further, they had to spend another $7,000 in transportation just to produce this income. Taxes and related costs thus took 55% of his and his wife's income, leaving them with only $18,000 for all their hard work and sacrifice of family time together.

Alex and his wife promptly quit thier jobs. As an alternative, they devised a far more productive life style:

(1) Alex and his wife and two sons all took part-time jobs.
(2) They set a ceiling of no more than $5,000 earnings per year for any of the four family members. Once that ceiling has been reached—the member quit working for wages for that year. Taxes are thus kept to a bare minimum.

For Alex and his family, the plan has been a smashing success:

(1) No one in the family works more than 4–5 months for outside wages.
(2) Out of their combined annual income of $20,000—they now pay less than $2,000 in taxes—meaning they have reduced their tax bill by a whopping 87%!!!! Moreover, they still have $18,000 in spendable income—as much as they had before—and with far less time and effort!!
(3) The biggest payoff of all is that the family now has 7–8 months a year of free time to do whatever they wish. They're actually having the time of their lives. Alex and his sons go hunting and fishing, the family goes hiking and picnicing and they have plenty of time for hobbies and other pastimes. In the last several years, they've begun to grow much of thier own food, put an addition on their home and build wooden furniture in their basement workshop—all of which has created non-taxable wealth far in excess of the $18,000 spendable income they receive from their part-time employment.

By reducing their earnings and spending more of their time working for themselves, Alex and his family have superbly thwarted the tax collector and are getting much more enjoyment out of their lives.

While the circumstances will vary from one individual to another, the reader should seriously explore the use of this technique for reducing taxes and increasing the level of prosperity. It really works!

(B) Barter more of your labor for goods and services instead of wages..

If directly producing your own necessities, such as food, housing, etc. is difficult or even impossible—then trade your labor for the goods and services you need. Keep your money earnings as low as possible which—as in the previous technique—will hold your taxes to a minimum.

However, since keeping your money earnings at a low level means that you will only be working part-time for wages—either a few days a week or a few months a year—you will have a great deal of free time available. If you are not using this free time to produce your own goods, then you can productively exchange your free-time labor for a variety of goods and services that you need.

There is nothing new about such a system of barter. It has existed since the beginning of civilization and in fact, until modern times was the most prevalent method of economic exchange. A farm hand would trade his labor for food and shelter, a seamstress would pay the landlord the rent by making clothes for his family, the rural physician would trade his medical skills for food and other objects from his patients, etc., etc. In recent times, there has been a dramatic resurgence of such bartering, and in the worsening economic situation—bartering is proving to be a superb method of acquiring many of the basic necessities and the practice is growing rapidly.

Alarmed at the possibility that some of the productive wealth of bartering may be escaping the tax net, tax officials have ruled that barter is subject to the same tax rules as money earnings. Benevolently, they have ruled that simple bartering or exchange of labor between relatives or friends will not be subjected to taxes.

For example, if your brother-in-law spent five hours of his time and labor helping you repair your back porch and you gave him half a dozen jars of canned tomatoes from your supply in the cellar for helping you—he would not have to declare the tomatoes as part of his taxable income. Even though the tomatoes were actually "earnings" for the labor he had expended—he would not have to pay tax on them.

Such heartwarming generosity, however, does not extend beyond the small circle of friends and relatives. If, for example, you agree to build a game room on the back of the dentists home in return for his fixing your children's teeth—then technically, each of you should declare the "fair market value" of the services or goods received in exchange for your labor and add this to your taxable income.

However, while such specific guidelines have been laid down by the taxing authorities, the problems involved in the evaluation of bartering are so overwhelming that enforcement of such rules on any large scale may well be unenforceable.

First of all, the whole tax system rests upon voluntary compliance by the individual, and depends upon the individual's keeping records and then paying the taxes. However, compulsory withholding of taxes from wages was instituted because the average individual did <u>not</u> keep sufficient records and because he frequently did <u>not</u> have enough money to pay the taxes when they came due.

It is hardly realistic to assume that the same individual will suddenly keep meticulous records every time he swaps a dozen eggs or a bushel of apples for an hour of casual labor.

Secondly, who will determine "fair market value?" Is a dozen eggs to be valued at the wholesale price or at the retail price? During the pullet season when eggs are cheap, or during the later season when they are more expensive? What is the value of a used table and chairs? 50% of original value? 20%?

The problems of determining "fair market value" on the vast range of goods and services in our society are mindboggling and the probabilities of controversy are endless. One of the major reasons for the creation of money was to give a definite specific value to each item. Once we move off of the money value system, we step into a no-man's land of values quite beyond the determination of the ordinary mortal and even that of the tax collector.

But even assuming that meticulous records are kept, and the fairest of market values determined, the individual comes out way ahead of the game by bartering his labor for goods and services instead of for money earnings or wages. Even with the payment of income taxes on these bartered earnings, he escapes the impact of Social Security taxes, sales taxes and the worst ravages of a host of other hidden taxes.

In general, by such bartering, the individual will reduce his overall taxes by at least 20–50%—which could spell the difference between subsistence survival and prosperity.

(2) USE ALL POSSIBLE DEDUCTIONS AND TAX SHELTERS.

In spite of the crushing burden of annual income taxes, many people do not take full advantage of the deductions to which they are entitled. It has been estimated that the average person could reduce his or her income taxes by as much as 10–20% if they would take every legitimate deduction available to them. Try the following suggestions for lowering your income taxes.

(A) Set up a record file just for taxes.

The biggest loss of deductions occurs through lack of accurate records. Immediately set up a record file—in a box, file drawer, or even just in envelopes. Set up a compartment for every category of expense that is deductible—medical, taxes, interest, contributions, etc. If you're not sure, refer to the I.R.S. Schedule A & B for the categories and label your categories from the schedule. If you're in business, use a Schedule C for a list of deductible categories.

Next, get into the daily habit of recording every expenditure you make, whether by check or cash and asking for receipts whenever possible. Then place each receipt into its proper compartment. If you had made a cash expenditure and gotten no receipt—say for a road toll or a parking fee—make a note of the amount and the date and place it in the file. Record every expenditure, no matter how small and file it.

Each year taxpayers lose hundreds of dollars worth of deductions that could have lowered their taxes. Setting up such a file will pay off in two ways: first, it will greatly simplify your task of preparing your return when tax time comes and second, you'll get every deduction to which you are entitled. While the law requires that you pay taxes that are due, there's no reason to pay one cent more than that for which you are legally liable.

(B) Do not overwithhold taxes during the year.

The average American taxpayer each year receives a tax refund of approximately $500–800. This means that the vast majority of employers are overwithholding taxes from the employees weekly paychecks. Some employees, under the mistaken impression that they are "saving" money purposely do not claim all of their dependents so that their tax refund will be even larger at tax-time.

When the employer overwithholds—the employee loses in two ways: first, the government pays him no interest on the use of the extra money it holds and he loses the use of it during the year. Secondly, by the time the employee finally gets the money back—inflation has eroded its purchasing power by 10–15%.

Very few people realize the actual extent of their losses through overwithholding. For example, the individual who received a $500.00 tax refund (because it was overwithheld) lost $46.90 in interest, plus an additional $70.00 loss through inflation (at 14% last year)—for a total loss of $116.90 out of the original $500.00!! At $800 overwithheld, the loss rises to $187.04! And if you're also receiving a state tax refund—you're suffering the same kind of losses.

Put still another way, if your taxes are being overwithheld, you're paying an additional penalty of 20–24% on all of the extra withholding!

So don't continue to overwithhold your taxes under the impression that you are saving money because you're actually incurring substantial losses. Go to your employer and have him lower your tax withholding.

(C) Be sure to use the new energy tax credits.

Here's one place where the taxpayer finally gets a break—so be sure to take full advantage of these new credits granted for weatherizing your home or installing solar, geothermal or wind energy.(1) If you weatherize your home to reduce heating costs —insulation, window caulking, storm windows, installation of a more effective burner or electro-mechanical ignition in your furnace—you can claim 15% of the first $2,000 cost—(or $300.00) as a credit. Bear in mind that this is a credit—not a deduction. A deduction is subtracted from your gross earnings —while a credit is deducted from your actual tax bill.

For example, on your $15,000 gross earnings, your Federal Income Taxes are calculated to be $2,322. If you are eligible for the $300 weatherization tax credit, you now subtract the $300 from the $2,322—lowering your tax bill to $2,022.(2) If you install mechanical systems to obtain alternative energy from solar, geothermal, or wind sources—you can claim 40% of the first $10,000 of cost (or $4,000) as a tax credit.

What these credits actually mean is that the government will give you a one-shot tax allowance if you take measures to reduce your consumption of traditional gas, oil and electric resources.

So at least consider weatherizing your home. Not only will you benefit from lower utility bills—but a portion of the cost will be covered by tax dollars. Full information is contained in I.R.S. Publication 903, Energy Credits for Individuals.

(D) Set up an Individual Retirement Account (IRA).

The new IRA, created by the recent tax legislation, is probably the only real tax shelter available to the average man or woman and everyone should take advantage of it.

Unlike previous plans, which tied the amount of contributions to the amount of income earned (15% of gross earnings)—you may deposit up to $2,000 a year regardless of your earnings. If you have a non-working spouse, you may deposit $2,250 a year, and if you and your spouse work, you may put $4,000 a year into an IRA account. If you earned less than $2,000—say $1,500— then your deposit cannot exceed what you earned.

The IRA is truly the working man's tax shelter. Whatever you deposit in an IRA comes right off the top of your earnings. For example, if you have gross earnings of $15,000, here is the situation:

WITHOUT AN IRA

GROSS EARNINGS . . $15,000.00   Federal Income Taxes . . —$2,322

WITH AN IRA DEPOSIT OF $2,000

GROSS EARNINGS . . $15,000.00
IRA Deposit. 2,000.00
Earnings Taxed. . . . . $13,000.00   Federal Income Taxes . . —$1,826

The $2,000 deposited in the IRA is deducted from your gross earnings, lowering the amount of taxable income to $13,000— so that you will pay $500.00 less in taxes. So of the $2,000 you put into the IRA, $500 actually were taxes that you would have otherwise paid. If your gross earnings are $25,000, the tax dollar portion of your $2,000 IRA rises to $700.

The IRA thus represents a unique tax-shelter opportunity for the average person to siphon off tax dollars into his or her own retirement income account.

The total amount of the IRA plus all interest, dividends and earnings accumulate tax-free and with compound interest over the years, can build substantial wealth for the individual.

Assuming even a conservative 10% interest or dividend earnings compounded over the years will give you an idea of the dramatic accumulation that takes place.

	TOTAL OF DEPOSITS AND ACCUMULATED INTEREST EARNINGS AT THE END OF:		
IRA DEPOSIT OF	10 YEARS	20 YEARS	30 YEARS
$2,000 EACH YEAR	$37,895	$157,883	$554,950

At the end of 30 years, for total deposits of only $60,000—the individual will have accumulated $554,950—nine times the amount deposited. This is because all of the earnings on the deposits are allowed to accumulate tax-free. At retirement, the individual will have to pay taxes on the money as it is withdrawn, but it will be at a lower rate.

The plan is a real bonanza for the taxpayer, but there are certain regulations which must be met:

(1) Deposits must be made in approved IRA plans—organized by banks, credit unions, brokerage houses, mutual funds, insurance companies, etc. The individual directs how the funds are to be invested, whether in common stock, certificates of deposit, money market funds, etc. but the money must be handled by an approved program.

(2) Minimum age for withdrawal of funds is 59½ and the maximum age 70½. If funds are withdrawn prior to 59½, the individual must pay taxes plus a penalty of 10% on the amount withdrawn.

Every individual should make an attempt to set up an IRA. Any amount up to $2,000 can be deposited and can even be made in installments through the course of the year—in some cases through payroll deductions. In the final analysis, it may even be worthwhile to borrow the money for an IRA deposit—and the interest on the loan is tax-deductible!

(3) GO INTO DIRECT MARKETING—THE BEST OF ALL TAX SHELTERS.

For the average person, there is absolutely no better tax shelter for reducing your annual taxes. Whether you have a full or part-time direct sales job, the tax benefits are more extensive than any other business. If you sell any kind of a product on an outside, direct sales basis, you can legitimately claim an incredible range of deductions:

(A) Home Deductions..

If you use a portion of your home—say a spare room, or part of your basement—as an office, display room for products, or any other function connected with your sales business, you take as a business deduction that percentage of your home so used. CAUTION: This portion must be used exclusively for business purposes. If it is also used for other living activities, it may be disallowed as a deduction by the tax authorities. It is important to note this restriction.

For example, say you use a spare bedroom for an office and display room and the room is 20% of the space in your home. Then you may deduct 20% of the amount of your mortgage or rent as a business deduction. The same applies to all other costs of your home such as heat, electricity, etc. 20% of all those costs can also be deducted as business expenses.

Secondly, if you operate from your home and you drive to a separate business or place of employment, that's considered to be travel between two business locations and is tax deductible. Since transportation to and from work constitutes 80–90% of all mileage driven—you can deduct about 90% of all automobile costs as a business deduction. That could save you $2,000–3,000 a year in Federal and State income taxes.

(B) Personal expenses, including entertainment and travel.

Since everyone you know or meet—including friends and

relatives—is a sales prospect, and since there are no geographical limits to where you might sell—a very substantial amount of personal entertainment, travel and personal expenses can be converted into business expenses which are tax deductible. Simply make a record of the date, the amount spent and get a brief, signed statement from someone to whom you made a presentation of your product.

The taxes you save will cover 40–50% of all your expenses.

(C) Income transfers to your children.

You can legally hire your children and deduct their salaries from your income. If a child is under 18 (21 if a student) he or she can earn up to $3,300 per year as an employee of a parent without being subject to any taxation. This means that you can pay each of your children a tax-free income of $3,300 and deduct this cost from your gross income as a business expense. This would save you about $800–1,000 on your annual taxes. Your children must, of course, be old enough and mature enough to be able to do the work you specify that they are doing.

(D) Deduction of gifts as a business expense.

Any gift you purchase as a business promotion or as a "thank-you" gift for a client or prospective customer—which could be friends and relatives—is tax deductible. The gift can be at any time or for any occasion such as birthdays, anniversaries, Christmas, etc., but there is a tax-deduction limit of $25.00 per year per person.

(E) Investment tax credits.

There is an additional 10% tax credit for any equipment you buy that is used in your business. This, of course, includes your automobile. After your taxes are compiled, you may deduct 10% of the cost of the equipment directly from your completed tax bill for that year.

For example, let's say that your taxes for the year are determined to be $5,000, and during the year you had purchased an automobile for $8,000. You may take a credit of $800.00 (10% of the automobile cost) directly off your tax bill, dropping the amount you must pay to $4,200.

(F) Partnership benefits.

Couples may operate as a partnership in a direct marketing business, bringing tax benefits to both. For example, since they are both in the direct marketing business, if they both have a separate additional job, they will be able to obtain deductions for each of their automobiles. If they are traveling together, expenses for both of them will be tax-deductible.

(G) Losses from your direct marketing can be offset against other income.

Let us say that from your part-time direct marketing business, that you actually made a profit of $6,000. When you add up all the business expenses you have recorded—for home, entertainment, auto, travel, children's salaries, etc.—they come to $15,000. The $15,000 is actually the same money you spent for living expenses, but because they are defined as business operational costs—on paper, you show a business loss of $9,000 from your direct marketing business for the year!

Since you suffered a "loss", not only do you not have to pay any taxes on the $6,000 you made—but you can deduct the $9,000 paper loss from any other income you had. If for example, you had a $15,000 salary from your regular job—this $9,000 loss can be deducted from that income—virtually wiping out all taxes you normally would have paid.

The tax shelter benefits of being in direct marketing are truly impressive. For the average man or woman struggling to relieve themselves of the crushing tax burden—it's definitely the way to go. It doesn't matter what the service or product you sell— Avon, Shaklee, Amway, Meadowfresh, Tupperware, Jewelry, Books, or any of a limitless range of products—just get into it.

With proper organization and planning, you can legitimately eliminate 50–90% of your annual income taxes!

(4) WORK OVERSEAS.

Prior to the last decade, hundreds of thousands of Americans worked abroad in all corners of the earth. Although the living and working conditions were often difficult, if not primitive—wages were high and taxes much less than in the continental U.S.—so that it was possible for these individuals, through thrift and hard work to return home after a number of years with a tidy nest egg for retirement or other purposes.

The presence of these workers overseas played a large part not only in the maintenance of American prestige abroad but in the sale of American products and technology—which greatly helped to effect a favorable balance of trade and a sound economy at home.

In the last decade, however, the tax authorities, embarking on the most precipitous rise of taxation in American history—withdrew the tax privileges of overseas workers and put them on approximately the same basis as domestic workers, despite the often higher costs and hardships of those in overseas positions.

Of all the industrialized western nations, the U.S. was the only one to so tax its citizens working abroad.

The results have been counterproductive and highly damaging to our position internationally. Not only have we lost thousands of jobs for Americans overseas through this policy of taxation, but the consequent loss of product and technology sales abroad have negatively affected our balance of trade and the soundness of our economy.

The new tax legislation of 1981, however, has now attempted to reverse this damaging policy, and in an attempt to revive American employment overseas, has again made foreign employment extremely attractive.

Beginning in 1982, any American working outside the United States will be virtually free of income taxes. The first $75,000 of income per year, plus $6,000 of living expense—for a total of

$81,000 per year—can be excluded from the payment of income tax. This exclusion will rise to $95,000 per year by 1986—so that for all practical purposes, the individual working overseas will be free of income taxes.

To qualify for this exclusion, the individual must be out of the continental U.S. for eleven months of the year and full details are available from any I.R.S. office.

So if you want to avoid income taxes—look for a job overseas.

(5) AVOID SALES TAXES BY BUYING OUT-OF-STATE.

Sales taxes, ranging from 7–9% are levied on virtually every product or service you buy, so that they take a healthy bite out of your income. Since such taxes are levied by the individual states (and often by counties and cities in addition) and since there is no such thing as an inter-state sales tax—it may pay you to do your shopping in another state—especially on large purchases. A resident of one state is normally exempt from another state's sales tax when he makes a purchase in the second state.

Often there is a difference even between counties within the same state. For example, residents of the county in which we live must pay a 7% sales tax on all purchases. However, in the next county, 12 miles away, the sales tax is only 4%, due to the lack of a county sales tax—and the merchants there do a thriving business from the residents of our county. 35 miles away is the border with another state and our local residents willing to make the half-hour drive pay no sales taxes on the goods they purchase across the state line.

Purchasing by mail from an out-of-state company is another way of avoiding sales tax since the point-of-purchase is literally the company office where they receive your check for the product, so that you are actually an out-of-state buyer and not subject to their state's sales tax. Make sure that you demand a sales tax exemption from the seller. Whether buying by mail or driving, you must of course calculate the cost of shipping or transportation against the savings in sales tax to determine whether or not you are coming out ahead.

In general, the greatest savings will be realized on large purchases and by those who live close to a state line and can conveniently cross the border for most of their purchases. In such situations, the average family could well save $400–600 per year in sales taxes.

(6) REDUCE REAL ESTATE TAXES BY DELAYING PAYMENT.

Real estate taxes have reached a crushing level throughout the nation and in some sections of the country, such as the northeast, they have virtually destroyed the concept of private ownership of property. Residents no longer really own their homes—they merely lease them from the community on an annual basis of tribute. If they fail to raise the ransom for several years in a row, they are unceremoniously stripped of their ownership and ejected from the home for which they may have worked their entire lives.

There are several counter strategies for fighting back against this growing confiscation.

First of all, do not improve the outside exterior of your property. Exterior painting or roof repair are normal maintenance and cannot be assessed as improvements for increase of your taxes. However, the addition of new siding, new windows, etc. are determined by many communities to be capital improvements and are used as a justification for raising your taxes. The rationale is that since your home is now worth more—you should pay more in taxes. One unfortunate soul in our own community made the unhappy mistake of taking a dilapidated old residence in the center of town and giving it an outside "facelift"—new siding, windows, and roof. When he was finished—after much work and expense—he had transformed a community eyesore into an attractive building that was of benefit to the surrounding neighborhood.

His reward? They tripled his real estate taxes. So if you're going to improve your home—do it on the inside where it isn't visible to the tax assessor. The punitive tax policies of our communities do not reward the efforts of citizens who upgrade the appearance of their neighborhoods.

Secondly—and more effective—is the technique of delaying the payment of your real estate taxes. In most communities, foreclosure of real estate for back taxes cannot occur until 3–4 years after the tax becomes due. In our area, for example, if you did not pay your real estate taxes for 1981, a tax foreclosure for these taxes would not take place until 1985—four years hence. Interest and penalties are added, up to a <u>maximum</u> (for the whole four years) of <u>25%</u> of the original taxes (or roughly about 6¼% per year).

For example, if your taxes for the year were say <u>$1500</u> and you did not pay them, over the next three years, <u>$375</u> (25% of the $1500) in penalties would be added so that if you paid them in the fourth year before foreclosure were to take place, you would have to pay a total of <u>$1875</u>.

Therefore, if instead of paying the real estate taxes, you took the $1500 and put it into a Certificate of Deposit in the bank, you could earn <u>13–15%</u> in compounded interest. Over a four year period at 15%, this would amount to approximately <u>$1,124,</u> which with your original $1,500 would now give you a total of <u>$2,624.</u> You now go in and pay your real estate taxes before foreclosure takes place. Subtracting <u>$1,875</u> tax bill from your <u>$2,624</u>—you're ahead by <u>$749!!</u>

Under the new tax legislation of 1981, you are allowed a tax-free interest exclusion of $200 per year ($400 if you're married), so that your interest earnings on the Certificate of Deposit are virtually tax-free.

In effect, <u>you</u> will have earned a tax-free <u>$749</u> on dollars that otherwise would simply have disappeared into the tax collector's treasure chest with no benefit to you. Analyzed another way, since you started with <u>$1,500</u> and you got back <u>$749</u>—you actually only paid <u>$751</u> in real estate taxes—meaning that <u>you reduced your taxes by 50%!!</u>

It is, of course necessary that you deposit the amount of tax money due into certificates each year to insure the security of your home. If you cannot make the deposit in a lump sum, then do it in installments as it is possible. But be sure to do it.

Tax foreclosure time periods and regulations vary from one community to another as do the penalties. But even if the tax foreclosure period in your community is only three years—you will still save 25–30% on your taxes, at 2 years, 15–20%.

Using this technique for reducing your real estate taxes can cut your annual bill 15–50%, so it's well worth investigating the specifics in your community.

SUMMARY OF ECONOMIC SURVIVAL TAX TECHNIQUES

TECHNIQUES	NET SAVINGS
(1) REDUCE YOUR MONEY EARNINGS AS MUCH AS POSSIBLE	20–90%
(2) USE ALL POSSIBLE DEDUCTIONS AND TAX SHELTERS	10–40%
(3) GO INTO DIRECT MARKETING— THE BEST OF ALL TAX SHELTERS	50–100%
(4) WORK OVERSEAS	100%
(5) AVOID SALES TAX BY BUYING OUT-OF-STATE	5–9%
(6) REDUCE REAL ESTATE TAXES BY DELAYING PAYMENT	20–50%
TOTAL POSSIBLE SAVINGS	5–100%

Since combined taxes today are the single greatest threat to our economic survival, the individual must use every legal means possible to reduce the overwhelming burden. The forgoing techniques should be extremely helpful in accomplishing that goal.

Recreation and Travel

—With the new low cost, no frills travel approachs, more Americans are traveling abroad than ever before.

RECREATION AND TRAVEL

Recreation and leisure are as vitally important to the well-being of the individual as are the proper food, housing and other basic necessities of living. Psychologically they are the safety valves that release one from the high tension pressures of work, money worries and the other problems of our highly complex society. A well-directed use of leisure into pleasurable recreational activities can also play a major role in lowering the level of drug usage, alcoholism and juvenile burglary and vandalism.

In spite of the increasing crush of economic pressures, Americans en masse—with a healthy insight into the therapeutic values of recreation and leisure—are stubbornly spending more of their dollars each year on fun and pleasure. If the economic system is going to deny them the fruits of their labor through the confiscation of taxation and inflation—at least they're going to get what pleasures life still affords them. It's a healthy—perhaps even a bit heroic—gesture of defiance in the face of increasing adversity and it's one of the expressions of "joi de vivre" that makes the American culture so splendid and vital. There's something strongly reassuring about a people who reject despondency and have the ability to laugh and play in the midst of crisis.

The extent of this escape from the harsh economic realities into the pursuit of pleasure can be measured by the explosive growth of the recreational industry. In the last five years alone, although taxes increased 100%, spending for recreation increased 150%—to nearly $250 Billion annually!!

This growing national pursuit of pleasurable recreation has

213

produced an incredible diversity of activities, encompassing physical sports, cultural affairs, sightseeing, educational programs, do-it-yourself projects, special interest tours and an endless range of unique and personally satisfying use of free time.

Approximately 10% of the average family's income—or from $1,200–2,500 per year is now spent on recreational or leisure time activities and the market economy has moved quickly to capitalize on this vertible flood of dollars. Billions of dollars in advertising are spent annually on the promotion of each new fad as it materializes and the range of special clothing, equipment, gadgets, kits and assorted paraphernalia available on the market is positively mind-boggling. While the cost of many of the current recreational activities is quite expensive because of the special equipment, clothing and services that may be required, there is also a vast range of inexpensive activities and pursuits that are equally as satisfying and pleasureable.

To reduce the cost of your recreational activities and stretch the dollars you spend for entertainment, consider the following approachs:

(1) MAKE RECREATIONAL ACTIVITIES FIT YOUR NEEDS AND BUDGET.

The biggest mistake people make in recreational expenditures is to equate the amount of money spent with the value of the activity. Frequently they will spend large sums in a matter of days or even hours on expensive trips or other activities and then feel vaguely dissatisfied. And often, on a whim, they will indiscriminately buy expensive equipment and other items for an activity and then discover that the activity really is not all that satisfying or pleasureable to them.

There are really two key principles to successful and satisfying recreation and leisure:(1) Whatever the activity, it should be a contrast, or "change of pace" from your normal routine. If, for example, your work or professional duties subject you to high-pressure mental tensions—leisurely hobbies or physical sports will probably give a pleasureable balance. If, on the otherhand, your work consists mostly of monotonous physical duties, you will find that mentally stimulating or competitive activities are a good counterbalance.

Your free time activities are as important to your psychological wellbeing as are your work or career activities and they should be just as carefully planned so that they make the maximum contribution to your overall life goals.(2) <u>Activities should be realistically adjusted</u> to the amount of time and money available. Once you have carefully determined the general types of activities that productively fit into your lifestyle or pattern of living—check out the activities in your community that will fit your free-time schedule and pocketbook. Many people are unaware of the vast number of activities available in almost every community that range from little or no cost to very expensive affairs.

While it would be virtually impossible in a single volume to list the total activities available, the following kinds of activities are not only pleasurable but will reduce the average family recreational expenditures by as much as <u>50–80%</u>, or an annual savings of <u>$800–2,000</u>.

(A) <u>Make your home a recreational center.</u>

Investment in the adapting of your home to recreation pays handsome dividends. The installation of a growing range of electronic equipment—cable T.V., videotape recorders, computerized games, etc.—can provide endless hours of pleasure for both adults and children alike.

Creating an outdoor recreation area in the backyard with barbecue pits, inexpensive above-ground swimming pools, gardens, and converting the basement into a game room or party room are further efforts in the same direction.

Utilizing the home itself as a recreational area can provide a wide range of pleasureable activities and the substantial savings in time, transportation, admissions fees, taxes, etc., etc. that are realized will quickly return the small investment necessary for making the home a major center of recreation and leisure.

(B) <u>Check out the free or inexpensive activities in your own community.</u>

Most local newspapers have a section which tells of the activities taking place in the community. There are frequently things that are entertaining and cost little to enjoy. For example, most college campuses always have something going on which requires little money. For instance, Charlie Chaplin Film Festivals, lectures, etc. Ethnic groups and civic organizations are constantly presenting festivals, folk-dancing and cultural displays. They're inexpensive and extremely entertaining. Also, visit the zoos, museums and other cultural displays. You're paying for them with your taxes—so take advantage of them. Equally important, they're all close to home, saving the costs of expensive transportation, motels, and other such expenditures.

(C) <u>Indulge in "do-it-yourself" recreational activities.</u> Some of the most pleasurable experiences of my life were the makeshift recreational activities we organized while my family was growing up. Between the duties of a full-time teaching position and maintaining a sizeable diary farm, for a number of years, I had very little leisure time and—with the size of my family—even less money.

But what little time there was available, we thoroughly enjoyed. At least several times a week, in the late afternoon, I would hook the tractor onto an old haywagon and the entire family would pile on top. We would go for a hay ride to the top of one of the nearby hills where we would have a cook-out and later, around a bonfire, we would sing and have a story-telling session until late in the evening. We often went hiking and camping in the nearby woods. We built lean-to's and Indian teepees and even a raft to sail on a nearby pond. In the winter, we built snow forts and had races down the hillsides on home-made toboggans. On weekends, we would pick out a different sight-seeing tour within a reasonable distance—the zoo, museums, a winery, a state park or an exhibition. One of our favorites was the drive along the Niagara River Gorge on the Canadian side and ending at the Falls itself. We would stop along the river bank and cook our meals on a portable barbecue while enjoying the magnificent sights and sounds of the river gorge.

On very few of these pleasant and vibrant recreational activities did we ever spend more than a minimal amount of money, but our leisure time was filled with truly satisfying activities and they are some of the most wonderful memories of our lives. In the final analysis, the secret of life lies in the warmth of shared experiences and happiness has really nothing at all to do with money.

The list of creative and satisfying recreational activities that can be done with little or no money is almost limitless. Try a few of the following:

(A) Get together a quilting party. The camaraderie and fun alone are worth the effort.

(B) Research a subject that interests you. Learning more about something you like is stimulating and productive.

(C) Organize a: barbershop quartet, a neighborhood band, a baseball club, a book discussion group, a community theater group.

(D) Form a social club of friends and acquaintenances for joint activities—picnicing, taking short trips and tours, community projects, cards and other games.

(E) Gardening or growing house plants.

(F) Try writing a book or painting a picture.

(G) Learn a new skill or craft. Get involved in handyman or "do-it-yourself" projects.

The activities possible are limited only by one's creativity and imagination. And surprisingly, often the most pleasurable and satisfying pursuits are those which cost little or no money.

By following the forgoing suggestions, the individual can put leisure time to a productive and satisfying use and dramatically reduce the amount of money spent on recreation.

(2) USE LOW COST OR NO COST APPROACHS TO VACATIONS AND TRAVEL.

In spite of the soaring cost of travel and vacationing, there are a number of unconventional techniques that can greatly reduce —and in some cases, even eliminate—the normally high cost of traveling. I have enjoyed extensive travel to many parts of the world and I have done so at a fraction of what it normally costs the average traveler. Again, if you follow the conventional wisdom and travel as most people do—you're going to pay the highest prices.

The following are some of the unconventional but highly effective travel secrets I've discovered over the years. If you want to get more fun out of traveling and spend less money, consider some of these techniques:

(A) On domestic automobile vacations—especially if the whole family is going—always carry an inflatable air mattress, a number of sleeping bags, and a portable barbecue set. Enroute to your destination, buy food in supermarkets and cook your meals out in the open at rest stops or any scenic spot that strikes your fancy. Not only is this great fun for the family, but by avoiding the restaurants you'll save an incredible sum of money.

The air mattress and sleeping bags have several potential uses. First, if you're in a remote area, they may come in very handy. If the weather is nice, you may very well be able to sleep outside in comfort. Secondly, if you stop at a motel and there are a number of children—as there were in my family—you can get by conveniently with only one room to rent. The same will apply if you visit friends or relatives who will put you up, but may not have additional beds available.

Before leaving home, check with the budget motel chains and get one of their national directories. Stopping enroute at one of their locations will save you as much as <u>40%</u> off the normal motel room cost and it will save hours of searching.

If you do stop to eat at restaurants, stop and have a big lunch rather than a later dinner. Often the same specials and dishes are available on the luncheon menu at a lower price than they will be at the later meal and you will save substantially on the food bill. We often took extensive automobile vacations and by using these approachs, we saved from <u>50–70%</u> over the normal cost of such vacations. Often the savings enabled us to participate in additional activities during the vacation that we would otherwise have been unable to afford.

(B) <u>If you're going to vacation or stay</u> in another city for <u>even a week—rent a room or an apartment</u>—instead of a hotel. Most vacationers would never consider such a possibility, but the savings are incredible. Even in the most expensive cities and crowded vacation resorts, it's a relatively simple thing to accomplish.

During a two-week vacation in Miami, for example, we used this approach with delightful success. Upon arrival in the city, I purchased a copy of the Miami Herald newspaper, and within hours, had rented a small bungalow a short distance from the beach. Even though I had to pay a <u>full month's rent</u>—the cost was <u>$340.00 less</u> than a two-week stay at a hotel. The landlord was delighted and so were we. Moreover, we had the full amenties of a home and were able to cook many of our own meals— saving even more money. We were close to the beach and the family had a marvelous vacation.

In still another example, my wife and I, one bitter February, decided, on a spur-of-the-moment impulse, to take a low-cost excursion flight to San Juan, Puerto Rico. We walked off the plane with no hotel reservations, and since it was the height of the season, all of the hotels—even at <u>$60–70.00 per night</u>—were booked solid. With the help of a friendly cab driver and the classifieds from the evening newspaper—an hour later we were comfortably settled in an immaculate little efficiency apartment <u>right on the beach</u> in one of the suburbs of San Juan. The rent?

A weekly sublet rate of $100.00—and even though we stayed only four days, that sum was still 60% less than our cost would have been at one of the hotels.

I have followed this procedure all over the world and saved amazing sums of money. In Madrid, I stayed in lovely apartments for less than $5.00 per night, in Lisbon in pleasant pensiones for less than $1.00, and in Rome, I've had quarters in sight of the Vatican for less than 30% of the cost of nearby hotels. In both the U.S. and abroad, the savings have always been at least 60% and often as high as 80%. As an additional bonus, I've had many delightful and unusual experiences which the average tourist seldom encounters.

I have always been puzzled at why more travelers do not use this approach since the advantages are so outstanding. It is far less expensive, there are no reservations to make or keep, and there are always available rooms or apartments to let. One need only review the local classifieds and contact the landlord. It's easier than you think and if you really want to vacation inexpensively—anywhere—try this approach.

(C) When in Rome, do as the Romans do. Americans, when traveling—particularly overseas—have a peculiar tendency to cling together in a group. They take their meals together in the hotel restaurant, ride together on the same excursion buses and side tours, shop together and in the evenings, they become a closely knit social group huddled together as if they were all members of a besieged wagon train in the middle of hostile Indian territory. Complete strangers, who back in the United States would ignore each other if they met on the street or in an elevator, suddenly develop a "it's us against them" comaraderie and begin making comparisons about the local environment and "back home."

While some of this behavior can be attributed to language barriers and a fear of getting lost in a strange environment, the result is that many Americans often travel to and from a foreign country in cultural isolation and miss many splendid experiences that come from simply "plunging" into the society on one's own—riding on the regular buses and trams, searching out the little side street cafes, arranging one's own side trips, etc. Equally important—and more to the point—leaving yourself in the hands of the tourist officials will cost you far more money than is necessary.

On a recent business trip to the Orient, for example, one of the popular day tours being touted by the tour operators to the group with whom I had flown over was a trip to a Buddhist monastery. The excursion cost of U.S. $28.00 included bus transportation to the ferryboat, a scenic two-hour boat ride to another island, a further bus trip across the island and to the monastery high up in the mountains. A tour of the monastery was then capped by a vegetarian luncheon and a return trip via the same route.

Instead of taking the organized tour with the group, I took a public bus to the ferryboat for only $.10 and bought a roundtrip ticket on the boat for only $1.50. Landing on the island, I bought a roundtrip bus ticket to the monastery for $.60 and spent another $.25 for the vegetarian luncheon.

The total cost of my excursion was only U.S. $2.55—less than 10% of what the others paid for the organized tour! Moreover, I had a marvelous time! Not only did I meet some unusual and interesting local people, but the experience of riding on the local buses, reviewing the boat schedules, and buying my own tickets gave me further insights into the local culture.

I learned years ago to avoid the costs of the tourist trap that often is the fate of groups on an organized tour. If you're staying in a tourist hotel—don't eat your meals there. Costs there are double or triple what they are out in the side-street cafes where the local natives eat. Leave the hotel and search them out. Not only is it a lot of fun and far less expensive—but the food is often better. In the same manner, use the public transportation systems and arrange your own side trips and shopping tours.

Everywhere in the world, there are two levels of prices—one for the tourists and one for the local natives. Whether it is Paris, Rome, Miami or Chicago, the natives spend much less than the tourists do for the same activities.

In brief—do as the locals do and you'll save 50–80% of the "on-site" vacation costs and this applies in the U.S. as well as abroad.

(D) Use student and senior citizen discounts to the maximum.
Students and senior citizens should always carry some sort of I.D. card identifying themselves as such. All over the world discounts of 10–30% are available on a range of travel services from transportation to lodgings, food and shopping. Since the nature of education is changing dramatically and many older individuals are now pursuing college degrees and advanced training—do not hesitate to identify yourself as a student if you're doing so—no matter what your age. If you don't have a formal I.D. card—have one made up. It can save you a sizeable abount of money.

Some years ago in the Soviet Union, for example, students were being given a discount of 80% on all travel costs. Booking a flight from Leningrad to Simferopol in the Crimea, I argued that even though I was 38 years old, that I was working on a master's degree at the University of Buffalo and was therefore technically still a student and entitled to the discount. (I did not, of course, point out that this had been an on-going part-time project over the past twelve years.)

After a heated debate by the incredulous officials and my furnishing evidence of my academic involvement—they conceded that I was still a student and gave me the discount— saving me over U.S. $250.00!

Since I have been a life-long studnet, continually involved in new courses and areas of learning, I always carry documentation of my status as a student. If you're involved in academic or technical learning—start claiming those discounts, and if you're a senior citizen, by all means make use of them. Before you pay for anything—ask if there is a discount. If there isn't—ask them to consider giving you one anyway. You'd be surprised at how often they will when you ask.

(E) Do a little homework before you buy travel arrangements. Nothing will save you more money than spending a few hours thoroughly investigating the costs of airline tickets, side excursions, hotel accomodations, etc. As already pointed out, you'll usually do far better working out your own lodging accomodations, food and side trips once you reach your destination.

But often the greatest expense of a trip is the cost of the airline ticket. And there is such a wide range of prices on tickets to the same destination—either through use of a different airline or via another route—that it really pays to spend some time comparison shopping. As a general rule, I have discovered over the years that with diligent research, I can shave 20–40% off the normal price first quoted to me. On a long distance trip, this can literally mean hundreds of dollars.

In your investigation, always check with a number of travel agents and make detailed comparisons of the prices, routes and times. Stress that you are seeking the lowest cost to and from your destinations. Also check with the airlines themselves and they all have toll-free numbers. Often, they are extremely helpful and since they know what the current situation is—may refer you to a better deal even when it isn't on their own airline. Finally, be certain also to check out the charter airlines for special excursion rates and group tours.

By spending the time to investigate all possibilities, you will invariably save yourself a considerable amount of money.

(F) Thoroughly acquaint yourself with the rate of currency exchange and financial customs of the country you are visiting. You can spend a lot of extra money unnecessarily if you don't concentrate on these details. Often the strangeness of foreign currency gives people the unreal illusion that somehow they are not spending real money and they tend to be less careful than if they were spending dollars with which they are familiar. Most Americans, for instance, overtip outrageously anyway. Foreign hotel and restaurant bills usually include a 15–20% service charge in the bill itself. Many Americans, not realizing this, add another 20%—so that they actually leave an incredible 40% tip for the service they have been given.

This lack of attention to such details, plus an easy-going generosity often has led Americans to be regarded as easy "marks" by unscrupulous vendors and tradesmen.

On one such occasion, I hired a taxicab in Athens, Greece to take me from my hotel to the airport, a trip I had made several times and knew the fare to be approximately $2.00. According to government regulations, meters in the cabs had two speeds: a slow speed for the first mile (giving a lower rate) and a faster speed and higher rate after the first mile.

As I stepped into the cab, the driver quickly appraised me and apparently concluding that I was an American from my clothing and my spoken English—reached over and flipped the meter at once to the second speed, thus effectively doubling my fare.

I realized immediately what he was doing, but said nothing and settled back to enjoy the ride through the city. At the airport, I handed him precisely the equivalent of $2.00 in Drachma, the Greek currency and no tip. He immediately began to protest,

"No-no, you have made a mistake—that is only half the fare. You still owe me that much more!"

"No—you have made a mistake," I said, getting a bit angry, "I'm a tourist—not a fool. You've tried to cheat me with your meter, and if you wish—we'll call a policeman and let him settle it."

He gave me a quick look, then scowling and muttering to himself, drove away down the airport exit.

While the vast majority of trade and service people abroad are sincere and scrupulously honest, not paying close attention to currency and local financial customs invites exploitation and unnecessary spending. It has been my observation that Americans probably spend at least 40–50% more money than they need to while traveling. Pay close attention to local financial customs—as the natives do—and you'll save a lot of money.

(G) When buying anything overseas—always bargain. The American culture has taught its citizens to pay whatever sticker price is attached to an item. Except for sales and distress situations, prices are not negotiable. The individual pays the price designated—or he does not get the item.

In most other parts of the world, however, the reverse is true —just about everything is negotiable. To the foreign merchant, selling is not a cut-and-dried routine—it is a highly developed art and he thoroughly enjoys the excitement of negotiating with a buyer. Often it is his only entertainment and the more heated the bargaining—the more he enjoys it. He sets a high starting price on an item and fully expects a potential buyer to challenge it and bargain with him.

Americans do not always understand this and when they simply pay the price asked—the merchant is quite taken aback. Of course, he will take the money and congratulate himself on his good fortune—but he feels a certain disappointment at the lack of bargaining and the American has paid a much higher price than was necessary.

Not only does bargaining lower the costs, but it is often a great deal of fun. I remember vividly a colorful cab driver in Cairo who, upon delivering me to my hotel one afternoon, suggested that he give me an escorted tour of the nightlife that evening, including the food, drinks and his personal services as a guide.

"Thanks," I said, starting to get out of the cab, "but I've already seen Cairo at night."

"Not with Alexander the Great you haven't!"

Startled, I hesitated. "Alexander the Great?"

"It's me," he beamed, his eyes sparkling. "I'm Alexander the Great!"

It was so absurd that I started laughing. "Oh, I'm sorry, I didn't realize—"

"Yes—it's me! And for only ten Egyptian pounds (U.S. $22.00)," he continued, "Alexander will show you the real Cairo!"

"Ten pounds?" He was such an engaging rascal that I was half considering it and knew that we were already bargaining. "Why that's piracy," I complained, "I would have to ransom my wife. I'll give you two pounds."

He gave an instant yelp, as if I'd physically wounded him.

"Two pounds? Two pounds? How will I support my ten children? How will I feed them?"

"All I'm buying is a short tour," I replied, "I'm not responsible for all of your past exploits."

"Because you are a nice American gentleman—I will make it only seven pounds," he conceded.

"And because you're Alexander the Great—I'll give you three."

We finally settled on four pounds, with which (since that sum represented a weeks wages for the average man) he was extremely happy. I had a really enjoyable evening at modest expense ($12.00) and we had both enjoyed the bargaining.

Probably the best summary I have ever heard was from a crusty old Englishman I met in Singapore who put it quite succinctly:

"Whatever they're asking, Yank—offer them a third and never settle for more than half!"

That's a pretty good rule of thumb, and even if you don't follow it precisely, at least get into the habit of bargaining if you want to save money on what you buy during your travels.

(H) Learn to travel free. There are two excellent methods of traveling at no cost that I have used with great success on a number of occasions:(1) Organize your own tour. This is easier than you think and it's a great way to go somewhere even when you don't have the money to do so. Let us suppose, for example, that you want to go to Paris, Rome or Las Vegas. Wherever it is—you can be certain that there are a lot of other people that also want to go to the same place. And you can also be certain that they are looking for the least expensive way to do so.

Since group travel is by far the least expensive way for most people to go—organize a "no frills" group tour. No special dinners, cocktail parties, side excursions, etc.—just basic transportation and hotel accomodations, with each traveler benefitting from the lower group rates.

The logic of such a tour makes it relatively easy to assemble a group of people and you do not have to be an experienced travel agent to do so. Essentially, you need to make only two basic arrangements:

(a) Airline transportation, and,
(b) Hotel accomodations.

Since you are not a professional tour group operator under the pressure of the need to make money—you have a number of distinct advantages:

—You can work with the smallest possible group—minimizing the hassle. Fifteen people is usually the minimal number necessary to qualify for a group rate—making it much easier to handle than the groups of <u>40–50</u> people in most commercially organized tour groups.
—Since you are not seeking profits and because yours is a "no frills" tour, you can eliminate all the headache and details of having to arrange parties, side tours, etc.

The procedure for setting up a group tour is relatively simple:

(1) Decide where you want to go and when.
(2) Get quotations on group rates to and from your destination. You can do this by contacting the airlines directly or even through a travel agent.
(3) Get group rate quotations on a block of hotel rooms in your destination city (or cities). You can do this by phone or letter, or again through a travel agent.

You'll find the airlines, hotels and travel agents all very cooperative. They're in business to make money and by organizing a group—you're a very appealing customer to them. In the case of the agent, he gets a commission from the airlines and hotels for bringing them customers, so he'll also be happy to talk to you.
(4) After you've assembled the rates for air flights and hotels— you now have a reduced package price to offer prospective group members. On both hotels and flights, you should have

gotten 30–50% off the normal rates for individuals, so that you have a very attractive price to sell.

Usually, once I had assembled a minimal group of fifteen people, I was given free air flights and room accomodations by the airlines and hotels as the tour group leader.

While this is no longer as common a practice as it used to be, there is no great problem. If you are not given your travel arrangements free, simply add your own costs to the groups total cost and distribute it among the individual members.

For example, let's say you're setting up a ten-day trip to Paris and the combined group cost for flights and hotels are $1,000 per person, then you calculate the following:

(a) Air flights & hotels (for 15 people) $15,000

Add your costs 1,000

Total for 16 people $16,000

(b) Divide the total cost ($16,000) by 15, so that the cost for the tour to each of the group (excluding you) is$1067.00.

You are thus traveling free of cost in return for your services in setting up the trip, and the other members are still getting a splendid reduction in their cost, so that it's a good deal for everyone.

Of course, be sure to specify that all other costs—meals, shopping, etc.—are up to the individual and not your responsibility. (5) Now go out and get members for your group. Again, this is a lot easier than you think. Talk to your friends and acquaintenances and tell them you're organizing a low-cost, no-profit trip and ask them if they want to join you. Put notices in church bulletins, local Pennysavers and even a small classified in the local newspapers. Everyone wants to travel and such projects generate a lot of enthusiasm. You'll be surprised at how quickly you can get fifteen people together who are willing to go to Timbuctoo or anywhere.

My wife and I have used this technique to travel to a number of memorable places. On one unforgettable such tour, we flew with a small group into the Soviet Union and after renting a number of Volga sedans, drove in an auto caravan the entire length of Russia, from Leningrad to the Black Sea. It was one of the most exciting experiences of our lives and everyone in the group felt it would have been a bargain at five times the cost of the tour.

So for traveling inexpensively, look into organizing your own tour. All it takes is a little work and a sense of adventure!(2) Pay for foreign travel by buying and selling goods. There are few foreign vacations or trips that you cannot pay for through the simple expedient of buying foreign goods at low prices and selling them back in the United States for enough profit to cover the cost of your trip.

No matter what part of the world you travel to—you will find incredible local bargains: silks and clothing in Asia, sheepskin coats and woolen textiles in Britain, perfumes in France, wood carvings in Africa, etc., etc. The range is almost unlimited and invariably, these products will bring at least 3–4 times their cost back home.

When returning from abroad, Americans are allowed to bring back $300.00 worth of goods duty-free. And that is based on what you paid for them in the foreign country—not the retail value in the U.S. You might have purchased $300.00 worth of silk cloth in Asia, but its retail value here might well be $1,-000–1,200.

Even if you bring in over $300 worth of goods, the usual duty is only 10% of the purchase price, so that you still have a price bonanza. The exception is where goods are from certain communist countries where the duty may be as high as 50%, because of trade restrictions.

If the cost of your trip was say $1,500—then by buying $300–500 worth of low-cost goods while abroad you can usually resell them at home for enough to recover your $1,500.

There are no definite types of goods that you should buy—but they should be artistically appealing or have a practical usage value. For example, I once purchased a magnificent hand-carved chess set abroad for $40.00. Back in the U.S., the set was valued at at least $250.00 and I was besieged with offers to buy it for that sum and even higher. Obviously, if I had bought, say 10 sets—which I could have done—I could easily have sold them and paid for my trip just with chess sets. On another occasion, I bought my wife five yards of beautiful Chinese silk cloth for which I paid only $3.00 per yard which here would cost $18–20.00 per yard if it was even available at all. Without difficulty, I could quickly have sold several hundred yards just in my local community at $10–12.00 per yard.

When purchasing such goods abroad, careful attention should be paid to the quality and the quantity of what you are buying. Calculate how much you need to cover the cost of your trip and give some thought to the appeal of the items, who will buy them and how much time and difficulty you may have in reselling them back home. I have never had any difficulty in disposing of the goods I purchased, but I spent considerable time weighing all of these points before I purchased and I believe you should give them the same careful consideration. Further, you don't have to carry all your purchases back with you. You can have them shipped at reasonable rates, although it may take 6–8 weeks to arrive back home.

Through the purposeful use of this technique, you can literally travel almost anywhere without cost. With a little planning, you can roam the world regardless of your level of income.

As a final twist on this approach, I recall a fellow traveler to Hong Kong who had carried this technique to the ultimate. On the evening of our arrival, I was astounded to discover that this witty gentleman had traveled from the States with nothing but the clothes on his back and two huge, empty suitcases.

A short time later, over dinner and drinks, he cheerfully explained this rather unusual traveling style.

"You see," he said, "I'm a salesman, and being well-dressed is important to my business. But in New York, a good suit is $350–400 and it costs me a fortune for clothes. Here I can get a top quality, tailored suit for 80 bucks. So I buy half-a-dozen suits, shirts, shoes—"

"And put them in the empty suitcases," I interrupted.

"Right," he grinned, "I'm all set for the next coupla years and I figure I'm saving at least $2,000!"

"Which pays for the cost of your trip?"

"Hell no," he replied, "I've got something else to cover that."

He produced a long written list from his inside pocket and spread it on the table.

"I've got requests from more than twenty people at the office," he explained, "so I've got a coupla days of shopping. But I'll make enough to cover the whole cost of the trip."

"That's great," I said, with a growing admiration for his creativity.

"It's better than that," he chuckled. "This is a business trip —so I can also get a tax deduction for the whole cost of the trip! By the way," he continued, ignoring my amazed look, "I did mention our company's electrical equipment, didn't I?"

"No, but I'm sure you will."

"Swell," he beamed, "I'll put down the details of our discussion later. Gotta keep a record of my business meetings for the taxman."

Somewhat later, I did a rough calculation of the financial details of his trip. Estimating that he would receive monetary benefits from three sources:

—$2,000 from savings on his own clothes purchases,

—$2,000 or more in profits from the purchases of goods for company associates,

—$1,000 in tax savings (assuming the cost of the trip to be approximately $2,000 and that he was in the 50% tax bracket).

I concluded that his gross benefits from the trip were about $5,000. Since his total expenses were only about $3,000 ($2,000 for the trip and $1,000 for his clothing purchases) he had not only covered the cost of an exotic foreign vacation and a whole new wardrobe—but he was ahead by at least $2,000!

I would call that a double home run!

Using the forgoing techniques will reduce your cost of traveling from 20–100%. With very little money, they have enabled me to travel around the world and to enrich my life with experiences that cannot be measured in terms of any currency. If you really want to travel—money is <u>not</u> a deterrent. Learn these secrets and use them.

(3) <u>LIVE AT A HIGHER LEVEL ABROAD: WORK LESS AND TRAVEL MORE</u>.

One of the final—and perhaps the most exciting—of inflation fighting techniques is to simply live abroad, where a small amount of dollars will buy you a much higher standard of living than they would here in the United States.

For example, on as little as <u>$7–8,000</u> a year—a bare survival level here in the U.S.—you can live <u>very</u> comfortably abroad and in a style that would cost you at least <u>$20–25,000</u> back home. In fact, some parts of Asia and South America, where $7,000 is roughly <u>six times</u> the average income—you can live <u>like a patrone</u> or a medieval baron!

In roughly <u>80%</u> of the rest of the world, <u>$7–8,000</u> or say <u>$600.00</u> a month, will place you in an elevated income status and the host country will be delighted to have you and your dollars as a resident guest. If you're worried about language barriers— don't be. English is rapidly becoming a world language and it is spoken in varying degrees virtually everywhere. Moreover, you'll find yourself in the company of a small, but growing number of American expatriates scattered throughout the world.

For example, at Lake Chappala, near Guadalajara, Mexico, there is a colony of over 20,000 American retirees and another 3–4,000 American artists in San Miquel de Allende, a beautiful old colonial Spanish village. You will find Americans in Costa Rica, the Phillipines, Hong Kong and even—until the recent crisis—Warsaw, Poland, where it is estimated that over 5,000 U.S. citizens were living on their Social Security pensions.

The number of places where you can live well on $500–600 per month is virtually unlimited. In most of Asia and the East Indies, you can live splendidly on that amount of money, with a comfortable house or apartment, excellent food, servants and all of your entertainment. In India, for example, on that amount you can live like a maharajah and the same is true of Thailand, Burma and Indonesia.

If you prefer, for that amount, you can have a tropical beach-front home or even your own lagoon in the exotic Seychelles Islands in the Indian Ocean or the Maldives off the southern coast of India.

If you like the Latin culture, throughout South America, you can live the life of a patrone in any type of a climate or culture that strikes your fancy, from the mountains to the seacoast, to the jungles, in villages or in magnificent cities. In Europe, outside of Germany, France and Scandanavia—which are quite expensive—you can live very well on a low income. In Portugal and Spain, delightful countries where $600 per month is about twice the average income, you can live in beautiful, cultured old cities like Lisbon or Valencia, or stay in a quaint seacost village along the Algarve in Portugal or the sun-drenched coast of southern Spain. The south of Italy, Sicily, Malta, Sardinia, and rural Ireland also offer unique cultural experiences and are well affordable on a monthly income of $600.00.

Whatever your cultural or climatic preferences—there are at least a dozen foreign locales that will suit your tastes.

For the average individual on a lower income level—whatever your age—you can live abroad with less effort and with far less money than it would cost you here for just a survival level of living. For the retiree, artist, writer, or just the ordinary sybarite —it's a marvelous way to go!

The specifics of the system are relatively simple:

(a) $1,000 will take you roundtrip to virtually anywhere in the world from the U.S.

(b) $500–600 per month, whether from Social Security, pension or accumulated cash will afford you a comfortable living in the country you have selected.

If you are retired, with a regular monthly income, such as from

Social Security or a retirement pension, you could well consider living abroad all year.

If you are of a younger age and still working for a living, then you might consider using this technique to live abroad perhaps six months out of every year. If such is the case, then you might try the following approach:

(A) As a working principle—$4–5,000 cash accumulation will give you a comfortable existence abroad for 5–6 months.

(1) $1,000 for your roundtrip airfare.
(2) Your remaining $3–4,000, or $500–600 per month will give adequate living funds during your stay overseas.

(B) To accumulate your $4–5,000, work the first 5–6 months of the year (or as long as it takes) at whatever type of employment is convenient for you.

(1) During your working time, live as inexpensively as possible, in order to accumulate your required money. Perhaps you can live with your parents, double up with a friend or find a job that will possibly give you your meals or your lodgings—such as working in a restaurant, hotel or vacation resort.
(2) Since you will be working only part of the year—thus lowering your gross annual earnings—be sure to have your employer decrease your tax withholding since you will be paying minimal taxes on an annual basis and you want this money to take with you. You don't want to wait until the following year for a tax refund on the overwithholding of your funds. You can accomplish this by filing enough extra exemptions to bring your withholding down to the proper level.
(3) Before leaving for overseas, investigate the possibilities of business activities in the area to which you are going—such as buying and selling goods, gathering material for a book, or magazine article, etc.—so that you can deduct all or part of your trip as a business expense and possibly earn a bit more money.

Living abroad part of each year not only dramatically reduces your cost of living, but it can add tremendous pleasure and excitement to your life. In addition to the exhilaration of being exposed to a different culture and life-style, it often opens up a range of social and business opportunities with which you would never have had contact had you stayed at home in Midtown, U.S.A. So for all of its appealing virtues—try living abroad!

SUMMARY OF ECONOMIC SURVIVAL TECHNIQUES IN RECREATION AND TRAVEL

TECHNIQUES	NET SAVINGS
(1) MAKE RECREATIONAL ACTIVITIES FIT YOUR NEEDS & BUDGET	50–80%
(2) USE LOW COST OR NO COST APPROACHES TO VACATIONS & TRAVEL	20–100%
(3) LIVE AT A HIGHER LEVEL ABROAD: WORK LESS & TRAVEL MORE	40–80%
TOTAL POSSIBLE SAVINGS	40–100%

Education

—Studies show that higher education is the route to economic success.

EDUCATION

There is no other aspect of our society today that more vitally affects the individual than that of education. Because of the sophisticated, technological structure of our culture—we are a diploma-oriented society and the lack of education, whether it be academic or technical—will have a punishing effect upon the individual's entire life. Statistics show very clearly that those with the academic and technical degrees and professional certificates earn at least twice—and often three or four times as much money as do the uneducated and unskilled persons.

Not only do the greatest financial rewards go to the educated, but they have far less unemployment, greater mobility, a better psychological self-image and a generally more satisfying lifestyle.

In brief, because it affects both your lifestyle and the level of financial existence for your entire lifetime—education and the acquisition of specific skills should be a prime objective of every individual. As we have stressed earlier in this book—the acquisition of any skill increases your productivity, which in turn increases your capital value (the total worth of your future labor in terms of money).

One of the major keys to the individual's survival over the coming decades (especially the overcoming of inflation)—will be to increase his or her productivity to the greatest possible extent. The answer to this is education—and we come now to highly successful techniques for acquiring such education even in the face of runaway inflation.

Higher education (i.e., beyond high school) can roughly be divided into two major categories:

(A) Academic and professional degree programs for training of such as teachers, doctors, lawyers, engineers, biologists, geologists, accountants, etc., etc. Such education normally takes place at a university or college over a 4–8 year period.

(B) Technical skills and crafts training for such as electricians, plumbers, mechanics, bakers, etc., etc. Such training may take place either formally at a technical school or institute or less formally through apprenticeship, on-the-job training or through a family enterprise. Still further, a vast range of craft and technical skills may also be acquired independently by a highly motivated do-it-yourselfer.

* It should also be here noted that the acquisition of such skills, even if not used as an enterprise—are invaluable in increasing your own self-sufficiency, which should be a basic element in your survival strategy.

The problem, of course, is that, like all other commodities today, the cost of education via traditional methods is soaring out of sight. In spite of the fact that the United States is the most highly educated and possesses the most widely developed educational system of any nation in the world—for the average individual, obtaining an education has become a financially devastating proposition. The cost of going to college has doubled in the last ten years and is now rising at an annual rate in excess of 11%!

For those beleaguered individuals and families despairing over the mounting cost of education, the following approaches can offer dramatic relief:

(1) GET YOUR COLLEGE DEGREE OFF-CAMPUS.

An off-campus degree is the same official, accredited degree you would normally receive as a result of a traditional four year

course of study at a college or university except that the degree
is usually earned through independent, off-campus work and
study.

While the requirements for an off-campus degree are the
same as those required for a degree earned on-campus—there
is a further departure from tradition in that the required credits
may be earned through proficiency tests, work experience, military experience, correspondence courses and past college credits if one has any. In several programs available to students
nationwide—the New York Regents Program and Hawthorne
University in Salt Lake City—an individual can earn a complete
degree just through testing alone!

Although these off-campus college degree programs are not
nearly as well known as they deserve to be, they offer the individual incredible advantages:

(A) Very low cost. Because credit may be obtained through
proficiency exams and for Life/Work experience, the student
literally saves thousands of dollars in tuition costs.

(B) Time. The student does not have the rigid time schedule
that is imposed upon the on-campus student. He may complete
his degree as quickly or as slowly as he wishes. If he secures
credit through exams and Life/Work experience, he can save
several years of time in getting his degree.

(C) Credit for Life Experience. It is possible to obtain credit
toward the degree from experience or knowledge gained from
various areas; military or work experience, traveling, reading,
hobbies or special interests, etc.

(D) Flexibility. The study program can be adjusted to individual
needs. Many programs also permit the student to make use of
a variety of learning situations such as on-the-job training, independent study, field work, private tutorial, etc.

(E) Use of prior credits. Credits previously taken at universities
or colleges, correspondence courses and a wide range of in-

service military and industrial programs may all be applied to the degree requirements.

(F) Open admissions. Most programs are open to all applicants and have no previous requirements, such as, high school diplomas, age, etc. The purpose of these programs is to make higher education available to many who would otherwise be unable to pursue a regular course of higher learning.

Of tremendous significance is the fact that the individual may pursue such a program without interrupting one's employment and income. The on-campus student's loss of income for four years must definitely be considered as part of the total cost of obtaining a degree.

The following chart, which compares on-campus degree costs vs. the off-campus degree costs illustrates the startling savings that can be realized.

FOUR-YEAR COMPARISON

	COSTS OF AN ON-CAMPUS PROGRAM	COSTS OF AN EXTERNAL DEGREE PROGRAM
TUITION	$5,400–15,000	$1,500–3,000
BOOKS	$800–1,600	$300–500
TRANSPORTATION	$2,000–4,000	–
SCHOOL FEES	$500–800	$300–500
TEST FEES	–	$400–700
LOST WORK INCOME	$20,000–30,000	–
TOTAL COST	$28,700–51,400	$2,500–4,700

From the chart, it becomes quickly obvious that the individual, through the off-campus approach, can reduce the cost of a degree by an astounding 80–90%!

While these off-campus, or external degree programs are not that well known to the general public—they represent one of the greatest educational bargains of all time!

The case of my own family will serve to demonstrate just how effective this approach can be. As a parent with eight children to educate, I was as concerned as other parents at how to see them through college. As a teacher, however, I was in a poor position to afford such a staggering financial undertaking.

The answer came through off-campus college programs. Starting with my oldest daughter, over a ten-year period, I counseled and directed each of my children in their chosen fields through independent, off-campus study. Today, six of them have either completed their degrees or will shortly. Two are engineers, one a geologist, one a business major, one a major in art history and still another a major in political science. Several of them, except for the taking of examinations, have never attended a class on-campus. Yet all hold valid, accredited degrees and two are going on to graduate school for advanced degrees. Not one of their degrees has cost in excess of $1,000!

By even the most conservative estimates, in the education of my children—I saved at least $120,000!!!

By no combination of earnings, government grants, loans, etc. could I ever have accomplished this in the traditional manner or at the normal costs of on-campus education.

This personal experience has been so invaluable and so successful in assisting my own children that I have counseled hundreds of other students into the New York State Regents Program and am currently the acting president of Hawthorne University in Salt Lake City.

While it would be impossible here in this short space to give all of the details of both these programs, complete information may be obtained by writing to the registrars of these universities (addresses given in rear index). For those interested in pursuing an off-campus approach to a college degree, these low-cost programs will be as valuable in reducing the time and tuition costs as they have been to me and my family.

As a final note, and of particular interest to women, is the recent development of college credit for competency in such vital homemaking skills as child care and counseling and financial management. Full details are available through Educational Testing Service (E.T.S.), Princeton, New Jersey (see rear Index).

So if you're wondering how in the world you can afford a college education—definitely investigate the off-campus programs.

(2) THOROUGHLY INVESTIGATE ALL AVAILABLE FINANCIAL AIDS.

The emphasis here is upon the word thoroughly. Each year literally millions of dollars in available financial aid for college students goes unused simply because people are not aware of the existence of many of these funds. In addition to the better known government aids—there is an incredible array of financial assistance from many little known sources such as foundations, industry, associations, etc. A few hours of intensive homework on these sources can pay handsome dividends and in some cases may reduce costs to the student by as much as 30–50%.

To help you discover the many possible financial aids, you should investigate three major reference resources that are available to you free of charge:

(A) "Five Federal Financial Aid Programs."

This publication is a description of major government aid programs, which you can obtain free of charge by writing to:

Consumer Information Center
Department SG
Pueblo, Colorado 81009

(B) "Scholarships, Fellowships, and Loans" by S. Norman Fein-

gold and Marie Feingold. This is a multi-volume index of a vast range of available grants, scholarships, fellowships, etc. and can be found in many public libraries for review.

(C) "A Selected List of Fellowship Opportunities and Aids to Advanced Education."

This is a publication listing all major financial aid sources and can be obtained by writing to:

Publications Office
National Science Foundation
1800 G. St., N.W.
Washington, D.C. 20550

A careful investigation of all available financial aids will almost invariably discover one or more offerings of assistance for which you are qualified and which will help to reduce your total educational costs.

(3) MAKE USE OF GOVERNMENT EXTENSION SERVICES FOR FREE OR LOW COST TRAINING IN TECHNICAL SKILLS AND CRAFTS.

Many Americans are not aware of the almost unlimited range of information and training in technical skills and crafts that are available in every local community under government auspices.

More than a century ago, as the nation expanded westward, there was a great popular demand for schools that would teach citizens technical homesteading skills in agriculture, mechanics and small manufacture. To accomodate this demand, the Morrill Land Grant Act of 1862 granted each state 30,000 acres of free land for every representative that state had in Congress. The Act required that the land be sold to create investment capital and that the resultant income be used to create a university for the teaching of these skills and crafts.

It was a magnificent concept and it has been uniquely successful in bringing invaluable technical education to generations of Americans. Today, every state has a land-grant university that offers training courses, workshops and seminars on almost every conceivable subject or topic. Whether it be auto mechanics, gardening, solar energy or whatever—programs are open to everyone and are either free or involve very modest fees.

To make such offerings available to citizens everywhere, whether rural or urban, a cooperative structure involving the states land-grant university, the federal Department of Agriculture and each county now functions effectively in every part of the nation.

Therefore, if you wish to learn any kind of technical skill or want information on any craft or subject whatsoever start with your County Extension Service. The Director will advise you of all available assistance on the subject area of your interest and this may take the form of course offerings, workshops, "how-to-books", cassettes, seminars, etc., etc. If they are not immediately available through his office directly, he can help you through the state's land-grant university. And behind all of this stands the enormous research and resources of the Department of Agriculture. In fact, this federal agency produces and maintains the most extensive inventory of "how-to-books" in the entire world. If you're in a hurry for information on anything in crafts or skills —and I mean literally anything—ask your local library for the latest edition of:

"List of Available Publications of the United States Department of Agriculture."

These thousands of publications are available free or for a very small charge.

While just the sheer volume of "how-to" information in itself is mindboggling—the further range and quality of the technical "hands-on" training through these extension services is also quite amazing. In those areas where such programs are known and utilized—they can have a startling impact upon the technical skill level of a community.

My own area provides a revealing example. The majority of my neighbors, who take maximum advantage of this low-cost technical education, can weld, repair machinery, build furniture, do plumbing, electrical wiring, etc., etc. In spite of the fact that it is one of the poorest counties in the entire Northeast—with a median family income well below the national poverty level— it also has a pool of trained labor with an amazingly high level of technical skill. This is due in large part to the unique technical education offered by the state and county extension services, which have cut the costs of such training to probably no more than 10–15% of the normal costs associated with such education.

In summary, the original land grant university concept and its present day extension services have created one of the most uniquely successful systems of education in American history and deserve much of the credit for our current competency in technical skills and crafts.

For a low-cost, effective approach to increasing your productivity and learning valuable new skills, by all means start making use of these marvelous extension services.

(4) CREATE YOUR OWN SURVIVAL LIBRARY AND HOME PRODUCTION CENTER.

As we have stressed continuously throughout this book—the ultimate solution to many of our current problems is a return to the principles of our former household economy:

(A) Greater self-sufficiency.

(B) Increased productivity.

(C) Avoidance of money.

Following these three principles can solve most, if not all, of the economic problems currently facing every individual. There are a growing number of books, magazines and articles designed to assist the individual in achieving these objectives and you should begin immediately to build your own little library of these invaluable "how-to" references. The secret to achieving greater self-sufficiency and productivity has always been a matter of acquiring the proper knowledge and tools—and having such a library at your fingertips is an excellent way to begin.

While books today are increasingly expensive, and many individuals will be restricted from extensive purchases because of finances, there are several outstanding publications that every individual should subscribe to as the core of their personal library:

(A) Mother Earth News
     P.O. Box 70
     Hendersonville, North Carolina 28739

This top-quality bi-monthly magazine is based upon and completely devoted to the three principles of self-sufficiency, productivity and money avoidance. It is a veritable goldmine of "how-to" techniques and tips for achieving these objectives and should be a part of everyones survival library.

(B)   New Shelter and Organic Gardening
Rodale Press
33 East Minor Street
Emmause, PA 18049

Both of these high quality magazines, which are published by Rodale Press furnish the reader with a continuous range of valuable "how-to" information for greater self-sufficiency and productivity in housing and home gardening. They are well worth the subscription cost.

(C)   Family Handyman
52 Woodhaven Road
Marion, Ohio 43302

A highly instructive bi-monthly magazine that offers valuable self-help information on the entire range of household needs from furniture to appliance repair to heating and energy-saving strategies. Here again, the basic emphasis is on helping the individual achieve greater self-sufficiency.

(D)   Popular Mechanics
P.O. Box 10064
Des Moines, Iowa 50340

This grand old publication has been a best selling staple in American homes longer than most of us have been around. It is a storehouse of technical information for those individuals seeking greater self-sufficiency in the repair of automobiles, appliances and a range of other household items.

(E)   Mechanix Illustrated
      P.O. Box 2830
      Boulder, Colorado 80322

A sophisticated, comprehensive publication for the "do-it-yourselfer," which also covers a range of auto mechanics, energy techniques, furniture construction and household improvement. As with the other forgoing publications, the basic theme is money-saving and greater self-sufficiency.

If you are on a small or limited budget, start with these publications for your home library. Add to them with other books, publications and newspaper articles as you come across them. If you have a particular interest in a certain craft or technical area—accumulate all the information and data on that subject that you can and put it into your library.

In conjunction with your home library, begin to accumulate tools and equipment that will increase your efficiency and productivity in the specific areas of your interest. For example, if you are interested in say the making or refinishing of furniture, then certain saws, sanders, routers, etc. will greatly increase the quality of your work and your productivity. If your interest lies in clothing, then a good sewing machine or a knitting machine is an excellent investment and will raise your level of professionalism.

Whatever the area of endeavor, knowledge and tools are the keys to increasing productivity. Whether you sell this productivity for money or increase your self-sufficiency by creating your own goods—you are beating inflation by raising the output of your labor!

Creating your own survival library and store of tools can dramatically raise your productivity and self-sufficiency—which in turn reduces your dependence upon money. I know of many individuals who have reduced their cost of living—in terms of money—by as much as 30–50% just through this process of increasing their household self-sufficiency with a home library and the proper tools.

So start to develop your home learning and production center—it will pay handsome dividends in the years to come.

SUMMARY OF ECONOMIC SURVIVAL TECHNIQUES
IN EDUCATION

TECHNIQUES	NET SAVINGS
(1) GET YOUR COLLEGE DEGREE OFF-CAMPUS	80–90%
(2) THOROUGHLY INVESTIGATE ALL AVAILABLE FINANCIAL AIDS	30–50%
(3) CREATE YOUR OWN SURVIVAL LIBRARY & HOME PRODUCTION CENTER	30–50%
TOTAL POSSIBLE SAVINGS	30–90%

Retirement

—and I know that after the years of dedicated service, that Willy Forbush will be as sorry to leave as we are to see him go.

RETIREMENT

For the individual reaching retirement age, today's economic situation poses especially difficult problems.

First of all, the retirement systems—including Social Security and the private pension funds—are in an increasingly shaky financial position. Secondly, the fixed assets of property and accumulated cash savings of our older citizens are particularly vulnerable to the ravages of taxation and inflation. For the retiree attempting to live on a fixed income in the midst of this constant and rising confiscation of wealth, the economic pressures are indeed severe.

There are however, positive and productive steps which the retiree can take to offset the worst effects of the growing squeeze upon personal assets and which will help to lower the cost of living.

(1) SELL YOUR PROPERTY TO CONSERVE YOUR WEALTH.

One of the finer parts of the American dream was that after toiling for a lifetime, raising the family and paying off the mortgage on the homestead—that one could retire happily and inexpensively to the security of a home that was fully owned and paid for.

Sadly, this is no longer true, for the system of taxation has largely destroyed this cherished concept of property ownership. Even if the retiree's home is fully paid for—and often it represents a large portion of his or her accumulated wealth—the unconscionable level of real estate taxes alone will confiscate a huge portion of the value of the property over the succeeding 10–20 years. In many sections of the country, particularly in the Northeast, the level is so punitive that it is financially impossible for older retirees to even remain in their homes after retirement. They often have no option but to sell their home and leave.

In addition to these confiscatory taxes, the annual costs of maintenance and repair of property places still a further burden upon the individual. Since the retiree's small income is largely income-tax free, real estate taxes do not even have the redeeming virtue of being a tax deduction as they are for the younger people still working.

Thus the costs of real estate taxes and repairs can absorb a large portion of the retiree's income if he or she attempts to retain home ownership.

Aside from the continual erosion of the retiree's wealth through real estate taxes and repairs—there is still a further hazard to the older person and that is the possibility of prolonged illness. Should one become infirm or disabled and require expensive medical or nursing care, the state can demand a surrender of the property to pay for the costs. Even if this does not occur and one enjoys a healthy and pleasureable retirement, the state will still take a sizeable bite out of the property value in the form of inheritance taxes when it is passed on to one's heirs.

To avoid this gradual confiscation through taxes and the burden of property maintenance, consider disposing of the property and keeping your hard-earned wealth for your own benefit and enjoyment. There are two excellent approaches that can be followed:

(A) Sell your property outright and rent your housing.
You are allowed a one-time tax-exemption of $150,000—so you will have no taxes to pay on the sale. If you have an average property value of $30–60,000, by putting the money into bank Certificates of Deposit or a well-managed money market fund— the interest received will probably cover most, if not all, of your home rental cost. You will be preserving your basic capital and protecting it from the ravages of taxation and avoiding the bur-

den and cost of property maintenance. Still further, you will have the mobility to travel and live wherever you wish.

It might, however, be a sound idea to put a portion of this cash —say 10–20%—directly into gold or silver as an emergency reserve against potential upheavals in the banking and monetary systems.

(B) Give your property to your heirs now rather than later.

If you wish to remain in your home and do not want to relocate because of your family—then consider giving them your property now in return for an agreement in which they will pay the taxes, keep the property in repair and allow you to live in the home as long as you wish. There are excellent reciprocal advantages to such an approach:

(1) It will free you from the burden of taxes and repairs, greatly reducing your cost of living.
(2) You can continue to live in and enjoy the home you worked for so long and hard. You will also continue to be close to your family and friends.
(3) By turning ownership over to your heirs now you will benefit them by avoiding inheritance taxes later. They can also deduct the real estate taxes they pay from their income taxes if they have ownership. Further, with the cost of property today, it is very difficult for young people to acquire a home and by such an arrangement, you would be greatly assisting them.

The specific details will, of course, vary with each situation, but I know of an increasing number of older people that are transferring their homes to their children, other relatives or friends under such an arrangement—either on a sale or gift basis. The advantages are such that it is well worth considering, and the details can be worked out to everyone's satisfaction.

Whichever of the two approaches are used, this technique can effectively reduce the overall cost of living for the retiree by a good 30–40%.

(2) <u>CONSIDER CO-OP LIVING WITH OTHER RETIREES</u>.

While most retirees do not wish to live with their children and prefer the privacy of their own quarters because of a difference in lifestyles—there are many advantages to the concept of cooperative living with other retirees.

In one specific situation with which I am familiar, a retired couple invited two other retired couples to share their spacious home with them. The three couples equally share the costs of taxes, utilities, food and maintenance in the home, and all are very content with the arrangement. Not only are they living in a comfortable and pleasant home—but they estimate that their individual costs of living are at <u>least 30–35% less</u> than they normally would be. The further bonuses of companionship and similar life styles make the arrangement an ideal one.

While certainly not all retirees will find such a concept to their liking, it is one well worth considering and there are many retired people that would find such a situation most appealing.

(3) <u>CONSIDER LIVING OVERSEAS</u>.

If you have a sense of adventure and want to live at a higher level on a lower income—then definitely consider living abroad, where you can reduce your living costs by <u>40–80%</u>. There are many of your fellow Americans already doing so and the government will send your Social Security checks to you anywhere in the world.

This is a marvelous time of life to see some of the rest of the world and it's easier and less expensive than you think if you do it in the right way. If you haven't already read the previous section on Travel, then refer to it for tips on how to travel inexpensively.

(4) <u>RELOCATE FOR A BETTER LIVING ENVIRONMENT</u>.

Relocation can often provide a much better living environment as well as lowering your cost of living. In general, there are specific factors that can help to produce a more pleasant and less expensive retirement:

(A) <u>A warmer or more agreeable climate</u>. Escaping from the harsher winter climate—such as that of the Northeast is not only better for your health—but it means savings in the costs of utilities, taxes, transportation, etc.

(B) A climate with a longer growing season will allow you to garden more and raise a greater portion of your own food—thus saving on a major living cost.

(C) Living in a small town where there is a much lower crime rate can also remove you from one of the major hazards increasingly faced by older people in the large cities of today.

(D) A less severe climate permits more outside physical and social activities for a more pleasant all around existence.

Quite aside from Florida, which automatically comes to mind as a retirement haven—there are many other areas of the U.S. which offer just as pleasant living and are somewhat less expensive. A few of these other areas that embody the four desireable factors mentioned above, i.e., better climate and lower taxes and utilities, longer growing season, less crime, and outdoor activities are:

—The Northern California and Oregon Coast area. This is a beautiful, scenic area of small towns and mild climate with a very low crime rate and modest cost of living.

—Northern Arizona and New Mexico. A warm, dry climate with many small towns, low crime and reasonable, outdoor living most of the year.

—Northwestern Arkansas. A marvelous, scenic area of quaint, small towns with a modest cost of living. A mild climate, low taxes and little crime make this area an ideal one for retirement.

—The Blue Ridge Mountain area. This area, which encompasses western North Carolina, eastern Tennessee, southwestern Virginia and part of West Virginia has some of the most beautiful scenery in the U.S., mild climate, small towns, and a lower cost of living which makes this a most attractive area for retirement.

—South and Southwest Texas. This part of Texas just north of the Rio Grande offers the retiree all the attractions of a warm climate, low taxes, small towns and year-round outdoor living.

There are, of course, still many other attractive areas of the country which offer pleasant retirement to the retiree—but these will give you a brief idea of some of the other possibilities besides just Florida. For the retiree settling into an area which affords the four basic features earlier outlined, the cost of living should be at least 20–25% less than his or her present situation.

(5) TAKE FULL ADVANTAGE OF ALL DISCOUNTS.

Many retired people do not take advantage of the discounts available to retirees on a vast range of products in stores and on services being rendered. Stay alert to all such offers and begin to make a list of the companies, organizations and agencies that offer such discounts and patronize those that do.

Whenever you are buying any product or service—get into the habit of asking whether or not there is a discount for retired persons. If you're told that there isn't—ask if they will consider giving one. You'll be surprised how many will do so if you ask.

If you actively pursue and get at least a 10% discount on most of the goods and services which you purchase, it will add up to a considerable sum of money through the course of the year.

(6) USE YOUR SKILLS AND TIME TO PRODUCE YOUR OWN GOODS.

Producing goods—becoming self-sufficient—is the surest and most effective way of beating inflation. And retirement is the best of all periods of life to become a self-producer! Not only do you possess the tremendous advantage of having unrestricted free time in which to do so—but you are probably more skilled in many areas than you were when you were younger. Possessing time and skill in any area is a superb combination for the production of personal, tax-free wealth for one's own betterment and enjoyment.

As a final plus to the producing of your own goods, there is the genuine satisfaction that is derived from purposeful and productive activity. Too often, and for too many persons, retirement becomes a period of despondent monotony, lacking in any meaningful activity. Continuing to use your skills and time in productive pursuits is one of the keys to a pleasant and well-balanced retirement.

There are several approachs to using your skills to increase your self-sufficiency and lower your cost of living:

(A) Produce as many of your own necessities as possible.

This might include growing food, building furniture, making clothes, repairing appliances or a range of other goods and services. Whatever you produce for your own use is tax-free and is that much less that you have to purchase—which lowers your cost of living.

If you can produce more than you need for yourself—you can sell or barter the surplus for other things you need—again lowering your overall money needs. Two retired widows who share an apartment in a nearby town are doing splendidly with just this approach. One has a gift for baking—turning out delicious cookies, cakes and whole grain bread that cannot be bought in any bakery. The other is a master seamstress who can quickly turn out any article of clothing. Not only do they supply their own clothing and baking needs, but they are easily able to sell or barter whatever surplus they care to produce. They are quite self-sufficient and they work only the amount of time necessary to supply their basic needs.

They lead a full and active life and often they will produce something not because of necessity, but more to oblige one of their large circle of friends and acquaintances.

Still another close neighbor is a retiree well into his seventies who had worked most of his life as an upholsterer. He is a talented and creative craftsman and as a hobby, he turns thrown-away trash into beautiful furniture and art objects. From discarded T.V. cabinets he makes magnificent cabinets and coffee tables. He turns old bottles and containers into exquisite lamps and broken, discarded old furniture he rebuilds and reupholsters into gorgeous new pieces.

While he creates these things mostly for his own pleasure, his reputation has grown by work-of-mouth and he has a constant flow of visitors to the little workshop in the rear of his home. Although what he earns from his hobby makes him more than self-sufficient, his greatest pleasure is in the creating of these products and he makes no great effort to sell them. In fact, on one occasion, he told me quite seriously that he had refused to sell a certain item to a customer because he did not believe the man would give it a good home!

Producing your own basic goods if possible, is thus an excellent way of developing self-sufficiency and lowering your cost of living.

(B) Barter your skills and time.

If you cannot directly produce your own necessities—such as food, clothing, etc.—then barter whatever skills or knowledge you have for the necessities you need. For example, if you were a bookkeeper, secretary, teacher, etc., etc.—trade your skills on a part-time basis for the basic things you need. Barter if possible, sell your time for money if necessary. One retired accountant I know makes a tidy extra income each year over a 2–3 month period helping people with their tax returns. This extra income fills his needs for the rest of the year. A retired secretary types out term papers for college students in return for maintenance of her home and auto repairs. Still another elderly woman keeps the books for a grocery store in return for the food she needs.

Whatever your particular skills or abilities—they have a value to someone else and they can be productively traded in return for the things you need.

Producing your own necessities directly or trading your skills not only will help you to become more self-sufficient, but conservatively can lower your cost of living some 20–60%.

(7) JOIN A RETIREMENT ORGANIZATION.

There are few groups in our society today that have more common interests, needs and objectives than retired people. Joining an organization or group that represents the interest of retirees will keep you abreast of developments that affect senior citizens and make a variety of valuable services available to you through the advantage of a group organization.

The largest and most active of such organizations is:

American Association of Retired Persons
215 Long Beach Blvd,
Long Beach, California 90801

Annual membership dues are only $5.00 and include an annual subscription to the regular News Bulletin and bi-monthly magazine, both of which provide a continuous flow of timely articles, stories and features of interest to older citizens.

A non-profit organization whose membership numbers in the millions, the A.A.R.P. is dedicated to helping senior citizens achieve greater independence and productivity in their lives. Members are afforded a variety of group benefits such as a non-profit Pharmacy service, motel and rental car discounts, health insurance and a range of other services. The Association also maintains a high-yielding money market trust to assist those members seeking a sound management of their investment savings. Finally, it also actively monitors and helps to influence legislation directly affecting the interests of senior citizens.

Thus, as a retiree, there are many advantages and benefits to joining a retired persons organization such as the A.A.R.P.

SUMMARY OF ECONOMIC SURVIVAL TECHNIQUES
FOR RETIREMENT

TECHNIQUES	NET SAVINGS
(1) SELL YOUR PROPERTY TO CONSERVE YOUR WEALTH	30–40%
(2) CONSIDER CO-OP LIVING WITH OTHER RETIREES	30–35%
(3) CONSIDER LIVING OVERSEAS	40–80%
(4) RELOCATE FOR A BETTER LIVING ENVIRONMENT	20–25%
(5) TAKE FULL ADVANTAGE OF ALL DISCOUNTS	10–20%
(6) USE YOUR SKILLS & TIME TO PRODUCE YOUR OWN GOODS	20–60%
TOTAL POSSIBLE SAVINGS	10–80%

Insurance

—Inspired by the phenomenal success of our Social Security System, I hereby propose a General Insurance Bill with payroll deduction of premiums so that every citizen will be properly insured!

INSURANCE

Insurance premiums today account for slightly more than $10.00 out of every $100.00 spent for goods and services in the nation. For the average family, that translates into an annual $1500–2000—a very considerable portion of their income.

In general, these insurance dollars are spent on four major types of coverage: life insurance, fire insurance, automobile insurance and hospitalization. While the premiums on each, like everything else in our present economic system, keep rising every year, it is possible to reduce overall insurance costs by 20–50% a year by making specific changes in your coverage:

(1) LIFE INSURANCE.

There are few legal documents less understood by the average person than a life insurance contract. In brief, for the payment of a given premium, the insurance company agrees to pay a certain sum to a beneficiary upon the death of the insured individual. In the past, the major reasons for purchasing a life insurance contract were:

(A) It created an immediate estate—$10,000, $20,000 or whatever the face value of the contract. If the insured was the breadwinner of the family, then for his or her spouse and children receipt of such funds would help compensate for the loss of income to the family.

(B) It covered the burial expenses of the deceased.

(C) In most contracts—such as whole life, endowment, family

265

plans, etc.—a substantial portion of the premium paid is for investment purposes. Beyond the small portion of the premium needed to cover the actual death risk—the insurance company invests the remainder of the premium and pays the insured an annual dividend on the use of this money. In effect, that portion is really a savings investment by the insured and over a period of years, a cash reserve or savings is built up through the contract.

Many people buying such life insurance contracts do not understand that they are paying higher premiums because only part of the premium is for "life insurance," while the other part is actually a monetary investment.

In today's economic picture, life insurance as a savings vehicle is a very poor investment. Most contracts—such as those mentioned previously—pay only 5–6% in dividends on the investment portion of your premiums, so rather than it being a savings—you are losing money to inflation.

There are several steps you should take to lower the cost of your life insurance premiums and get the full value from the money you do spend:

(A) Buy only "term" life insurance.

With a "term" life insurance contract, you are paying only for the actual "life insurance." There is no investment portion and you get nothing back—but the premium is 50–60% less than that of a whole life, etc. contract. If possible, get a "group term" life policy through your work, a club, organization, etc. which will cost you even less than an individual policy.

(B) Adjust the amount of life insurance to your age.

If you are younger, with a family, carry a larger amount of life insurance—$20,000–$30,000—to protect them. At a younger age, term life insurance is very inexpensive and is a real bargain in the insurance field.

If you are older, your need to create an estate for your family is largely diminished—so carry a term policy just large enough for burial purposes. When my family was young, I carried large amounts of term insurance, but today, with all of them now adults, I carry only a small group term policy through my university alumni association.

(C) If you have other than a term policy—convert it.

If your current life insurance policy is other than a term policy —convert it to greater advantage for yourself. Every policy (other than term) has a built up cash reserve under which you have three options:

(1) You can take out the full cash value plus accumulated dividends. If you have carried the policy for a number of years, the amount could be substantial. Take this cash and put it into bank Certificates of Deposit which will earn you 2-3 times more on your money than the current 5-6% you're getting in dividends.

With regard to the policy, you can do one of two things: Take out the cash as a "loan" and continue to carry the policy. The interest rate on the loan is only 5-6% and you do not have to pay the loan back. All that happens is that, in the event of your demise, the amount of the loan (plus accumulated interest) is subtracted from the total payment to your beneficiary. If you had taken the policy out years ago and at a young age—this would be the best course if the existing premium is lower than the term premium at your current age. The second course is to simply cash in the policy completely and take out a new term policy at a lower rate.

(2) The second option on the policy is that you may use the cash reserve to purchase a lesser amount of paid-up insurance. This is also a very attractive money-saver, particularly if you are older, have been paying premiums for years and would like to stop paying. Let's say, for example, that you've been carrying a $10,000 policy for the last 15 years and that at this time you have a Paid-Up option for $3,500. You could convert the policy to a totally paid-up one for $3,500, have sufficient burial coverage and never again have to pay a life

insurance premium! Such a decision depends, of course, on your specific needs and decision—but it is one of your options.

(3) The third option on your policy is that you may take the cash reserve to extend the face amount of coverage on the policy for a given number of years without paying any further premiums. I used this provision very effectively to cover my children during the years that they were growing up.

As each of them was born, I took out a small whole life policy upon which I paid the premiums until they were five or six years old. I then discontinued payment, and used the cash reserve to extend their coverage until they were 18 years old —at which time they took out their own adult policies.

By following the above practices in your purchase of life insurance—you can effectively reduce your costs by 50–70% and still get the same effective coverage you are now getting.

(2) FIRE INSURANCE.

The most effective form of fire insurance is a combination Homeowner's Policy which covers your building, contents, general liability, theft of contents, and is generally 20–30% less expensive than the purchase of coverage individually on these areas of risk. In recent years, these policies have also been made available to those renting as well as those owning property.

In purchasing fire insurance, there are several areas of potentially enormous loss to the insured which the insurance company and agent often does not point out to the insured:

(A) The 80% Co-insurance Clause.

Most fire policies contain an 80% Co-insurance Clause which literally means that the insurance company is covering 80% of the fire risk and the insured is assuming the other 20%. Therefore, if the individual does not maintain coverage to a full 80% of the value at the time of a fire the company will only pay a portion of the claim even if the loss exceeds the amount of the policy.

During an inflationary period, if coverage is not revised upward every few years—your property can quickly become underinsured, opening you up to serious insurance losses in the event of fire.

Some three years ago, I had the misfortune of gaining first hand knowledge of just such a situation. Several days after Christmas, while my wife and I were away visiting one of our daughters, our home of more than twenty years was totally destroyed by an inside fire of unknown origin.

The following morning, the first traumatic shock we suffered was the sight of the smouldering rubble that had previously been our home. The second one was dealing with the insurance company. Fortunately, aware of the inflationary impact upon fire insurance coverage, I had just the previous year increased the coverage some 30% so that at the time of the fire, I was right on the borderline of the 80% co-insurance requirement. Nonetheless, the ensuing negotiations were strongly reminiscent of the Geneva Disarmament Conference.

Ultimately, after more than three months of heavy infighting, I finally collected what my policy said I should have in the first place. I would strongly urge every reader to pay close attention to that 80% Co-insurance Clause.

(B) Make a detailed inventory of every item in your home.

In the event of fire, it is not sufficient to simply give an estimate of the items lost. The insurance company will insist upon a detailed account of every single item—brand name, cost when new, age and exact description and value—before they will pay the claim. Off-hand, could you just now identify the items on the shelf of your bedroom closet? Give a detailed account of all the items in your dresser drawers?

That is precisely what you will have to do if you have a fire— and if you can't—you'll suffer serious losses in the collection of insurance money. Begin immediately to make a room-by-room detailed inventory of your belongings. You'll be amazed at how much value you actually possess and the odds are 10 to 1 that you're vastly underinsured. 90% of all American households are underinsured on their contents and would suffer serious losses in case of fire.

Another alternative to an inventory list is to take photographs of every room from which a list could be compiled. After completing a list and/or photographs—file them for safekeeping somewhere outside of your home. Hopefully, you'll never have to use them, but if you do, you'll be very happy that you did.

With fire insurance therefore, get a Homeowner's Policy and pay heed to the 80% Co-insurance Clause and a contents inventory.

(3) AUTOMOBILE INSURANCE.

For the average person, automobile insurance premiums represent a healthy annual outlay and account for a large percentage of the dollars spent on insurance. There are, however, some effective ways of cutting your costs by as much as 20–60%. Where possible, try the following:

(A) If you live in a city—try to establish a residence address or "domicile" for automobile purposes in an outside rural area or small town. Insurance there is 40–50% less than it is in a city. Perhaps a relative or friend living in such an area can accomodate you.

(B) Try to car-pool to work and list your vehicle as "pleasure only" for insurance purposes. This will save not only on transportation costs, but insurance as well. If your car is listed as driving only 10 miles to work, the premium is substantially higher. Over 10 miles, the premium skyrockets.

(C) If your car is relatively new and you must carry collision insurance—carry $250–300 deductible rather than $50–100 deductible. Your objective is to insure against a major loss, not small accidents and the higher deductible is considerably less expensive.

If your car is four years old or over—drop the collision insurance altogether. All you'll get is the book value if it's destroyed and you can write it off on your income tax as an uninsured loss. The coverage you're getting generally isn't worth the high premium you're paying.

(4) HOSPITALIZATION INSURANCE.

Hospitalization insurance is generally so expensive that on an individual basis, the premiums are virtually prohibitive for the average person. Fortunately, many people are covered under a group plan through their place of employment.

If you're one of the individuals who do not have group insurance through employment, the best advice is to join some club, association, organization or other group that does offer its members some kind of group hospitalization. Recognizing the need, a growing number of clubs and other organizations are developing group plans and with a little searching, you should be able to find one. It's well worth the effort, since group plans are at least 50% less expensive than an individual plan.

SUMMERY OF ECONOMIC SURVIVAL TECHNIQUES IN INSURANCE

TECHNIQUES	NET SAVINGS
(1) LIFE INSURANCE	50-60%
(2) FIRE INSURANCE	20-30%
(3) AUTOMOBILE INSURANCE	20-60%
(4) HOSPITALIZATION	40-60%
TOTAL POSSIBLE SAVINGS	20-60%

TECHNIQUES OF SURVIVAL—A SUMMARY

It should by now be overwhelmingly obvious to the reader that the real threat to our economic well-being in the present society is the use of money (or paper currency we call money).

Money may be the medium of exchange—but it is also the medium of confiscation. As long as you continue to conduct your economic affairs through the use of money, you will be subject to the seizure of your wealth through ever-increasing levels of taxation and inflation. Money per se is the major and really only vehicle through which the massive transfer of wealth by the political leadership can actually be accomplished.

While the avoidance of money as a practice may be totally contrary to the conventional wisdom which we have been taught to believe—for the individual in our present society, it is the surest way to economic survival and freedom.

These forgoing techniques, which represent the accumulated experience of a lifetime are guaranteed winners in the struggle for economic survival. Because they emphasize the key principles of self-sufficiency, productivity and avoidance of money— they will enable the individual to retain more of the wealth created by his or her labor and productivity.

In the current economic squeeze, they are effective defenses against the ravages of inflation and taxation. In the coming years, no matter what the upheavals with which we are confronted—they will be equally effective in guaranteeing the individual's economic survival.

Whether the individual employs several, many or all of the forgoing techniques—to the extent that they are used, they will ensure a richer and more productive existence in the future. For the reader who wishes to adapt these techniques to a more highly refined and organized plan specific to the readers own needs and objectives, we shall now proceed to the outlining of a personal survival strategy.

PART III

OUTLINING A PERSONAL SURVIVAL STRATEGY

HOW TO OUTLINE A SURVIVAL STRATEGY

In the preceding sections, we have examined the basic economic concepts and how their use in the present society has led to the economic oppression of the individual and a serious national crisis. We then carefully reviewed effective techniques which will enable the individual to offset the worst effects of our runaway taxes and inflation.

At this point, the reader may be content to simply employ some of the strategies from Part II and go no further. In that event, he or she will still benefit substantially from whichever of the techniques that are used and be much better off economically than before.

However, for the reader who wishes to carry these economic survival strategies to the highest level of development and success—then some further hours of time and effort should now be invested in actually drafting a personal survival plan for future reference and guidance.

The man with a road map usually gets to his destination more quickly than someone who doesn't know which route to follow. And the person with a detailed plan is much more successful than one who simply reacts to situations as they occur and forgets or misses opportunities that might have made the solution to problems a little easier.

So drafting at least a rough outline of future strategy is not a waste of time—it is a worthwhile investment in your future well-being. By having specific facts and options that relate to your personal situation in a written outline for reference—it will greatly facilitate the process of decision making and problem solving in the future.

The following suggested outline is one which I have used with enormous success over the years and which consists of four basic charts which I keep in my files and to which I constantly refer. The reader may wish to use these as a guideline for preparing his or her own individual plan:

(1) A MONEY "FLOW CHART".

You should begin immediately to keep a monthly "flow chart" of where you spend your money each month. Even though you may already be a cautious spender and feel that you manage your money quite prudently, you will be surprised at what you will discover from this flow chart.

For example, when I first began to keep such a record many years ago, I was shocked to discover that small, miscellaneous —and often unnecessary—expenditures accounted for nearly 20% of all the money I had spent the previous month!! Often these were the seemingly insignificant expenditures of under $1.00 that went almost unnoticed in the larger spending for food, shelter, etc. But in the end, these trickles amounted to a sizeable sum of money. This discovery had an important impact upon my future spending habits.

The average person is quite undisciplined in the control and spending of money. Ben Franklin once made the wise observation that—

"A small leak can sink a large ship."

A money flow chart is a simple and valuable device for locating the "leaks" in your own ship. Bear in mind that you are getting ready to go to war—a war for your survival—and you will need all the ammunition you can get. Your flow chart is the first line of defense against the enemy.

(2) A "NEEDS" ASSESSMENT.

By compiling a list of your "needs" (and/or that of your family) in the areas of food, shelter, clothing, education, vacations, etc., you will develop a much clearer idea of the objectives you must reach in fulfilling these necessities.

(3) A PERSONAL ASSET ASSESSMENT.

By compiling another list of your assets—and this includes not only your material possessions, but all of your abilities, special talents, unusual knowledge, etc.—you will begin to recognize that you often have far more assets to sell or trade than you realized.

(4) AN INDIVIDUAL STRATEGY OUTLINE.

From an analysis of the first three lists or charts, you will be able to develop a general working outline to follow in securing the things you need for a fuller, more satisfying existence.

While the preparation of the forgoing charts may at first seem like a lot of unnecessary paper work—rest assured that they will play a vital role in developing a successful survival strategy and their importance cannot be over emphasized. The few hours you will spend in creating and maintaining them will pay you dramatic dividends in the future.

On the following pages are suggested outlines you may wish to use in compiling your own lists and strategy outline. They are the same ones I have used throughout the years, and while I have altered and expanded upon them many times, they have proven to be invaluable to me and they occupy a place of honor on the wall of my study.

MONEY FLOW CHART

A monthly "money flow" chart can be set up quickly and simply. The important thing to remember is that every expenditure, no matter how small, should be recorded. At first this may seem bothersome, but it really takes only a few minutes each day and after a short time of conscious effort, it will become a routine habit.

A painless way of keeping this record is to carry a small notebook and jot down each cash or credit card expenditure as it is made. Then once or twice a week record these on the chart from your notebook. Once a month, refer to your checkbook and record on your chart the expenditures you have paid by check. This will give you a complete record. I have found the following chart to be most helpful.

MONTH OF _____

MONEY FLOW CHART

31	30	29	28	27	26	25	24	23	22	21	20	19	18	17	16	15	14	13	12	11	10	9	8	7	6	5	4	3	2	1	
																															DATE
																															FOOD
																															GAS
																															HOUSING (rent or mort.)
																															INSURANCE
																															CLOTHES
																															ELECTRIC
																															HEAT
																															AUTO (supplies, repairs)
																															SCHOOL
																															RECREATION
																															PHONE
																															MEDICAL & DRUGS
																															PERSONAL
																															TAXES
																															SAVINGS
																															CLEANING
																															GIFTS
																															HOME SUPPLIES
																															HOME REPAIRS
																															ALLOWANCES
																															BOOKS
																															EMERGENCIES
																															JOB EXPENSES
																															OTHER
																															MISCELLANEOUS
																															TOTAL

NEEDS ASSESSMENT

A "needs" assessment is an important part of your survival strategy. Just the developing of such a list or chart will have an impact on your thinking, for we often confuse "needs" and "wants" until they are indistinguishable from each other and this clouds our judgment.

For example, I may "want" custom tailored suits, a Maserati sports car and filet mignon—but I don't "need" them to live comfortably and well. A suit off the rack, a Ford or Chevrolet in good mechanical condition and a variety of high-protein, low cost foods will all give me the same survival comfort—if not the same social status. All too often we confuse our basic needs with artificial status symbols created by a sophisticated and all pervasive advertising industry. A substantial amount of the money we spend is for things the industry wants us to buy and not the basic items we need.

In developing a "needs" assessment, consider what you and /or your family actually needs each month to live comfortably. The securing of these "needs" should be the first and primary objective. Anything beyond that is a bonus and even a luxury. As you begin to use and further develop this chart, you will come to recognize that much of what you formerly considered "needs" were really "wants". This does not mean that you must live in total austerity and discard many of the things you genuinely enjoy, but understanding the difference—that these things are not necessities—will give you greater control of your consumption in the future.

The following suggested outline may be of value to you in

developing your "needs" assessment list. Try to estimate as closely as possible your actual needs for each month. In effect, it is very similar to a projected budget. While this list will undoubtedly change as time goes on, it will give you an excellent idea of what you must accomplish for the forthcoming month.

NEEDS ASSESSMENT

Your needs for the month can be roughly divided into two categories: (1) Fixed expenses, and (2) Flexible Expenses.

NEEDS CHART

MONTH OF _____			
FIXED EXPENSES		FLEXIBLE EXPENSES	
HOME MORTGAGE OR RENT		FOOD	
INSURANCE (Home, Auto, Life, Health)		CLOTHING	
TAXES		GAS	
INSTALLMENT PAYMENTS		ELECTRICITY	
DUES		TELEPHONE	
CHURCH		HEATING	
OTHER		HOME IMPROVEMENTS	
TOTAL FIXED EXPENSES		HOME REPAIRS/	

FLEXIBLE EXPENSES	
MAINTENANCE CAR REPAIRS	
MEDICAL & DENTAL	
CLEANING, LAUNDRY	
ALLOWANCES	
SUBSCRIPTIONS	
SCHOOL EXPENSES	
SUNDRIES, TOILETRIES, COSMET- ICS	
RECREATION, ENTERTAINMENT	
GIFTS	
OTHER	
TOTAL FLEXIBLE EXPENSES	
TOTAL MONTHLY EXPENSES	
CURRENT MONTHLY INCOME	
BALANCE (+ or −)	

PERSONAL ASSET ASSESSMENT

The purpose of compiling a personal asset list is two-fold: to give you a more accurate picture of your actual wealth and secondly, to use it as a "resource" list in helping you to secure the necessities listed on your "needs" assessment. In short, you will use your "assets" to fulfill your "needs".

Your personal asset chart should cover two specific areas: your material assets and your skills and special knowledge. This second area is extremely important and for many people, it constitutes the bulk of their real wealth or "capital".

In preparing a list of your material assets—list everything you own, no matter how small, worn-out or seemingly trivial. Such items can often be fixed up and used, and if you no longer want or need them, they can often be fixed or sold. Everything has a value to someone. If you have never before listed all your belongings—it's high time you did, because such a list is important to you in several ways. First of all, you will be surprised at the value of what you possess. Secondly, if you ever have a fire, you will absolutely need such a list to collect your insurance. If you have no insurance, you will be able to deduct the loss from your income taxes.

The vast majority of people have never made such a list of their material possessions and as a result have only a vague idea of their actual worth and in case of fires and other disasters, they suffer large and unnecessary losses by not having made such an inventory. Rest assured that neither the insurance companies nor the tax collectors lose any sleep over your failure to keep such records.

You may want to use the following suggested outline, or develop one of your own. You may also wish to group certain items, such as cooking utensils, etc. rather than listing each item individually. Try to estimate the value of each item—not on what you paid for it—but on what its current replacement value is today. For example, a hand meat-grinder which we purchased some years ago for $15.00, now would cost over $40.00. Of course, if I were to sell it, it would not bring as much as a brand new one, but it is still probably worth $25–30.00—substantially more in terms of dollars than its original purchase price. Use your own best judgment for each item on your list.

PERSONAL ASSET ASSESSMENT

LIST I—MATERIAL ASSETS

ITEM	NUMBER	HOW OLD	CONDITION	ORIGINAL PRICE	CURRENT VALUE
CASH ON HAND					
MONEY IN BANK ACCOUNT					
EQUITY IN HOME OR PROPERTY					
LOAN OR CASH VALUE OF LIFE INSURANCE					
STOCKS OR BONDS					
FULL OR PART OWNERSHIP OF A BUSINESS					
AUTOS, OTHER VEHICLES					
MACHINERY, EQUIPMENT					
TOOLS (List Them)					
FURNITURE (List All Items)					
HOME FURNISHINGS (List All Items) (Linens, Drapes, Lamps, etc.)					
APPLIANCES (List All Items)					
DISHES, COOKING UTENSILS (List All Items)					
FOOD					
CLOTHING (List All Items)					
SPORT OR RECREATION GEAR (List)					
KNICK-KNACKS, TOYS, ETC. (List)					
BOOKS (List)					
SUPPLIES (Of Anything—List)					
TOTAL VALUE OF ALL MATERIAL ASSETS					

The equity in your home or any other property is the market value minus the amount of any mortgage or loan you may owe. For example, if your home has a market value of $50,000 and you owe a mortgage of $30,000, your equity—the amount you own—is $20,000.

Every life insurance policy has a loan or cash value depending on how old the policy is. This is an asset available to you and the amount can be determined from the table on the policy. If you cannot determine this value yourself, ask your agent to advise you.

LIST II—SKILLS ASSETS

After completing LIST I, you may have been surprised at the total wealth in the material possessions you already have. Now in LIST II, it will quickly become obvious that even greater wealth exists in your skills assets—your future time and labor times the level of your skills. If you will recall from Part I that by using a simple formula, a person could determine his or her capital value.

In compiling LIST II, we shall now use this formula in greater detail to arrive at your current "capital value"—a very important part of your assets. Since the vast majority of people have never before compiled such an evaluation of themselves, the following suggestions will be extremely helpful:

(1) Take the number of working years you estimate you have left × 2000× the rate per hour you are currently earning.

For example, if you are 40 years old, earning $8.00 per hour, and will probably work another 25 years:

25 × 2000 (hrs. per year) × $8.00 = $400,000.00.

Your remaining "capital value" is a total of $400,000.00. In our planning strategy, we shall later break this down to a weekly or monthly level.

If you are already retired, you still possess valuable skills that can be used, even if on a part time basis. Estimate the amount of time you might comfortably devote to the use of such skills, times your remaining life expectancy and make the same calculations.

For example, let us say that you are a 65-year-old woman with an expertise at making clothes. You could comfortably spend, say 20 hours a week and the minimum value of your work would be $5.00 per hour. Your remaining life expectancy is at least 13 years. Then your calculated "capital value" would be:

13 × 1000 (hrs. per year) × $5.00 = $65,000.00.

If you are unemployed, calculate what your capital value would be at your current job or trade if you were working. Even though you are not working now, your future time and labor has a great value and part of our planning strategy will be to put your skills to work in the future.

No matter what your age or circumstances, calculate your current capital value and put it into your list.

(2) List every skill or ability that you possess, even if you only regard it as a hobby or something unimportant. All abilities and skills have value and may in some way be turned to great productivity in the future.

For example, a retired woodsman in our area was recalling a few years ago how as a boy he had made a little wooden instrument that simulated a turkey call.

He laughingly dismissed it as a pleasant childhood memory—but with a little encouragement, he made several for his friends. Today, he now earns a tidy little sum each year supplying local hunters with these unique little gadgets and he is thoroughly enjoying himself.

A local widow who had taken a course in calligraphy (elegant hand printing) nicely supplements her social security income by designing the menus for a number of restaurants and beautifully prepared invitations for weddings, parties and other special occasions. Still another elderly gentleman, a retired master carpenter, is in great demand as a consultant by "do-it-yourselfers" throughout the area.

The examples of someone using a special skill or knowledge are almost limitless and you should list every skill that you have, no matter how unimportant it may seem at this time.

LIST II—SKILLS ASSETS

(1) Calculate your current capital value.

This should be done on the basis of your present working status. If you are unemployed, determine what that value would be if you were working. If retired, but could work part-time, as previously discussed, calculate that value.

Current Capital Value$ _____

(2) Special skills and talents.

Do you possess special abilities in something you are not currently using to earn a living? For example, can you weld, sew, keep books & records, do carpentry, teach, make things, etc. etc. No matter what the skill or whether or not you ever did so for a living—make a complete list of these abilities in this section.

(3) Training and education.

List all education and training you have had. Did you finish high school? College? Have you taken any special courses or on-the-job training of any kind? Every one of these are definite assets that can be used as such or improved upon to increase your productivity. List all of them, no matter what the subject or area.

(4) Hobbies and special knowledge.

List any and all hobbies or areas of special interest which you pursue. You may well have acquired an expertise through these activities that can be most profitable. Do you have a special knowledge in any subject or area? List it in this section.

Completing the forgoing asset list is not an idle exercise and it has several very practical purposes.

First, it will force the reader to consciously evaluate him or herself and may bring to mind abilities and skills that have been forgotten and unused for a long time. However, an individual is the sum total of all of his or her experiences and everything that has ever been learned is an asset.

Secondly, such a list can be most valuable in planning your individual survival strategy—to which we will now proceed.

AN INDIVIDUAL SURVIVAL STRATEGY

From the forgoing sections of this book, you now have all of the necessary tools needed to devise an individual survival strategy which will fit <u>your</u> specific needs and objectives:

—In part I, the major economic concepts of capital, productivity, money, taxes, inflation, etc. were defined in detail in order to show the origins of our present economic situation.
—In Part II, inflation-beating techniques in all areas of economic need were presented in order to give you specific methods which you can use effectively in your own battle plan.
—Now in Part III, you have created three valuable reference charts specific to your own situation: a money-flow chart, a "needs" assessment and a personal asset assessment.

In brief, you now have the three primary requirements for a successful "battle" strategy—knowledge of the problems, effective weapons and an assessment of your personal strengths and abilities.

You are now ready to outline a battle plan for your future economic survival.

PLOTTING YOUR STRATEGY

In creating an outline for obtaining your economic necessities, it is best to set up a separate section for each area, such as food, transportation, etc.

As you outline each area, keep uppermost in your mind the three basic keys to economic survival and prosperity:

(1)Avoidance of money. In obtaining any of your necessities —money should only be used as a last resort when you cannot satisfy your needs in any other way. The less you use money, the lower your exposure to inflation and taxes.

(2)Self-sufficiency. With any goods or services you need—can you make it or do it yourself? If you can't—do you have goods to barter or services you can swap in exchange for what you need? This is where your asset assessment will be most helpful.

(3)Increased productivity. Can you boost your productivity— either in a present skill or by learning a new one? The extra or surplus productivity can then be bartered or sold in exchange for what you need.

Following these three principles, by combining techniques from Part II with an intelligent use of your assets from your assessment chart—you can develop an excellent survival strategy designed to meet your specific needs.

Your monthly cash flow chart will then help you to check your progress as you put the strategy into action.

The following is a sample outline in the area of food. A similar

293

outline should be drafted for each of the other major areas—
housing, transportation, etc. This particular outline is an actual
working sheet from one of my son's files for August, 1981 and
is a good illustration of the strategy for a typical four-member
family. It clearly demonstrates the effectiveness of the strategies
previously discussed.

MONTHLY FOOD STRATEGY

NEEDS	ESTIMATED COST	STRATEGIES	SAVINGS
FOOD FOR TWO ADULTS, TWO CHILDREN	$400.00	(A) *USEABLE TECHNIQUES FROM PART II* (4) BUY INSTITUTIONAL FOOD (6) AVOID CONSUMER TRAP (7) GROW YOUR OWN FOOD (B) *FROM ASSET ASSESSMENT* (1) BARTER OF UNUSED TABLE FOR 20 DOZEN EGGS @ .89 PER DOZEN (2) ALTER BAKERS SUIT IN RETURN FOR BAKED GOODS AND BREAD	 $30.00 80.00 80.00 17.80 48.50
	$400.00	TOTAL	$256.30

ACTUAL COST $143.70

   Against the estimated cost of $400.00 for the monthly food
bill, he used three of the strategies from Part II. In discount
buying of certain staples from wholesalers, he saved $30.00 and
since he shops only once a month with a carefully prepared list,
he saved another $80.00. Vegetables from his garden saved still
another $80.00. From his material asset list he discovered an
unused table which he was able to barter with a farmer in return
for all of his eggs for that month. Finally, from the skills asset
assessment came the final savings. Since his wife was adept at

sewing and alterations, the local baker supplied them with bakery goods in return for having one of his suits altered. They thus
reduced their need for money by $256.30 or a savings of 64%
on their food bill for that particular month.

This result is not unusual and can be duplicated month after
month in every area by setting up outlines and following the
same strategies.

Prepare a similar monthly outline for each of the major areas
of need—housing, clothing, transportation, etc. After you have
a blank outline:

(1) Estimate the total cost in that area for the next month.
(You can get this from the "needs" assessment you have already prepared.

(2) Examine the techniques from Part II and determine which
of them you might be able to use. Enter them on your outline.
Examine your assset assessment to determine if you have
available goods, skills or services that can be bartered or exchanged in return for what you need. Enter these items on
outline also.

(3) Proceed to follow the strategies from your outline
through the course of the month. Record the savings on your
outline sheet as they occur through the month.

(4) At the end of the month tally up your savings and compare the actual cost for that economic area with your original
estimate. You will be surprised and pleased at the results.

While all of the forgoing may seem like a lot of extra work—
in reality it will take you only a few hours each month. The asset
assessment, once prepared, needs little further attention, except
to add a new skill or item as it is acquired. It remains, however,
as a very valuable reference chart for your future use.

The "needs" assessment and strategy outlines, once you have
prepared a few, take only a few moments of your time at the
beginning of each month. You can prepare master blank sets
and run off copies on a duplicating machine. Then all you need
do is fill them in each month.

The only other work involved is a few moments spent recording data through the course of the month and tallying up the
results at the end.

Once you have developed these habits, it takes very little time.
The results, however, are truly impressive. Working with these
charts and strategy outlines, you develop a precise control over
your entire economic situation. You know exactly where you
stand at any time—and exactly where you are going. Not only
can you effectively combat the destructive effects of our present
economic situation—but you will have created a survival strategy that will enable you to survive virtually any form of economic upheaval over the coming decades.

Economic survival over the coming decades will not be a
matter of luck—rather it will be the result of knowledge and
careful planning. Hopefully, this manual will have assisted in
both and given the reader helpful insights for devising his or her
own successful survival strategy for the difficult years ahead. If
so, then this writing has served its purpose and the effort will
have been adequately rewarded.

INDEX

The following is an index of products, services, magazines and information that will be of great value to the reader in each of the areas listed.

BARTER

—Barter Magazines

Barter News
P.O. Box 3024
Mission Viejo, CA 92690

The Traders Journal
P.O. Box 1127
Dover, NJ 07801

Both of the above are direct barter magazines for those who wish to barter with others around the country.

—Barter Clubs

International Association of Trade Echanges
5001 Seminary Road, Suite 310
Alexandria, Virginia 22311

A national organization of barter clubs throughout the U.S.

CONSERVATION

Mother Earth News
P.O. Box 70
Hendersonville, North Carolina 28739

A bi-monthly "how-to" magazine that will be of great assistance in the area of Conservation. The magazine also has a barter or "swap" section.

OFF-CAMPUS DEGREE PROGRAMS

—Off-Campus Education

Regents College Degrees
Cultural Education Center,
Rm. 5D45
Albany, New York 12230

Hawthorne University
External Degree Program
1121 So. Redwood Road
Salt Lake City, Utah 84104-3706

—College Credit For Competency In Homemaking Skills

Educational Testing Service
Princeton, New Jersey 08541

Women interested in gaining college credit for such experiences should write to E.T.S. for full details.

FOOD

—Magazines

Organic Gardening
Rodale Press
33 East Minor Street
Emmause, PA 18049

An excellent "how-to" magazine for the growing of food in home gardens.

HOUSING

—Home-Building Schools

Cornerstones
54 Cumberland St.
Brunswick, Maine 04011

The Owner-Builder Center
1824 Fourth St.
Berkeley, California 94710

Heartwood Owner-Builder School
Johnson Road
Washington, Massachusetts 01235

Northern Owner-Builder School
Plainfield, VT 05667

Shelter Institute
Bath, Maine 04530

Owner-Builder Center
2615 6th St.
South Minneapolis, Minnesota 55434

All of the above offer "hands-on" home building instruction to first time self-homebuilders. Write for full information.

—Magazines

Family Handyman
52 Woodhaven Road
Marion, Ohio 43302

New Shelter
Rodale Press
33 East Minor Street
Emmause, PA 18049

Excellent "how-to" magazines for the home owner and builder.

TRANSPORTATION

—Magazines

Popular Mechanics
P.O. Box 10064
Des Moines, Iowa 50340

Mechanix Illustrated
P.O. Box 2830
Boulder, Colorado 80322

Both excellent publications for self-efficiency in mechanics and a range of other household requirements.

RETIREMENT

American Association of Retired Persons
215 Long Beach Blvd.
Long Beach, California 90801

The largest association of retired people in the United States. A non-profit organization dedicated to helping older people achieve independence and a productive retirement. Write to above for full details.

ABOUT THE AUTHOR

Dr. Alfred Munzert has a rather extraordinary background. A communication specialist with a command of six languages, he is an international traveler who has served with the U.S. State Department in Russia, been a technical training consultant to the Italian and Portuguese governments, and developed accelerated training programs throughout the world. In addition to having raised a very large family, he is also a highly accomplished teacher, lecturer and writer, with more than a dozen best-selling, self-help books ranging from intelligence testing to communication skills to economics. He now devotes his full time to writing, lecturing and traveling and is well into another book on his unusual experiences inside the Soviet Union.